Culture and the Cuban Revolution

CONTEMPORARY CUBA

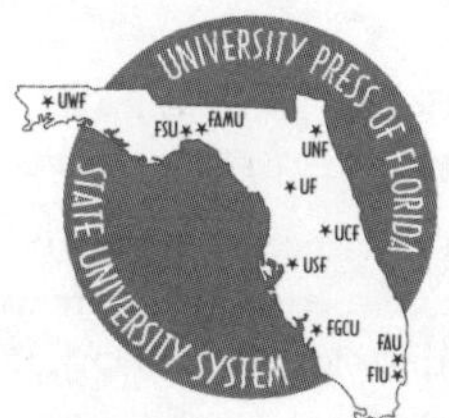

Florida A&M University, Tallahassee
Florida Atlantic University, Boca Raton
Florida Gulf Coast University, Ft. Myers
Florida International University, Miami
Florida State University, Tallahassee
University of Central Florida, Orlando
University of Florida, Gainesville
University of North Florida, Jacksonville
University of South Florida, Tampa
University of West Florida, Pensacola

Contemporary Cuba

EDITED BY JOHN M. KIRK

A multidisciplinary series focusing on balanced, current, and provocative aspects of Cuban history, culture, society, and politics. Of special interest are works that examine the dramatic changes in Cuba since 1959, such as the role of the military, the nature of economic reforms, and the impact of foreign investments, human rights treaties, and tourism on the island.

Afro-Cuban Voices: On Race and Identity in Contemporary Cuba, by Pedro Pérez-Sarduy and Jean Stubbs (2000)

Cuba, the United States, and the Helms-Burton Doctrine: International Reactions, by Joaquín Roy (2000)

Cuba Today and Tomorrow: Reinventing Socialism, by Max Azicri (2000)

Foreign Relations in a Post-Soviet World, by H. Michael Erisman (2000)

Culture and the Cuban Revolution

Conversations in Havana

John M. Kirk and Leonardo Padura Fuentes

University Press of Florida

GAINESVILLE · TALLAHASSEE · TAMPA · BOCA RATON

PENSACOLA · ORLANDO · MIAMI · JACKSONVILLE · FT. MYERS

06 05 04 03 02 01 6 5 4 3 2 1

Library of Congress Cataloging-in-Publication Data
Kirk, John M., 1951-
Culture and the Cuban Revolution: conversations in Havana /
John M. Kirk and Leonardo Padura Fuentes.
p. cm.
ISBN 0-8130-2078-6 (alk. paper)
1. Arts, Cuban—Interviews. 2. Arts, Modern—20th century—Cuba—Interviews. 3. Artists—Cuba—Interviews. I. Padura, Leonardo. II. Title.
NX525.A1 K57 2001
700'.92'27291—dc21 2001016167

The University Press of Florida is the scholarly publishing agency for the State University System of Florida, comprising Florida A&M University, Florida Atlantic University, Florida Gulf Coast University, Florida International University, Florida State University, University of Central Florida, University of Florida, University of North Florida, University of South Florida, and University of West Florida.

University Press of Florida
15 Northwest 15th Street
Gainesville, FL 32611-2079
http://www.upf.com

For Margo and Lucía
in Halifax and Havana

"I've always found very useful that observation of the American filmmaker Nicholas Ray, who said that, while there is no formula for success, there is one for failure—trying to make everybody happy. I think any art that makes everybody happy runs the risk of being a failed art. That is the challenge which we all have to face."

FERNANDO PÉREZ

"I think that right now our culture has tremendous responsibility toward the Cuban people and toward the government. We artists in Cuba—and indeed in any place in the world—have the obligation to ask questions, while the politicians have to respond."

JORGE PERUGORRÍA

Contents

Foreword

There must be few people who have not heard of the "Buena Vista Social Club" success in recent years—an extraordinary story in music and marketing. Yet there are also many other aspects of Cuba's dynamic cultural scene, in the film industry, art, dance, jazz, and, increasingly, literature, that also deserve wider recognition. Clearly, this small country has produced a lively cultural expression that goes far beyond its relatively small geographical size. Cuban culture—whether it be practiced on the island or abroad—truly casts a large shadow around the globe.

This book seeks to offer some insights into this exceptional culture. Admittedly it is a relatively small sample (just thirteen cultural protagonists were interviewed over a two-year period), yet its value lies less in this fact than in what the interviewees actually say. Too often we tend to believe that Cuban cultural expression is one-dimensional and dogmatic, revolving solely around parameters laid out by the Cuban government four decades ago. Yet this interpretation is vastly outdated—and distorts both expectations of Cuban reality and our own aesthetic sensibility. The world has changed dramatically in the past four decades—and so has Cuba. It is therefore wrong to expect Cuban cultural figures to think the same as they did in 1960—or practice the same cultural discourse. The need to move on, to accept that Cuba in the new millennium is extremely different from the country of more than forty years ago, is thus clearly extremely important. And unfortunately, political concerns do their best to get in the way.

Another related observation is that there is no such thing as "capitalist" or "socialist" culture—particularly in these days of globalization. Gloria Estefan's music is well known in Cuba, rap music from New York is the inspiration for many Cuban *raperos,* and commercial U.S. films (mostly of horribly mediocre quality) continue to be shown on Saturday nights on Cuban television. But the pendulum also swings the other way: the greatest concert given to date by the Buena Vista crew was at Carnegie Hall, Alicia Alonso's rapturous welcome in New York and San Francisco in recent years reveals tremendous respect for the grande dame of international ballet, and Silvio and Pablo are still revered in folk circles. As Grammy-winning musician Chucho Valdés notes correctly in this book: "Music is never socialist or capitalist. It is simply music, a form of art that belongs to humanity." The same can be said of other cultural expressions in Cuba, as this book of interviews attests.

The objective of the book is quite simply to offer some personal insights into contemporary cultural expression in Cuba, and to invite people to reflect upon its worth. To a certain extent the huge success of the Buena Vista phenomenon has prepared the way, with the documentary and CD (nominated for an Oscar and a Grammy, respectively) revealing the nature of this extraordinary Cuban talent. The interviews found in this book develop this central thrust, allowing some of the protagonists of the Cuban cultural scene to review a variety of topics related to their trade. They clearly have a wealth of experience (with the exception of Perugorría, all have been active on the Cuban cultural scene for at least three decades), a fact that allows them to reflect on the "good old days," which for several of them were a depressing experience indeed. By the same token, it also provides them with an ability to assess sweeping changes that have taken place in Cuba in recent years, and which all see as being extremely positive for national culture.

Together their views provide a series of invaluable insights into one of the world's most dynamic, and multifaceted, cultures of today. Hopefully the day will come when cultural expression will flow unimpeded across both sides of the Florida Straits—certainly the world will then heave a collective sigh of relief. In the meantime here we see some thoughtful and talented protagonists of the Cuban cultural scene analyzing their reality. Their comments will please some, infuriate others, and—hopefully—cause readers to think about the mere ninety miles of open sea that inhibit this process.

John M. Kirk
Series Editor

Acknowledgments

This project–carried out on the proverbial shoe-string budget over two years—was not easy. In addition to a lack of funds there was also the matter of tracking down the subjects and getting them to find the time for the interviews, some of which required several sessions. Clearly this was not high on their list of priorities, and to make matters worse, many were often out of the country on international projects and engagements. And finally the interviews had to be translated faithfully, checked several times against the original interview for tone and nuance as well as meaning, and all loose ends tied together. It was not easy.

Much of the credit for ensuring that the interviews took place should go to Estrella Morejón, of the International Relations division of the Cuban Union of Writers and Artists (UNEAC). From the outset she saw the value of this project and provided tremendous support to it. Estrella worked the telephone tirelessly, encouraging reluctant interviewees to subject themselves to the ensuing sessions, and providing encouragement at moments of frustration. Mark Rushton helped to edit the original English translation. Lisa Kirk was an invaluable research assistant—in Havana and Halifax—helping to prepare questions for the interviews and hunting down bibliographical references. Susan Fernández of the University Press of Florida has been consistently helpful, supporting this project, and the "Contemporary Cuba" series in general. Finally, appreciation is due to these thirteen exceptional cultural protagonists, who gave generously of their time (some on several occasions) so that the project could go ahead. To say the least, their cooperation was invaluable.

Needless to say, we are fully responsible for the final product—and Kirk for the accuracy of the translation into English. We hope that readers will find it provocative and interesting, and that it will contribute to the debate on this vibrant culture.

Prologue

John M. Kirk

On a personal level, this book of interviews has proved a fascinating project. Before beginning the book, I had already been in Cuba on several occasions since my first visit in 1976. I had also published several books on the island's political history and, of course, felt a profound admiration for its culture. This began in the late 1960s when I first came across the work of novelist Alejo Carpentier. Since that time I had developed a somewhat amateurish interest in several areas of popular culture: I had several records of Silvio Rodríguez and Pablo Milanés; I had seen Alicia Alonso dance at the García Lorca Theater in Havana; I could identify works by the talented artist René Portocarrero; I had heard some pieces interpreted by Leo Brouwer and Frank Fernández; and I'd seen a fair amount of Cuban cinema.

I was also aware of the other side of that cultural treasure trove. In the early 1970s I had written my master's thesis on the "engagée" literature of Vargas Llosa, and I was well aware of his denunciations of censorship in Cuba. I had been shocked by the horrible way in which the poet Heberto Padilla had been treated. I had also engaged in some limited correspondence with exiled writers Guillermo Cabrera Infante and Reynaldo Arenas, whom I had invited to participate in an academic conference held in Canada in 1989 to evaluate thirty years of the Cuban Revolution. (This invitation had not been a notable success: Arenas had sent several letters to newspapers, the "president" [*sic*] of Canada, and local university presidents, and he had written two articles for the *Miami Herald*—all to condemn the conference.

Cabrera Infante sent me an extremely forceful letter, informing me that to invite him to this academic conference "would be the same as inviting a Jew to come and celebrate Hitler's birthday.")

My perspective, therefore, is that of a Canadian academic, raised in England, with a relatively good grasp of the dynamics of Cuban culture. In 1997 I suggested the concept of this book to Abel Prieto, at that time president of the National Union of Writers and Artists of Cuba (UNEAC). The great cinema director Tomás Gutiérrez Alea had recently died—a person for whom I held the highest personal regard.

The plan was simple: to interview leading figures on the Cuban cultural scene who had left a lasting mark over these four decades. Everyone interviewed is clearly identified as a Cuban "star." We have chosen people who remain on the island basically because they are the clearest and most accessible proponents of Cuban culture. At the same time I feel it desirable, and indeed necessary, to complete the picture with interviews of Cuban cultural figures who live in exile, and I would encourage colleagues to pursue such an initiative. They, too, have an important role in the complex and multitalented equation of Cuban culture.

Because of the popular mythology surrounding Cuba, I should begin by saying that at no moment was any kind of limitation placed on this project concerning either the people whom we wanted to interview or the questions we wanted to raise. Leonardo Padura and I prepared the list of subjects to interview and the questions to ask. There were several sessions between Padura and myself negotiating over the subjects, points to raise, and division of labor. At no time did we consult anybody in the government about the project; rather, it was a personal effort on both our parts. It was not easy to coordinate extensive interviews with figures of this caliber: they appear to be constantly traveling abroad with remarkably tight schedules in Cuba, and the last thing they want is to have a journalist and an academic pester them with long interviews.

There are two weaknesses in this book. One is the glaring lacuna of an interview with the great *cantautor* Pablo Milanés. We attempted to interview him on several occasions, but his busy concert schedule abroad made him extremely difficult to tie down. He also had major health problems and was hospitalized twice during the course of these interviews. We would like to recognize, however, his leading role in the development of Cuban culture over these past four decades.

The other has to do with the limited number of women interviewed. While Alicia Alonso and Nancy Morejón are widely known in international ballet and literary circles, respectively, it is clear that in the other areas of culture those spaces are dominated by men. This is unfortunate, and it speaks volumes about the "glass ceiling" that women encounter. At the Seventh Congress of the Federation of Cuban Women in March 2000, the organization's president, Vilma Espín, spoke of "flagrant discrimination" faced by women who seek executive positions in Cuba. The situation of women in Cuba is significantly better than that of their counterparts in most of Latin America (45 percent of Cubans involved in the science sector are women, as are 49 percent of judges, 72 percent of those working in the health sector, and 58 percent of university graduates). Yet there are only 20 women in the 150-member Central Committee of the Communist Party, only 2 in the 24-member Politbureau, and only 3 women ministers in the 34-member Cabinet.

The cultural field also reveals these limitations, since it is clear that women are badly underrepresented. They have faced fewer barriers in literature and dance than in cinema, where their potential has clearly been limited. Nevertheless, the constraints of machismo have made it difficult for women (and to a slightly lesser extent homosexuals) to receive the recognition that they deserve. And this is reflected in the subjects chosen, since there are few women who have made—or rather, have been encouraged (allowed?) to make—a significantly representative contribution.

Both Padura and I had concerns as we started this project, since it was far more difficult than we had expected. Nevertheless, what is found in these pages is the direct result of our efforts alone, in combination with thirteen world-class cultural figures, who generously gave of their time. At no time, I repeat, did anybody pressure us in any way. We had complete freedom in all stages and facets of this project. That said, it is important to remember that all the stars interviewed belong to the Cuban cultural "establishment," in that they enjoy support, prestige, and official recognition. (For the record, Leonardo Padura interviewed Leo Brouwer and Jorge Perugorría, and I interviewed Alicia Alonso, Nancy Morejón, Roberto Fernández Retamar, Frank Fernández, and Fernando Pérez. We both participated in the remaining interviews, with Padura taking the lead in all six cases.)

After completing the interviews, and having read them through on several occasions, we would like to draw out several key themes. In this introduction I would therefore like to summarize my impressions on this intensive, and extensive, work.

What is clear is that Cuban culture—like so many other facets of political life of this country—has far more depth than one would expect to find of a country of just 11 million inhabitants. To take but one example—the importance of the Cuban cinema—it is clear that the contribution of Cuban cinema goes far beyond the extremely limited budget of the Cuban Film Institute (ICAIC). Indeed, the annual festival of new Latin American cinema now is of continental importance.

Similarly, Cuban music leads that of all other Latin American countries. From the original *trovadores* to the army of *salseros* who now are as popular in Miami as in Havana, Cuban music casts a gigantic shadow throughout the Americas. Who has not heard of the Latin jazz of Grammy Award winner Chucho Valdés? Or the haunting ballads and contemporary commentaries of Silvio Rodríguez and Pablo Milanés? Connoisseurs of classical music will recognize the names of pianists Frank Fernández and Jorge Luis Pratts and guitarist Leo Brouwer, as both performers and composers. They have added another vital dimension to the image of Cuban music. The Oscar nomination for *Fresa y chocolate* (Strawberry and Chocolate) and the Grammy awarded to the Buena Vista Social Club and Chucho Valdés are hardly accidental. Rather, they are indications of the extremely high quality of contemporary Cuban culture both on the island and abroad.

At the same time it is only fair to say that literature—especially after the period known as the "quinquenio gris" (literally the "gray five-year period"), starting in 1971—had fallen on hard times and was mediocre at best. In the 1990s, however, it improved dramatically, and there are few literary competitions in the Spanish-speaking world where Cuban writers are not among the prize winners. Cuban theater has also developed notably and is now in the vanguard of cultural change, questioning many established parameters. In particular Abelardo Estorino's work has been well received, both in New York and Miami. The enormously successful U.S. and European tours of the Ballet Nacional de Cuba under the direction of the legendary Alicia Alonso need little comment. Likewise, the plastic arts have matured notably: the Havana biennial festivities, a remarkable "happening" in the avant-garde community, are well known internationally, while the paintings of Roberto Fabelo command astronomical prices abroad.

In synthesis, cultural life in Cuba is once again flourishing, despite the many economic difficulties that the island has had to face in recent years. Or perhaps these same problems have forced the country to seek out new formulas in order to survive. Whatever the reason, it is clear that things in the cultural sphere are going extremely well.

There can be no doubt that the revolution has placed an extraordinary emphasis on cultural expression and has sought to place it at the service of the people. The poet Nancy Morejón has referred to this process: "One can note there the tremendous potential which we came to see in ourselves. The revolution opened doors for us and allowed an enormous social mobility. Many walls that blocked communication were demolished, and taboos were cast out." Leo Brouwer, whose career began before the revolution, has explained the original dream of those first years: "I have always said that period was one of unforgettable catharsis. Until that moment, artists involved in cultural pursuits had been struggling to reaffirm a nationality that Batista had denied, a deeply rooted nationality led by figures like Carpentier, Fidelio Ponce, Abelia, Amelia Peláez. When the revolution took place, this need to define ourselves and to defend ourselves took on a new meaning, and it now became one of collective spirit, of love, of pledging ourselves to build something new." As is only natural, the active participants in the cultural world swiftly took advantage of this new context, and in so doing became even more nationalistic.

Because of these elements, the least surprising aspect of these interviews is the strong sense of national identity that can be found in all the people we interviewed. Without exception, these intellectuals identified fully with the nation, *their nation*. All are considered official figures, nationally recognizable in cultural circles. But many others have suffered censorship, and some have been persecuted. For all, however, Cuba is their home. And even though they enjoy ample international recognition and could live far better in Miami or Madrid, they remain in Cuba because they prefer to live there. All state that they feel wholly Cuban.

This concept of *cubanía* (poorly translated as "profound pride in being Cuban") is almost impossible to define or to explain, but it is a quality that can be felt—indeed, almost touched—in the work of the people interviewed here. Perhaps one of the greatest achievements of the Cuban Revolution is precisely the result of having developed this sense of identity, and these widely held patriotic values, throughout the country. In this way, then, they have brought up to date the important cultural substratum that originated in the nineteenth century in the work of Heredia and Martí and were passed along to Lezama Lima, Wilfredo Lam, and Alejo Carpentier.

Another aspect that I found revealing was the humility of these major figures of Cuban culture and the relationship that they share with the Cuban public. Everyone interviewed here has enjoyed considerable international success, and most have also had success in their own country. But most are also from poor origins (scarcely two or three are from middle-class families), and several of them are from the countryside. It is worth noting that, to use an old cliché, they have not "forgotten their roots," and they identify with "the people," however one defines that term.

Since they all experience the daily rigors of life in Cuba today, the singers, artists, dancers, actors, writers, and artists interviewed here see themselves as cultural workers rather than as superstars. Several of them, of course, have very large egos—as one would expect from people accustomed to hearing applause. At the same time there is a genuine awareness that they have an obligation to contribute to the nation's cultural development, to "pay back" the fruit of their talents to the Cuban public. In essence, most of them began with nothing, and therefore any artistic success is the direct result of the support received from the people and the Cuban system. Most accept their role as standard-bearers of the government's cultural policy. Many also recognize numerous errors made in the Cuban government's cultural policy. Several, for example, were very critical of the government's handling of the Padilla case in 1971, and nobody interviewed here defended the official policy in that sad episode.

They do not limit themselves to criticism of that particular incident, however. Nancy Morejón and Leo Brouwer, for example, criticize the government's decision to prioritize the idea of culture for all, which Morejón says led to "the accompanying practice of justifying mediocrity, often in the name of a supposed form of equality." For his part Silvio Rodríguez, the leading exponent of "official" Cuban music, criticized the centralization of the media and called for the right to more information. Abelardo Estorino, the most famous dramatist in Cuba, also remembers with some bitterness the repression of religious adherents and homosexuals—a practice which was commonplace in Cuba for many years. In sum, there is a fair amount of concern at mistakes made by the cultural apparatus during the revolution.

Perhaps the person who best expresses the experience of the Cuban intellectual in this revolutionary society is Nancy Morejón. A black woman from humble origins, she is a clear illustration of the transformation of Cuban culture in the 1960s. She holds what she terms "a profound sentiment of the need to contribute, to give back—speaking in intellectual terms—the benefits that were given to me. . . . It is very important to me to be useful." At the same time she speaks openly about the challenges she feels need to be addressed by Cuban intellectuals and artists. She believes that it is necessary to be rigorous in criticizing social problems found in Cuba—but without forgetting government support these past four decades. It is precisely because of this support that Cuban culture has developed and prospered and become extremely connected to the people. Besides, she emphasizes the need to remember the peculiar context of Cuba: "We must take into account our reality as a country under siege, but one that has never been alone. We must always remember the hostility to which we have been subjected."

Morejón, who was subjected to official neglect during the "five gray years" (when her poetry was deliberately not published), offers constructive criticisms of the process and appeals to society to pay less attention to values determined by "the market" (read "dollars"). At the same time she calls for a greater and more rigorous appreciation of Cuban reality: "I feel that Cuban writers today are demanding things that simply cannot be conceded in a period like this, since we are facing difficulties as critical as the Bay of Pigs invasion or the Missile Crisis." For her the revolution "has to exist, to survive." As a result in her opinion—shared in this instance by the government, but not necessarily by all the intellectuals interviewed—it is necessary to have reasonable expectations, not to exceed the limits.

This need to participate, combined with the complex nature of reality in revolutionary Cuba, has led the intellectuals to develop an acute awareness of their role as a cultural symbol. This does not mean, however, that they have forgotten many of the political errors committed by the revolutionary government, especially in cultural matters. As will be seen, several of these important figures have suffered at the hands of the cultural bureaucrats. In some cases they were deliberately ignored, and their work was not published for many years; some lost their positions; many saw people they loved and respected punished. Censorship was their companion. And all have had to assume the challenge contained in the slogan "Within the revolution, everything is possible; outside it, nothing is," often without knowing where the dividing line lay—especially since the line could be moved at any time. Clearly it was not an easy matter to be a cultural figure under these circumstances.

Perhaps the best examples of this extremely harsh treatment at the hands of the cultural commissars are Pablo Armando Fernández and Antón Arrufat. From the outset Pablo Armando held a remarkably open perspective on the Cuban process: "I was in the Soviet Union in 1960, and what I saw there really scared me. And because I criticized the Soviet Union here, I was publicly chastised. In good Cuban, they told me not to say such crap." His close friendship with Heberto Padilla and his support for the poet when he was released from detention caused him many problems. He spent nine years working in the print shop of the Academy of Sciences, fourteen years without publishing anything in Cuba, and another thirteen without leaving Cuba. The case of Antón Arrufat is somewhat similar: in the late 1970s he was harassed by the bureaucrats. Suddenly his work was interpreted as being "suspicious," and as a result he was sent to work in a library on the outskirts of Havana, where conditions were humiliating. The lack of vision and the treatment meted out to so many intellectuals were truly unpardonable.

Even leading figures such as Silvio Rodríguez were affected by official censorship. In the late 1960s, he was suspended from Cuban television and prohibited from singing the song "Fusil contra fusil." Supposedly in the name of ideological purity he was criticized for recognizing the importance of the Beatles' music—at a time when the commissars had decided that they represented the worst of western cultural decadence. And both he and Leo Brouwer were criticized for their unrevolutionary appearance, largely because they wore long hair.

All of this today seems laughable. Yet it was a serious enough matter at the time for Cuban intellectuals. There were tense moments for both the revolutionary process and the singers and writers, since they had to learn how far to go before incurring the wrath of the bureaucrats. Those same bureaucrats, it must be remembered, wielded a lot of power.

Although Pablo Armando Fernández now believes that all of this belongs to the past, he remembers vividly the censorship that existed and the self-censorship that many writers practiced after the Padilla case exploded and in the wake of repressive campaigns against homosexuals. Roberto Fernández Retamar, for many years president of the internationally recognized Casa de las Américas, also condemns in this book the excesses committed in the name of the revolution—the UMAP camps of the late 1960s where homosexuals were sent to be "reeducated," as well as the decision not to publish certain writers because of a lack of trust in their revolutionary credentials. He also criticizes the decision not to mention exiled writers in literary anthologies, dictionaries, or even reviews—as if they had never existed.

Retamar, seen by many abroad as the most trustworthy spokesperson of the official cultural position, has spoken openly about the failings of this cultural policy: "Naturally, over a period of forty years we have committed many errors. Those errors should be recognized—and rectified. . . . That writers should have been excluded from a dictionary of Cuban literature for nonliterary reasons is simply an error."

As is evident, many of the persons interviewed here have horror stories with regard to the ideological excesses of cultural policy. At the same time all expressed great admiration for the work of the current minister, the writer Abel Prieto, who as president of the UNEAC had fought against such prejudices. As a result, without exception, all expressed their belief that the situation for intellectuals had improved in recent years: "Things have changed. For example, Cuba is now publishing books that would have been unthinkable in the 1960s and 1970s. I no longer see the sinister, indeed evil, examples of twisted policy that we witnessed in earlier periods, such as the persecution of homosexuals," noted Pablo Armando Fernández. In music and the cinema, a similar comment could be made.

All the subjects interviewed here spoke freely about limits on their work. Nobody asked to speak "off the record" or cut references to censorship after reviewing a transcript of their interview. Frankly, this surprised me, because I believed that there would have been a greater fear of official retaliation. Of course, a healthy and necessary skepticism can be seen in some. After all, who has not reacted with skepticism after seeing the government's angry reaction to the films *Alicia en el pueblo de Maravillas* (Alice in Wonderland) and *Guantanamera*? After all, they were interpreted as being "counterrevolutionary." As a result, although all the intellectuals here respect the great cultural successes of the revolution, they are also in favor of demanding greater space to express themselves. Indeed, many think, citing the example of Carlos Varela's masterful song "William Tell," that it is time to take control of their own cultural discourse.

Since most of the figures interviewed are established, with a long cultural record, I had expected to find a more official reaction on their part. There are one or two interviews where an unswerving loyalty to official policy can be seen, where virtually no questions are raised. Most of the people interviewed, however, claim the need to express their own voice, seeking independence from whatever may be considered necessary by officialdom. This commitment goes beyond strictly political beliefs. The film director Fernando Pérez expressed it in this way: "What defines us as a group is that we try to produce a form of cinema that has repercussions on society, that can contribute to the definition of concerns that we have—not just as individuals, but also as part of the collective society at large. And because of this, even though we might employ the most diverse of styles, we have developed a form of cinema that seeks to deal directly with our reality. We are not producing a form of cinema with a defined political program or one designed to educate our population." Rather, the goal of cultural figures in Cuba is to produce something that speaks to Cubans about "our history and our reality, our way of life."

The image projected outside Cuba is that the State (always in capitals) controls everything. It is the Big Brother of all totalitarian systems, which insists that absolutely everything be done as it sets out. Of course, I am not so ingenuous as to believe that there is no basis for this interpretation. At the same time, the freedom of expression that I found in these leading cultural figures was far less limited than I had imagined.

It is very clear that the Cuban Revolution has evolved greatly, in the same way that we all have. More specifically, it is important to recognize that Cuba has changed more in the last five years than in the previous thirty. I am referring to the Cuba of the "paladares" or home restaurants, joint ventures with foreign capital, farmers' markets, self-employed workers, and packed churches. And also the new Cuba where the dollar rules and where prostitution and minor corruption have reappeared. As a result, we should not be surprised that cultural policy of the late 1990s should be so different from that of years past. This does not mean, unfortunately, that there are not still "hard-liners" seeking to limit cultural expression, nor functionaries determined to protect their sinecure by criticizing any work they might consider the least bit unorthodox. By the same token, we should not live with cold war stereotypes: the new millennium is far removed from the 1960s.

The necessary prism through which to analyze this cultural reality should not therefore be the lamentable Padilla case, although forgetting it is not a wise policy, either. Rather, the fairest approach nowadays is to seek a balanced overview, emphasizing both positive and negative aspects. There is no doubt that in recent years Cuban culture has clearly opened up dramatically to new realities, which in turn are parallel to the new reality of life on the island. It is necessary to retain a healthy skepticism about these changes, while allowing the writers and film directors to express that vision. We also need to accept that this is indeed their vision and not seek explanations about "new strategies of manipulation" by the government.

One has only to see films such as *Fresa y chocolate, Guantanamera, La vida es silbar* (Life Is to Whistle), or *Lista de espera* (Waiting List) to understand that Cuban intellectuals are not a flock of sheep who go wherever they are led by the cultural commissars. And as a result there is much official resistance to confronting openly this new reality. The new, extremely vigorous literature being produced also points the finger, uncompromisingly, at recent developments in Cuban society, expressing major concerns. In addition, many songs by Carlos Varela, los Van Van, Pedro Luis Ferrer, and even Silvio show that there are many worries—and a great deal of anguish—about the new reality.

It is therefore not by chance that several of the subjects interviewed here speak openly about these problems. Who has visited Cuba in recent years and not seen the gulf between those who have dollars and those who eke out a living on a peso salary? Indeed, there are major differences between those cultural figures who sell their work abroad, are paid in dollars, and have their manager, their agents, their sophisticated studio or office and those who depend completely on an income in pesos. There is a clear division based upon the possession of dollars in Cuban society, and cultural circles are no exception.

But there are other social concerns, too. Nancy Morejón, a black poet, outlined her displeasure with the way in which black Cubans were presented in the media: "We also need to see black characters somewhere other than in films about slavery. We badly need something more contemporary and more pertinent." She also believes that market values have had a major impact on Cuban society and that it is necessary to reconsider many phenomena that are part of the revolutionary tradition. "Some people here say, 'Don't talk to me about the race question.' But we do have to examine this again, because it is an important matter here in Cuba."

As will be seen from the interviews, there is widespread concern about social and racial divisions in Cuba today. The awareness of the many social gains of the revolution has slowly weakened as a form of life has been imposed without the previous egalitarian policies. Referring to the new rules of the game since the demise of the socialist bloc (which in Cuba has led to the inversion of the social pyramid in recent years and the dramatic impact of foreign tourism), Morejón outlines her fears: "It is a reality that in many ways is upsetting, in part because it was so unexpected. We need to be audacious if we are to function properly in this new context. . . . It is fair to say that we have been surprised by the kind of tourism that has sprung up in certain sectors. It has been painful for us in many ways."

It is also important, however, to recognize the (justified) pride in recent cultural work in Cuba—and a determination to keep it from the hands of the functionaries. In undertaking this research, I found a broad awareness of the errors committed in the name of ideological purity, in defending the revolution. In this regard, it is at all times important to remember that

Washington maintains (some forty years later) the "Trading with the Enemy" Act and that official policy is to overturn the Castro government. The sad litany of U.S. government–sponsored assassination attempts of the Cuban president, the 1961 invasion, and the economic blockade speak volumes about Washington's hostility. Significantly, everyone interviewed here expressed complete confidence in the capacity of the Cuban people to resist foreign pressure. It is precisely to achieve this end that they rightly demand greater freedom of expression and government faith in them.

One person to develop this line of thought very clearly was the actor Jorge Perugorría, who starred in *Fresa y chocolate* and *Guantanamera*. He referred to the criticisms Fidel Castro made regarding this latter film: "I disagree with the idea that this is a counterrevolutionary film. I wish that I could have the opportunity to meet Fidel and tell him that and to explain why I feel that way. I believe that it was a mistake to reduce the film to that idea, because it is definitely not the goal that Titón set for the film, nor is it the result of the finished product itself."

In tying these loose ends together, it seems that the key word to define the approach of the subjects of this anthology is *maturity*. While they understand the origin of the limitations under which Cuba lives—on a personal and societal level, as well as those of the government—these cultural figures are not easily intimidated. Moreover, they know that, since 1993, developments in Cuba have been heading in a very different direction, one that cannot be turned back. As Jorge Perugorría explains: "Within the cultural context of Cuba, many things have changed, as one would expect, largely because the world has changed a great deal, as has Cuba. It is therefore logical to suppose that intellectuals in Cuba will also have changed, and this has been the case." The result of this process is a cultural expression that reveals a profound confidence in itself, as well as a mixture of concern at this process of change and an underlying sense of pride in its achievements.

As we weigh up more than four decades of the Cuban revolutionary process, it is important to ponder the opinions of these cultural figures, all of whom have lived in an extraordinarily intimate relationship with their country. Without exaggeration, the final analysis reveals an extremely rich culture: wherever they live and whatever political opinions they may hold, Cubans have every reason to feel proud of the many successes of their compatriots interviewed in these pages. It is hoped that this impressive culture will continue to develop, overcoming the many material and ideological limitations and seeking new—and fully deserved—triumphs.

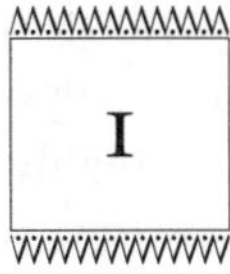

Silvio Rodríguez

Folk Music, Revolutionary Style

Silvio Rodríguez is the founder and leading exponent of the "New Troubadour" movement, and his folk songs are enjoyed throughout the Spanish-speaking world. Silvio is one of the few artists capable of filling enormous theaters and stadiums with the mere presence of his voice, his guitar, and, above all, his compositions.

For an entire generation of Cubans and Latin Americans, he symbolizes the glorious years of the Cuban Revolution. Clearly he has identified himself with the political process on the island to such an extent that, for many, he is the top singer of the revolution. His work, widely supportive of events on the island these past four decades, is today a kind of artistic chronicle of this period. At the same time his work has made few artistic concessions, because if anything defines the essential work of Silvio, it is this mixture of a political message and its high artistic quality.

Silvio is controversial. He is one of the few artists in Cuba who has dared to confront the public with his ideas. Some Cubans see him as intellectual, distant, and cold; others consider him passionate. His views are well publicized, from his defense of revolution's goals to his criticism of its defects. So vigorously has he defended the revolution that he has been appointed a deputy in the Cuban Parliament.

At the same time, the artistic trajectory of Silvio Rodríguez in many ways summarizes the history of the transformations faced by Cuban intellectuals these past four decades. Indeed, he too has been faced with censorship, and indeed at one point he was forbidden to perform. Silvio and his work bear in their souls the traces of a long process in Cuba in which intellectuals have always sought to explain and validate their opinions in the political reality of their country. Silvio, however, who insists in defining himself as a "necio" (poorly translated as being silly, perhaps naive), has put up with a lack of understanding, and has resisted attacks upon him. Yet he has emerged victorious and today is one of the most highly regarded cultural figures of the Cuban Revolution.

. . .

Give us a self-portrait of Silvio Rodríguez before he became a famous musician.

I am the son of two peasant parents from extremely humble origins. My mother's family worked processing tobacco. The families came from two small towns in the Province of Havana that were close to each other. My mother's family was from San Antonio de los Baños, and my father's was from Vereda Nueva. In the 1950s they moved to Havana [city] looking for work, especially my father. In between these rural and urban experiences, I'd say that I was a normal kid. It is afterwards that exceptional things start to happen. When I was twelve, the revolution overthrew the Batista dictatorship. And I began my adolescence roughly at the same time that major changes began to happen in Cuba.

I've made that analogy on several occasions, because I think it is very appropriate in my case. This transformation of a child into an adolescent and the social transformation of our society happened at the same time. Afterwards I kept on studying and, while still a youth, participated in various activities that encouraged this social transformation. For example, when I was only fourteen years of age, I joined the national literacy campaign as a volunteer teacher. That was in 1961, at the time of the Bay of Pigs invasion. I also volunteered for the first work brigades to go and cut the sugar cane. In short, I began to participate in this new social process at the same time that I was going through adolescence.

A little later, in March 1964, I signed up for the first group of those doing their year of obligatory military service, as it was called at that time. That first period was very hard indeed, since it reflected harsh military conditions. I did my military service with great political consciousness, however, since I was a young kid who identified completely with the revolutionary process. Without any doubt at all, though, I later ran into the harsh reality of our country, and as a result several of my beliefs changed after the three years and three months that I served in the armed forces.

Had you already begun to draw before you began your military service?

When I joined the armed forces, I already had some experience sketching. I had been a designer and had drawn a fair bit. I had also received some experience as a journalist in the journal *Mella,* which the Young Communist League published. I had also written some stories when I was fourteen years of age, and when I entered the army I already had all this experience. Several officials began to use my talents to contribute to different military publications. Eventually I came to the journal *Venceremos,* a publication of the western army, where I worked for almost a year as an illustrator, in between regular military duties. I spent my last year in the army working for *Verde Olivo,* the official journal of the armed forces.

But it was also in the army when I began to compose songs, basically as a means of relieving the boredom of military life at night. At that time I used to read a lot, but I needed something else to channel my energy into. There was always someone in the camps who had a guitar, and I used to borrow it and strum away, since I'd never owned one of my own. I felt so good doing this that soon I was playing every day. Finally I decided to buy a guitar, since I was using the one I had borrowed more than its owner was. That first guitar cost me sixty pesos. Afterwards I began to play all kinds of songs that were in fashion: calypso music, boleros, everything. Later I began to feel very comfortable with the guitar, and soon I was composing my own songs.

It is obvious that there was a strong artistic vocation that, some way or another, was going to make its presence felt. Is this the result of your upbringing?

I had an uncle who played the bass and drums in the Mambí jazz band in San Antonio de los Baños. He is the only musician I remember from my family. But I didn't see him a lot, although when I turned seven years old he gave me a drum and taught me to play the basic rhythm used to accompany bolero music, the rumba, and things like that. It is likely that my interest started through that. But it is also true that there is a lot of interest in music on my mother's side of the family.

When my mother was young, for example, she used to sing with one of her sisters. Once she told me that they didn't pursue this interest, because of the prejudices that their parents had, since at that time to be a professional musician was seen as the worst thing in the world. They also used to sing in a trio with a friend of theirs who played the guitar, and used to go to people's houses to sing. None of that ever came down to me, although without a doubt my mother's voice has been a major influence. From the day I was born, she used to sing to me. When she washed the dishes and cleaned, it was always there. And she had a wonderful voice, tiny but well developed, in tune, and with lots of musical ability.

Then, when I was seven or eight years old, I began to study piano with a lady who lived on our block. It seems that one day I arrived at her house and began to play the piano, and apparently I struck up some kind of melody. Anyway, she asked my parents if she could teach me for free. Apparently I made a lot of progress in just a few months, but this was at a time when I was more interested in playing on the street with friends than in sitting in front of a piano. Shortly before joining the army, perhaps due to some sort of frustrated commitment, I again tried to play the piano. I even sought out a teacher. But then I was called up and so had to leave the piano as well as my studies in painting, which I had started at the San Alejandro art school.

And what happened with those songs that you wrote in the army?

Some of them I sang in a duet in music festivals that the armed forces organized. By the time I was demobilized, I had composed dozens of songs. By chance one day I arrived at the house of an important musician, Mario Romeu, who conducted the orchestra that played often on Cuban radio and television. He listened to my songs and took an interest in them, and it was he who first put me in front of the television cameras.

Was it during this time that you met up with the people who worked at the journal El Caimán Barbudo?

No, I'd known many of them from before, because they had worked with me at *Mella:* Guillermo Rodríguez Rivera, Víctor Casaus, Félix Guerra. I then met Jesús Díaz and Wichy Nogueras after I was demobilized. I'd heard of Jesús before I met him because the others talked to me about his short stories. It was about this time that he sent his book to the Casa de las Américas literary competition and won the prize in 1966 with *Los años duros* (The Hard Years). I also met Guillermito in that group. He had some problems with his nerves, and perhaps because of that he could never get his work together. It was a shame, because he was a brilliant writer.

El Caimán was founded in April 1967, and I was demobilized in June. I remember that perhaps the first interview that I gave was to Wichy for *El Caimán.* Without a doubt, the group of people who were associated with the journal helped me to be more connected with the writers of that time.

How did the cultural atmosphere of the 1960s help to define you in artistic terms? Was it lucky for you to be developing as an artist in such an important decade as the 1960s?

When I look back several decades later, I definitely think so. When you're a young kid, you have lots of illusions but lack any sense of perspective. You think that you're changing the world but without knowing if you're really doing so. In our case, fantasy and reality fused perfectly because we had in front of us the reality of our revolution, with all of its changes, and this made us aware that we were living through a truly significant period.

And the poets with whom you used to hang out—Raúl Rivero, Guillermo Rodríguez Rivera, Luis Rogelio Nogueras—did they have any influence on your songs back then?

In stylistic terms, I wouldn't say so. But in regards to the ethics and aesthetics that good songs need to have, I think that definitely it helped me a lot to bat ideas about with them. To take one example: At that time there was a real obsession with colloquial expressions among young poets. And the more that poetry resembled the language of the street, the better. The use of metaphors took on another significance, and the more diluted its impact within the syntax of a poem, the better it met its aesthetic objective.

We used to sit at the Coppelia ice cream parlor and talk endlessly about literary matters. It helped me a lot that they were all university students and had an ordered view of literature—the history of literature, its various periods, the writers who came from those periods, the basic themes and styles of those writers. I had none of that. It therefore helped me a lot to participate in those conversations, and as soon as I heard about a book or an author, I immediately went to look it up.

I remember in particular one conversation that I had with Guillermo Rodríguez Rivera in which he told me that there were many words that should never be used in a song. Nobody used the words *shoe* or *screw* or *tool.* They were words that were in fact excluded from songs, which in fact had a limited lexicon. That was an idea which, when I realized its implications, made me react very strongly. And so I began to put all sorts of words into my songs. About that time I wrote "This Age Is Giving Birth to a Heart," which was at first seen as a pornographic song. This phenomenon of the language gives some idea of the extraordinary world that was opening up to us. It was now possible to include all kinds of words in our songs. Nobody else had done that, and to a certain degree it made its mark on the way I regarded my work.

Was there any deliberate effort to break with the past?

That was exactly what we did. I attempted specifically to reject the idea that the words found in a song were some kind of idyllic language, conditioned by certain words or expressions. Without any doubt, all of this process is due to the contact that I had with those young poets who were so interested in experimenting with new approaches, and writing a form of poetry that was as contemporary as possible.

And how did your connections with the world of Latin American protest music come about?

This occurred after the Casa de las Américas cultural institute had opened the door to young Cuban folk singers and put us in contact with musicians, writers, and artists from all over the Americas. And so whenever its director, Haydée Santamaría, wanted to entertain the jury members for the Casa de las Américas literary awards, she'd call us up. And that's how I met people like Roque Dalton, Paco Urondo, Mario Benedetti, and many others. We were fortunate that Casa de las Américas had such a strong ethical position toward culture, definitely based upon ideological concerns, since at that time there were no other cultural institutions that did anything like this.

Speaking of ideology, how have you evolved politically since you left the army?

Well, this has been a real roller coaster for me. There are several elements to be considered. There is a clear break between the Silvio who left the army when he was twenty years old and his counterpart one year later, who had crashed headlong into a different reality. In the army I had lived in the midst of an immense collective spirit, where all of us had worked toward the same goals, something which led to my developing a sense of belonging to the collective.

A year later, however, I was on my own in the midst of a major personal transformation and for reasons that at times seemed extremely simple. Perhaps what most changed me was the loss of a feeling of an almost womblike security that I had felt in the army, even though I had never really adapted to military life. Afterwards I fell into the world of radio and television, where there were clearly different interests, and people behaved in a manner that was completely distinctive, too. At times there exists a sense of solidarity because of the sector you're in, but in reality there is also an extremely strong individual sense in everybody, and I was just not prepared for that.

I threw myself into this new stage of life with great candor, and at first the experience was very hard for me. That was the first abyss that I had to climb out of, a process that lasted several years. During that time I felt that I was falling, falling, until I touched bottom when I went to sea after signing up with the *Playa Girón* fishing boat. When I came ashore I was a very different person, since while I was at sea I had lots of time to reflect on where I was going. As a result I returned with clearly defined ideas.

Why did you decide to leave everything behind and go to sea?

I have always been a voracious reader of books written about the sea. I had read much of the work of Jack London and Conrad. I remembered well *The Voyages of Sinbad the Sailor* and Melville's *Moby Dick,* and I had all these stories at the back of my head. It was only when I was five years old that I saw the sea for the first time, and until that time I had always been intrigued with the sea. The only body of water which I had seen before that time was the river near my home town. And I remember clearly the impression that I had the first time I saw the sea.

That impression has always been a subliminal message for me, as well as the desire to know what was beyond the sea, to see the other side. . . . My favorite dream had been to head northward, to Greenland and visit the Arctic. I wanted to see whales and walruses. To see what I had read about, nothing more and nothing less. And so that's why I signed up on the *Playa Girón* (which was supposed to be headed for Newfoundland). That is precisely where I wanted to go. However, as we left port they sent us fishing to Africa. . . .

An important event in your career was the founding of the Experimental Sound group at ICAIC (the Cuban Film Institute). How did you come to meet Leo Brouwer, and what did it mean to you to work alongside him?

I had heard about him. I knew that there was a guitarist named Leo Brouwer, and possibly I'd read something about him in the press. Besides, he worked at the ICR (the Cuban Radio Institute as it was called then) at the time that I was demobilized and began to work there. One day I bumped into him, and I was greatly surprised because I expected to meet an older man when in fact he was more or less of my own age.

I really got to know him when I was beginning to have problems at the ICR. One day Leo came up to me and told me that he knew that I was having problems and that I could count on his support completely. I remember that he arranged for us to meet at the Habana Libre Hotel because he didn't want to talk with me at the ICR. He gave me just one recommendation: to write down in black and white everything that was happening to me. "Write it all down," he told me, "and send it to whomever you want. And, if you need signatures to support you, I'll be happy to sign it for you." And that's how I came to get to know him, first as the human being and later as the artist. Later, almost right away, he began to adapt some of my songs into orchestra scores for his wife at that time, the singer Yolanda Brito.

As an artist, however, I never thought that I could touch Leo. I always considered myself as being extremely lucky to have him around and to have him take an interest in my songs. Then one day Alfredo Guevara called us to a lecture he was giving on a trip that he'd made to Brazil at the end of 1968, when he'd been fascinated by what he'd seen at a film festival. After the lecture he asked Leo and me to stay behind. He then told us of his desire to create a Sound Experimentation Group at ICAIC, because he'd seen that here in Cuba there was a similar movement to what he'd witnessed in Brazil. Our cinema industry needed a group of people to take charge of the soundtracks for the movies, and he thought that, under Leo, we should form that team. It was not until April 1, 1969, however, that Leo and I were transferred to ICAIC. We already had a series of names of definite members, such as Pablo Milanés, but soon started to hold the meetings to decide who else would be members of the group.

And all of this is prior to the formation of the New Troubadour movement?

Yes, because quite some time before the New Troubadour movement started there had already been a group of troubadours, and indeed a sense of our generation's interests in this form of protest folk music. Usually the date of February 18, 1968, is given as the official date when a group of troubadours with these interests was presented publicly at Casa de las Américas by Haydée Santamaría. That night Pablo Milanés, Noel Nicola, and I performed, while in the audience Eduardo Ramos, Martín Rojas, and Vicente Feliú were also present, and we asked them to sing with us.

For many, that performance had been seen as the continuation of the festival of protest music that had been held the previous year. However, we didn't have any songs that could be seen as having a "social" message, which in general were songs with an anti-imperialist message. Pablo had written "I Saw the Blood of a Child," I had composed two or three more, and Noel had one or two as well. But among all of us we didn't have more than ten songs of that nature. Our songs did, however, deal with other social problems and had a vision of the world that was different from the normal material. It would be fair to say, though, that at that moment we did not have an extremely precise aesthetic definition.

Tell us about your experiences with censorship and self-censorship.

I think that they are in essence examples of the same phenomenon. In my own case I have always felt the need to challenge any form of censorship and to do the same with the fear which springs from self-censorship. Whenever

I am afraid of something, the first thing I try to do is not to behave like a coward. I have also reacted in this way. But all of this is more complicated, because we have drawn up a neat framework of what censorship is, when it is in fact far more complex.

When I think back to some of my reactions to this phenomenon, I laugh at them. When I see reactions of young people today, I feel tremendous empathy with them because it reminds me of myself. For example, if a young singer approaches me and says that he's concerned with his work since he hasn't had one of his songs prohibited for six months, I feel great fondness for them. It is clear that it is a human reaction that transcends epochs, political systems, several processes. It revolves around the need to prove oneself by means of challenging these limits.

And did they ever prohibit any specific songs? I remember that people spoke about "Summary of the News."

I wrote that song when I was at sea on the *Playa Girón,* and when I returned to Havana the conflict with the ICR was not quite over. But those songs were not suspended. . . . I was! In actual fact, the only time in my life that they have told me that I couldn't sing a song was with "Rifle against Rifle." I remember that it was Manolo Rifat who passed on the news to me, and he did so with tears in his eyes, because he knew well that it was a crime. But he had to follow orders apparently given by a commission of the Central Committee of the Party whose job it was to approve songs, poems, and anything that had to do with Che Guevara. Apart from that, nobody has ever told me that I couldn't sing something. There was, however, a circular that came around stating that I was suspended from national radio and TV, and of course my songs were also banned.

And what caused this suspension?

I think that it was because of a series of unrelated events, all pretty silly. The suspension came about when they were making a television program, and I was asked what I thought about the Beatles. We had already had a rehearsal for the program in the afternoon, when the same questions had been asked and when I had given more or less the same answers. But there was an inspector from the head office present at the evening show. He was officially called a producer, a title that was used to hide his function as a spy. His name was Alberto Batista, and I learned recently that he was now living in Miami. Amazing to see the changes that life brings! He saw the entire rehearsal, and saw that on the actual show that night I said the same things that I have also said about the Beatles.

The following week, when we were going to record some songs for the program, I was summoned to meet with the ICR boss, who was waiting for me. I was questioned about my reply on the previous program, to which I replied that I had answered the question raised. That I had not answered anything that I'd plucked out of the air. Then he told me that I couldn't talk that way about the Beatles. . . .

To tell you the truth I didn't understand any of this, because the crazy period—roughly 1964–65, when there was a terrible official reaction here against the Beatles—had passed. But he then told me that I was suspended. It's not a lie to say that the decision didn't really bother me that much, because singing was not that important to me, and I've always preferred to write songs for others to sing. But in his diatribe against me, this particular functionary went too far, stating that from then on I could have nothing to do with the revolution. I was mad, really mad, because nobody—absolutely nobody—had the right to exclude me from the revolution. . . .

In the end the solution that they came up with was to suspend me. They didn't kick me out of the ICR, and they wanted to keep on paying me, but I refused to take any payment. And that's how the legend started about my treatment with the State. It's been magnified a great deal. It's been said that I was jailed by state security officials, and that I'd renounced my membership in the Young Communist League in order to practice *santería*, and that's why they had suspended me. And that's because nobody could imagine that it was in fact my opinion on the Beatles that had caused all this fuss.

However, it is often thought that the 1960s were a period of great creativity, of openness, especially in comparison with the 1970s, when we can see culture being turned into dogma.

I don't agree with that. I believe that the 1970s were in fact kinder than the 1960s. Remember, for example, that in the 1960s we had the "revolutionary offensive."

Agreed. But you should remember that the 1970s was a time when they marginalized or prohibited Lezama Lima, Virgilio Piñera, Antón Arrufat and so many writers, dramatists, painters. . . .

Well, I see your point. Because it is the people who publish and make our history, and not those who sing, dance, and produce cinema, I understand your argument. Personally, however, I think that the 1960s were a more difficult period, among other things because it was the time when the class conflicts in the country reached their peak. And it was a class struggle to the death. The mountains of Cuba were full of counterrevolutionaries, there was the Bay of Pigs invasion, and the Missile Crisis. . . . It is true that in the

1970s they tried to turn culture into dogma, but there is a major difference between what an official tells you to do in your work and what you actually do. I have no doubts that some intellectuals will indeed have paid attention to these orders and might have wanted to ingratiate themselves with officialdom, emphasizing the positive qualities requested. But nobody can be forced to do this. At least explicitly in their work.

And how did the 1970s turn out for you personally?

When I returned from my voyage on the *Playa Girón,* I joined the Experimental Sound Group, which by then had been officially formed. I began to study again, to work with members of the Group, and to compose music for the cinema industry. It was a time when we were still marginalized from radio and television, although there was a time in 1972, or perhaps 1973, when we were invited to make a television program. So we went along to the studios. However, as soon as the functionaries saw that we had hair down to our shoulders, they informed us that, if we wanted to appear on television, we would have to get our hair cut. We responded by walking out the same door that we'd entered. And so, while we were suspended from television, it was the Cuban film industry through which our work became known. I remember how Santiago Alvarez used us a lot in his weekly news bulletin at ICAIC. In fact, he used any pretext to have us participate, and many films had our music. The attempt to marginalize us was as futile as trying to block out the sun with a single finger.

Which was your first concert outside Cuba? How did the path toward fame and international popularity start out?

My first journey abroad was rather unsuccessful in developing fame and popularity. Indeed, just the opposite occurred, and it almost cost me more suspensions back here in Cuba. This happened in 1972, when I attended the IV Meeting of Political Songs in Berlin, along with Augusto Blanca and Eduardo Ramos. When we arrived there, we found that the Germans shared a strongly pro-Soviet perspective on the revolution and on Che's ideas. (They were clearly opposed to Che, and claimed that he was an adventurer.) And since I began my concert with "Rifle against Rifle," and finished it with the same song, I was not particularly well received by the audience.

My second trip abroad, once again representing Cuba, was to Chile, thanks to Gladys Marín, secretary general of the Chilean Communist Youth League, who interceded with its Cuban counterpart. This all came about because Gladys was a good friend of Chavela Parra and also a good friend of mine. When the Parras first came to Cuba, accompanied by the Quilapayún musical group, there were some people who spoke very badly of us—people in the Young Communist League and ICAP (the Cuban Institute for Friendship with Peoples). They told the Chileans not to meet with us, since according to them we were hopeless cases. They said all sorts of things about us. . . .

But one day Chavela showed up at the house, and when I saw her I immediately recognized her. I asked her what she was doing there, and she told me that she wanted to meet me since they'd told her so many bad things about me that she wanted to come and prove it for herself, since she couldn't believe that anybody could be that bad. And that's how my conversation with Chavela started, and how our friendship did, too. Just over a year later, Noel and I traveled to Chile as part of the official Cuban delegation attending a congress of the Chilean Communist Youth League.

This took place in September 1972. I didn't travel outside Cuba again until 1974, when I went with Noel Nicola to a meeting in the Dominican Republic that was called "Seven Days with the People." It was attended by the crème de la crème of people in the protest song field, from Daniel Viglietti, Ana Belén, and Víctor Manuel to Pi de la Serra. It was there that I got some indication that my music was being appreciated outside Cuba. For example, there was a debate in the local press about who my composition, "Song for the Chosen One," was dedicated to. They were trying to determine if it was about Che or somebody else. During the festival itself there was a lot of media attention on my work.

It was at this time that I began to realize that my songs had become fairly well known and that they were appreciated. Then, in 1975, I went to Mexico with an enormous artistic delegation from Cuba, and we played in the magnificent old auditorium in Mexico City. But it was in Guadalajara, after the show had finished, when a number of young people came up to me and started talking about my songs—which they knew very well—that I realized my music was heard outside Cuba and by people of my own age or even younger.

How many albums have you recorded, and which of them do you have a particular soft spot for?

I'm afraid that I'll tell you what everybody does: that I love them all, because albums are like one's own children. . . . Some of them do have a special importance, and especially the first one, "Days and Flowers," where I recorded a good number of my songs. To record that album was extremely difficult, since I recorded it in 1975, when I had already been composing for about a decade. It was a real headache to choose twelve songs from all those that I'd composed, and all those that I liked. And so I came up with a mixture of songs that I'd composed on the fishing boat, like "Playa Girón" and some other more recent songs. That record is still a favorite for many people, and I can quite understand that.

Then there's another album, "Women," which I'm extremely fond of, because it was the first one on which I'd used a guitar. Also important is "Unicorn," since it marks an important point in my career. Another important album is the first that I made with Afrocuba, "Causes and Fates," because there is a well-developed objective on the album, largely due to the impressive talent of Afrocuba. From my perspective, that album is a turning point: it had a major impact, and caused a wave of interest.

What has been the influence upon your work of North American music?

It has had a great and varied impact. I have always stated that my interest in melody stems in part from classical music, from composers with wonderful melodies such as Tchaikovsky. But it also comes from having listened so much in my adolescence to the work of Johnny Mathis, songs which had such effective, beautiful, and precise musical arrangements. I was also influenced by the music of Elvis Presley, and I remember myself when I was seven or eight years old standing in front of a mirror with a plastic guitar, playing "Don't Be Cruel" while listening to Radio Kramer. The first image I have of anybody playing the guitar was of Elvis, and it has always stayed with me. And then of course there was so much excellent North American and British music. It was later that the influence of Bob Dylan reached me. He is a great poet and artist, with an enormous power of seduction in those early songs such as "Blowin' in the Wind" and especially "With God on Our Side" which, from the structural point of view, is perfect. I have greatly enjoyed much North American music, and of course the influence of jazz is also noticeable.

For many years your work has had an extraordinary international boom, one which has brought you some economic benefits. How does a person with the economic privileges that you have live in today's Cuba?

In terms of material conditions, I live better than many Cubans, but not as well as I could live outside Cuba. On a human level, I live with the goal of composing music that is useful to my people, trying to leave behind some tangible good that may be of use to others when I disappear. There are various projects in this regard that I am working on. One of them is the recording studio "Ojalá," which was built to a certain degree in order to show that a work of this nature could be undertaken. We have now started a new studio, which is called "Abdala," and to which I have contributed financially. More important than the financial support, however, is that the original idea was mine. Because I considered it to be so important, I was very involved in seeking support for the concept, including at the highest government levels, and tried to convince people of both the need and the utility of this project.

Do you believe that, despite all the difficulties that have resulted from the current economic crisis of the country, this has in fact been of some benefit to the country? I am thinking, for example, of the space for debate and for ideas which now exists. Do you think that this has grown?

Without doubt these spaces have opened greatly, because in essence I believe that the political will for them to increase has always existed. This is especially true among people who have participated in these discussions all along—and not among those who have allowed us (or not, as the case might be) to participate in these debates. . . . But in all fairness some important improvements have taken place, even in the press, with the publication of "La Gaceta de Cuba." I also believe that Abel Prieto, at first from the presidency of the National Union of Writers and Artists of Cuba (UNEAC) for several years, and now as Minister of Culture, has played an important role in creating these spaces for the debates to occur.

At the same time, I believe that we are a great distance from exhausting this space. For example, one of the things that has always bothered me is the lack of communication and of information in Cuba. It really bothers me. Why can't I have access to what other people say? I would like to learn more about the opinions of people who don't think along the same lines as myself, because that helps me to reflect, and maybe it will help to improve me, to make me understand things. . . .

One of the defects that all socialist systems have had is precisely that. Why do people say that there is more freedom in a capitalist system than in a socialist one? It is precisely because, whatever the reason may be, there always exists in socialism the pretext that can be used to restrict certain freedoms. I am a complete socialist. But I would be far happier if we who live in a socialist system could really say that we are freer than those who live under different systems. That is the kind of socialism which we should be constructing.

In recent years Cuban culture has clearly grown in importance, both in its diffusion and in its quality, and has come to form a part of the contemporary social debate of Cuba. Do you think, however, that declarations—such as those of Fidel

Castro on the film Guantanamera—mean a step backwards in this process of critical openness in Cuban art?

I believe that what Fidel said about the film may well mean nothing more and nothing less than his own opinion about the film, an opinion which of course he has the right to express. What I do indeed hope is that this does not mean any limitation upon the spaces and the territory that have been won. If that were the case, I would definitely not be in agreement, and I believe that many people would also be opposed.

What do you believe about the current national and international boom in Cuban music and salsa in particular?

In the first place, I think that it is a blessing that in these uncertain times in so many regards, young people have adopted our music. This is clearly an indication of the depth of our identity that speaks for itself. Within this process there are some aspects that concern me about this particular context. For example, there is an overemphasis on a musical phenomenon that was first created here, later was re-created abroad, and was then returned to us as a foreign reflection of our own Cuban culture. From the theoretical perspective, there may indeed be some questionable aspects of this boom, since behind the current fashion there are people behind the scenes who are promoting its commercial aspects. This is the result of the fact that a space has been created for foreign businesses to export this form of music to countries where it is seen as exotic.

But I also believe that it was inevitable for music, and indeed salsa music, to become more complex in the way that we have seen. All these musicians here are graduates from art schools, all know how to play jazz, the majority of them are virtuosos, and in essence many of them have wanted to do jazz for a long time. In arranging and composing their music, they show clearly their ability as virtuosos, indeed, to the point where sometimes they go overboard, and as a result the audience doesn't understand precisely what's going on in musical terms.

I've seen, for instance, some groups with three complete sets of percussion. From a spatial perspective, this is crazy, because it goes against the need for occasional silence: all you hear is nonstop noise. It is often a form of music that seems to be struggling desperately against silence. And you realize that this is an experimental process, as it searches for new forms. Indeed it has to pass through this phase before getting back on track.

It is not coincidence that in almost all of Europe there is such a notable acceptance for musical groups that play a more traditional format. It is because music is understood a lot better there, even though they may add interesting arrangements and harmonies. But there is also a basic respect for the spatial quality of the music, which allows you to understand and enjoy it, since the aesthetic enjoyment of music stems precisely from the contrast that the listener can pick out.

What is happening nowadays is that, as time goes by, the true values will remain behind. Note, for example, that it is the fundamental work—by people such as Adalberto Alvarez and Juan Formell—which survives and is respected. It may not be with any spectacular or splashy nature, and its popularity may rise and fall. But the fact is that its power remains. This does not mean that their music has not evolved—because it clearly has. Formell is a great innovator, and his innovations are related not only to the sound of his orchestra but also to the harmonic cycles and the forms of harmony that he employs. He is a musician who still needs to be studied. And in the case of Adalberto, too, we should examine both his renovation of the overall sound and the form of his compositions.

For many years, people tried to understand the hidden meaning of your "Blue Unicorn." After a long silence you said that it was a metaphor for El Salvador. How did this identification come about?

What happened is that there were so many interpretations about the meaning of the Unicorn. So many people asked me about it, trying to understand the mystery (which, I think, is the most beautiful aspect of that text) that at a time when the war in El Salvador was at its peak, I mentioned it to draw attention to what was going on in that country. I tried to establish the connection in a very deliberate fashion, in order to get people to focus their attention on the war that was going on in El Salvador. And it was for that reason that I created the entire fable around the issue of the unicorn.

I think that we've talked about almost everything, although there is one thing that we haven't clarified. . . . Precisely what was it that was so terrible about the Beatles that you said on that television program that led them to kick you out?

Well, I said what I've always said: that for me the Beatles were extremely important musicians. For me, the most important thing that they did was to break down the barrier between so-called popular music and refined or cultured music. Perhaps others had done so before, but the first artists to succeed in this transgression were the Beatles. I also said that I loved their complex arrangements, the way that they had rescued certain folk music forms, and that they had been an important point of reference for me and my work. More or less what I've always said.

2

Antón Arrufat

A Writer Whose Heart Is Still Beating

Few people have experienced the changes in Cuban cultural life more intensely than Antón Arrufat. It is curious that all of this should have happened to an exquisite writer who tried to make his literature into a kingdom in which there lived only imagination and poetry. Reality, however, more stubborn than the desires and wishes of mere mortals, forced itself into Arrufat's life, turning him into a creature besieged by his time, his history, and his circumstances.

He was born in the warm city of Santiago de Cuba and was educated in a Jesuit college. He spent several years in New York during the 1950s and returned to Cuba in 1959. Since then he has lived Cuban cultural life with great intensity. Sometimes this has been as a joyful participant, a simple writer, but he has also been an implacable judge and a victim. His biography thus follows closely the twists and turns along the path of Cuban cultural policy during the revolution. In this process, in essence a savage struggle, Antón has emerged—like Hemingway's famous protagonist—beaten, marked by a thousand scars but never defeated.

Although I have known Antón Arrufat for several years, and I have always taken an interest in the political and cultural conflicts in which he was involved, I have never dared to interview him. I have now had the opportunity to hear from the perspective of this writer about the dramatic events as they unfolded in his life. The cultural process, as it affected him, reveals the contradictory and at times tragic situation of an intellectual who sought only to live and write within the historical and geographical margins of Cuban culture and within the revolutionary process.

Arrufat is enormously talented as a poet, narrator, and dramatist. He is the author of the controversial drama *Los siete contra Tebas* (The Seven against Thebas), censored since 1968 when it was determined to be a counterrevolutionary play. Nowadays, however, Arrufat enjoys public recognition, although for many years he was considered by officials as one of the most controversial protagonists of the island's cultural atmosphere. This label cost him nine years of absolute ostracism. To show how much things have changed in Cuba, it is worth noting that he was awarded the prestigious Carpentier Prize by the Cuban government at the Ninth International Havana Book Fair in February 2000.

Because of this context, I don't believe that it is an exaggeration to describe this interview as exceptional. It is the testimony of a man who, saved from the ravages of hate and resentment, looks over his life. Some fifty years ago, he notes, "To be a writer here was nothing important." Soon afterwards, as his own story shows clearly, it was transformed into a responsibility that swept along mere individuals.

. . .

Can we start with your memories of your youth, your early studies, and the years that you lived in Santiago de Cuba?

I was born there in 1935. I was born under the sign of Leo, which often produces very headstrong individuals who, if they fail, commit suicide. I studied at the Jesuit school until I was eleven years old, and I was already writing by that time. While the priest was lecturing, I wrote a novel about people struggling for independence in the last century. One of the books that most influenced me when I was a child was *La manigua sentimental* (The Sentimental Revolt) of Jesús Castellanos, which nobody cites today. It was somewhat surprising for a boy that young to have read it. I think that my mother gave it to me.

I lived in Santiago until 1947, when we came to Havana. Until that time my father had been a salesman, selling clothes in the province of Oriente. The owner of the business, a Spaniard named Ciriaco Sánchez, sent for him and set him up working in a department store called La Industria, which was on Prado Street beside the Hotel Saratoga. We moved to an apartment above the store. My father later went back to work as a traveling salesman. He was killed in a train accident in 1956.

Is the name Arrufat originally from the Arabic?

No. I thought that it was a Catalán name, but on a trip that I made to

Spain I was told that it was originally from the Aragón area, but that later it had passed to Valencia and then to Castellón de la Plana. My paternal grandfather arrived in Cuba from Sitges, or rather he came in the stomach of his mother, who left from there, and he was born in Santiago de Cuba.

Did the city of Santiago de Cuba have a major impact on your cultural development and with your sense of identifying your origins?

It doesn't have anything to do with my cultural development, although it clearly offers many early memories and life experiences. At the Dolores school, for instance, I learned what it was like to be ordered around and categorized. But I also walked through the streets, I played baseball there, and many of those early experiences are reflected in a couple of my works.

Afterwards I returned to Santiago on several occasions. My mother died in 1953, shortly after the attack on the Moncada garrison, and there was a terrific silence in the city. Around that time my family drifted apart and my father—who had returned to work in Oriente Province because things were not going well in Havana—sent me to live with my uncle and aunt in the old Arrufat house on Heredia Street. I spent a year there and finished my studies at the Sagarra school, which had been founded by a Santiago teacher who had his own ideas about educating children.

Were you particularly religious at the time? Are you now?

While I studied with the Jesuits, I was very religious. I was even an altar boy, and at all the parties and feast days they used to dress me up as the pope. I remember that we used to have large parties at Christmas.

After that early attempt at novel writing, when did you start writing again in a more professional vein?

After that early novel on the struggle for independence, I began to write poetry. The best pieces were written around 1954 or 1955. After arriving in Havana in 1947, I began to meet several writers here. This created a problem at home, since at that time I was finishing high school, and my father wanted me to be a lawyer. One day, after seeing how uninterested I was in my studies and how often I missed classes, he asked me if I preferred to be a lawyer or a writer. I told him that I wanted to be a writer. This idea of becoming a lawyer was some sort of family ambition, one which nobody had been able to achieve.

My father wanted me to save the Arrufat family from the dishonor of not having any lawyers in the family. When I assured him that I wanted to become a writer, he asked me: "How do writers prove their ability?" I answered that it was a matter of time. He then told me that writing paid terribly and had no importance in this country. And he offered me a challenge: I was to write something, which he would then try to publish. He had friends at the newspaper *Diario de la Marina,* and if they agreed to publish it, then we would talk again about my literary vocation. I then wrote a piece about the paintings of Wilfredo Lam, who had just opened an exhibit here.

At that time there was a page for young people at the paper edited by Gastón Baquero. Since my father knew many people with businesses on Muralla Street, he talked with them about the article. And one Sunday it was published. My father then called me, and we sat down at the dining room table. He told me very honestly, "Well, they published your article. Now you can do what you like." That was one of the most profound conversations that I had with my father, with whom I rarely spoke about serious matters, since I had a better relationship with my mother.

In what year, then, did you become a writer, with your father's blessing?

That article came out in 1954. Afterwards I began to publish in several newspapers, like *Excélsior* and the *Diario.* Virgilio Piñera, who was in Argentina at the time, read one of those articles [on Kafka], and wrote to José Rodríguez Feo telling him about this young writer with a very strange name whom he should hire to write for the journal *Ciclón.* Around that time I was writing a ridiculous essay on Rimbaud. I also had several friends who were writers, like Luis Marré, and I often went out with him at night. We would sit down on the Avenida de las Misiones and discuss literature. I used to read a lot, and I already possessed that passion to write that comes from within oneself and that is strengthened when you speak with other writers.

When I finished my essay on Rimbaud, I sent it to a competition organized by *Ciclón.* This occurred after the separation of Lezama and Rodríguez Feo, when Rodríguez had insisted on publishing two issues of the journal written by him alone. The idea was to produce a caricature of *Orígenes,* and in fact Lezama called it the "apocryphal *Orígenes.*" One day Rodríguez Feo called me at my sister's house, where I was living at the time, and asked me to go and see him. When I arrived, part of the future team of writers for *Ciclón* was already gathered: Luis Marré, Manuel Díaz Martínez, Guillermo Cabrera Infante, Daniel Jordán. . . . I can't remember if Severo Sarduy or Calvert Casey were there. Piñera wasn't. That was in December 1954.

After the second issue of the journal, in 1955, I became a writer with the journal. The first piece that I published there was an article on existentialism. At that time I considered myself something of a philosopher. Around that time the composer Natalio Galán, with whom I wrote an opera, cast my horoscope, and when he finished he told me: "It says here that you will not be a philosopher, just a would-be amateur one." Faced with this evidence, I turned my hand to other interests.

Several people have claimed that the 1950s were a sterile period for Cuban culture. What is your opinion?

I personally don't think that there have been any really sterile periods in Cuban culture since the nineteenth century, largely because of the strong Spanish influence. We have a literary continuity, and although there have not always been major international figures, we have always had good writers and poets here. I believe that in the nineteenth century there was a period of somewhat pretentious poetry, but even then, if you study it well, there were two or three important figures.

The 1950s were the gestation period for future literary movements. How can it be termed sterile if it changed so many things in Cuba? Instead, there is a continuity. The revolution expressed, especially in the early years, the frustrated desires of the previous generation. Besides, one should not forget that in the 1950s notable figures like Lezama Lima, Virgilio Piñera, and Alejo Carpentier were writing, Alicia Alonso had started several dance initiatives, and there were painters like Lam, Amelia Peláez, Portocarrero, and Mariano. In the 1950s there was also a fair amount of theater in Cuba, a very strange development in this country. And finally there were many young writers, myself included, who were developing our skills and later would be called "the generation of the fifties." So I do not accept the idea that in the twentieth century there was a sterile period for Cuban culture, much less during the decade that led to the great flourishing of culture in the 1960s.

When did you publish your first book?

My first book was published in 1962 and was called *En claro* (Stating Things Clearly). It was a collection of poetry that I had been writing since 1955. It was published in a rather strange fashion, perhaps because it was the last private edition during those years. Ballina published it in his small collection called *La Tertulia,* in which he had already published some texts and for which Fayad Jamís designed the covers.

This particular publication has a curious story. Ballina first called me to write the prologue for a series of nineteenth-century Cuban poems that he was interested in editing. Several people have seen it as rather strange that I would write a prologue for this particular collection, but at that time it was something that I was interested in, since there was a renaissance of interest in all sorts of Cuban culture. You have to remember that we lived in a country that often overlooked its own cultural talent. Indeed, one of the most important achievements in the spiritual order of the revolution is to have made us examine ourselves once again. In part, the international isolation that began with the U.S. blockade and a number of developments later made us look to our roots. Anyway, returning to Ballina. . . . After I had done the prologue, he proposed publishing a book of my poems in his collection. I had some thirty or forty poems written, and I chose from among them for the book. He then informed me that it would cost some 250 pesos to publish the book. I don't remember if he paid or if I did. I do remember that Raúl Martínez did the cover—it is a white cover with a blue shaded area.

I had gone through a similar experience with the staging of my first play in 1957. I remember hiding behind a tree and jumping out to sell tickets. I now had to do something similar to sell my book to the bookstores. I went to many stores and was almost always told, "This won't sell." I would ask them to accept the book on consignment. They then displayed it, and some even dared put it in their store windows. I used to visit the stores to see if anybody was buying it. Some people did buy it, and slowly the book began to disappear from the bookstores' shelves. With the money that I got from the sales, and some of my own savings, I managed to raise the 250 pesos to pay for the publication costs. The important thing was that it was well received by the critics, and it led to my being considered part of the "generation of the fifties" of Cuban poetry.

Prior to the publication of this collection you had begun to work in the theater?

Yes, in 1957. I already knew Virgilio Piñera, and I had published some poems in *Ciclón* which I had never used in my poetry collection because I didn't really like them. They were in the neoclassical vein, and the first thing that I wrote for the theater was also a neoclassical piece on the Medea myth, imitating the style of Seneca. I wrote it in a small hotel room where I was living on Monte Street, on an old typewriter that was falling to pieces. The only thing remaining from that play is a letter of Rodríguez Feo to Virgilio Piñera. In it he states that I had gone to his house to read him the piece and that I was such an arrogant and proud writer that I wouldn't accept the slightest piece of criticism from him. That I had left abruptly and left him still talking!

Afterwards I wrote *El caso se investiga* (The Case Is Being Investigated) in 1957. I met the theater director Julio Mata, who presently lives in the United States, and he asked me to write a play for him. He wanted to stage Virgilio Piñera's *Falsa alarma* (False Alarm), but since it only lasted an hour, he wanted me to complete the program with another play of about the same length. At that time the theater of the absurd and the works of Ionesco had started to be known, and Julio Mata had staged *The Bald Soprano* and *The Lesson*.

It was a time when the small literary drama groups were being consolidated here. A director and a group of actors would get together almost anywhere and adapt to the available space. And, surprisingly, people came to these small-scale productions. What particularly caught people's attention, naturally, was the sexual element. The first play to be staged was *La ramera respetuosa* (The Respectful Whore), which Morín directed. In one scene the actress comes onstage partially dressed and sits on the bed. This awoke a lot of curiosity, since Cubans are very prudish, somewhat uptight, almost medieval. . . . That continued until the 1961 literacy campaign, when women left their houses and girls went up to the mountains and began to sleep with the peasants.

Returning to the theme, I did write the play that Julio had asked me for. I enjoyed writing it because it is one of my most amusing works. They printed flyers for the debut and placed them in stores throughout the city. They called people on the phone to announce the play, and announcements were published in the local newspapers and cultural bulletins. We even printed some posters, all of course with our own money. Virgilio contributed. I'm not sure where he got the money. I also put in some money, and again I'm not sure where I found it, since at that time I lived on twenty cents that my family gave me. . . .

We tried to sell the tickets ourselves, because at the Lyceum (at the corner of Calzada and Eighth Street), where it was staged, they didn't allow tickets to be sold. It was an elegant club, with cultured ladies, and since they wouldn't allow us to sell tickets on club premises, we had to do so outside to recoup the money that we had spent on staging the play. Virgilio and I hid behind the plants in the garden, and when somebody passed by, such as José Antonio Portuondo, we would jump out in front of him and ask him to buy a ticket. This type of theater was attended by a particular type of audience.

And that's the story of how *El caso se investiga* was staged. It played for two or three days and was savaged by the critics. Luis Amado Blanco and René Leal pulled it to pieces. It's rather strange to note that the next time it was performed, it was well received. To a certain degree it was a rather surprising work in which, when a character asked something, he received a reply that had nothing to do with what had been asked. I imagine that, because it was so different, it surprised many people.

How important for you was the friendship of Virgilio Piñera?

It is curious. He has come to mean more to me since his death than when he was alive. His memory is so important to me. It is clearly more important to me now, which is a curious turn of events. He always told me: "I am twenty years older than you, and I will die first—since that's how nature has decreed it." He was always bothered by the issue of time. Occasionally he denied its very existence, sometimes he affirmed it, and at other times he paid it no attention. He was not the first important writer that I knew, since I had earlier met Lezama Lima, with whom I came to develop a good friendship after several years of dealings with him. But when I met Virgilio in 1955, our friendship started almost immediately. We were both friends of Marré and often went out together—to the theater, art exhibits, or just walks around the city. We used to like to go to a tiny park in front of the church in Guanabacoa, where we would sit down to talk, tell jokes, make fun of everything, or talk about what we were writing at the time.

I never appreciated just how important Piñera was, however, until after his death. I think it was because of the way he dealt with me. He liked to compete in literary terms. He didn't like to present himself as the great teacher, and he never placed himself in the position of lording it over me because of his established reputation. Rather, he treated me like his equal, and through conceding that sense of confidence in me, allowed me to criticize his work. He would then laugh and make fun of me, or he would get angry. Because he insisted on this relation of equality, I never really appreciated just how important he and his work were until after his death.

Besides this, I should also point out what Rodríguez Feo termed in his letter my "arrogance." I can remember how, when I was in school, the priests used to tell me: "Arrogant child, kneel down and pray, and ask forgiveness for your pride." I was a difficult child who neither permitted anything nor pardoned anything either. I must have been exceptionally dogmatic and horribly boring. Nobody was allowed to contradict me. Whenever people tried to contradict me at home, I used to have an attack, literally foaming at the mouth and falling to the floor in convulsions. The living room at my home even had a white circle on the tiled floor caused by my bile. And so then a doctor would come and inject me with a relaxant so that I would calm down. Later that arrogance moderated or became somewhat more restrained; it remained, however, and I still suffer from it. I think that it was because of that pride, and because of the manner in which he dealt with me, that our friendship remained.

But Piñera was like that, not just with me, but with everybody. He always liked to compete, and we young ones reminded him of that aspect. I think that he became livelier when he was with us. He was always concerned with what we were writing and wanted to read our work; he was never indifferent to that. He would ask, "Are you writing anything now? What is it?" And then, of course, you had to tell him about it. He would then ask, "How many pages does it have?" He was always concerned with the size of a work, and it seemed that on the basis of that he judged its significance. And that influence stayed with me, since I always ask people the same thing. He, however, wrote short texts and was always worried about getting writer's block. It was one of his greatest concerns. Besides, he would often tire of one work that he was writing and then start another. Maybe that is why he wrote in so many literary genres and why he left so much of his work unfinished. Any kind of continuous work used to bore him.

Why did you go to New York in 1957?

I went for family reasons. My father died in a train accident, and with the insurance money that they paid—I think that was about 500 pesos—I bought a ticket to New York, where I had a friend who had invited me to visit. I felt very down, very alone at the time. I had nowhere to live in Havana, no home or family. My sister had recently married, and I didn't want to bother her.

I lived in New York for three years. I published some pieces in the newspaper *La Prensa*. I also spent a lot of time with friends like Humberto Arenal and Oscar Hurtado. But I never felt at ease there, because of the question of language. Besides, cultural life is very difficult for a foreigner in that city. It is a very closed world, as is the case with cultural life in general, like in Europe, too, where it is also difficult to get ahead.

What else did you find in that city? How else did it influence you?

Well, really, New York meant a lot to me. For the first time in my life I saw an original painting, since in my time the National Museum was closed and the Museum of Fine Arts had not been finished. When I arrived in New York, I went immediately to the Metropolitan, where I saw the works of Van Gogh that I so admired and that until then I had only seen in reproductions: *Man with Sunflowers* and his self-portrait. For the first time I saw original paintings by Bosco, the famous painting of Saint Anthony. But it was also important to have the experience of living in a really splendid city, in many ways the capital of the twentieth century, with its many theaters and museums, with a truly intense and prodigious lifestyle.

I worked there in a bookstore in the Village that was owned by an extravagant Italian named Gaetano Masa. He was a pleasant fat man who had made his fortune in the business, and he closely resembled the image that one has of nineteenth-century booksellers. His bookstore was thoroughly disorganized, and he seemed to spend the whole day on Fourteenth Street eating hamburgers and hot dogs. People would arrive and say, "Masa, I've written a book." He would then tell them that he'd publish it—before he had even read it! He had a publishing company called Las Américas Publishing where a rather interesting Puerto Rican writer whom I met, Arturo Parrilla, worked as editor.

One day Gaetano proposed to me that I should edit an anthology of Spanish American poetry, and I immediately accepted. After that I worked in his bookstore two or three times a week. Working there actually meant talking with him, allowing him to tell me about his life in Italy. Behind this image of a good-hearted soul, however, there was a shrewd businessman who made a fortune selling books to Columbia University. He wanted the anthology of poetry precisely because he hoped to make a great deal of money selling it to students. I began to prepare the anthology, but never finished because it was interminable. He asked me to begin with Ercilla's "La Araucana" and to continue with Balbuena. I got as far as Sor Juana Inés de la Cruz just as the Cuban Revolution took place, and so I told Gaetano that I was returning to Cuba. . . .

In early 1959, Guillermo Cabrera Infante formed the journal *Lunes de Revolución,* and Virgilio Piñera—who was already working for *Lunes*—wrote to tell me that I had a job there. At that time I did something typical of me: I immediately packed my bags, got on a plane, and came here. I returned to New York a few months later, but only to pack up my books.

What did you find in Cuba when you arrived here in 1959?

I found the beginning of a revolution. For the first time I saw the "bearded ones," the revolutionaries who were all over the place, covered in rosaries and religious medals. I began working almost immediately for *Lunes de Revolución* and fell into the midst of a whirlwind. I took part in the demonstrations and heard many shots being fired. There were still sharpshooters in Havana who shot from the rooftops. It was a magical situation, the birth of something that was seeking to burst forth. Really, they were extraordinary years for me. Everything was changing around me, and I was changing with it. What had been important before no longer was. Morals began to change. People started to support each other, at least in human terms. The mental structures changed, people began to lose interest in money, and you could almost get by without any at all. People also lost interest in the clothes they wore. It was enough to have one pair of pants, a shirt, and a pair of boots. And people liked these changes.

It was a sort of generalized joy. There were long speeches on television. At that time government decisions were made on television, and people sat down at home to see and hear the future changes. There were constant marches in the street. People joined the militias in immense numbers, and there was shooting practice. We were attacking everybody. I personally attacked Lezama in the newspapers and Jorge Mañach, too. I attacked everything that bothered me. There was an enormous freedom to do anything you wanted. And you could use the newspaper, the official newspaper of the July 26 Movement, to attack any figures you wanted, regardless of their prestige. I can imagine how poor Lezama, when he woke up and was told by his wife that there was an attack against him in the revolution's paper, must have trembled. All the power that you can imagine was in our hands, and it was used joyfully and irresponsibly. That gives you a taste of what I lived through in those early years.

What was the importance of Lunes de Revolución for Cuban cultural history?

Well, *Lunes* definitely deserves a proper public study, something that has never been done, and it deserves to be rehabilitated. I know that some attempts have been made at the University of Havana, where there have been some theses on *Lunes,* but it has never been properly evaluated for what it was, namely, one of the great creations of the Cuban Revolution. The revolution has no right to feel embarrassed by it, nor should it abandon *Lunes,* since for the first time in Cuba they printed some five hundred thousand copies of a cultural magazine.

For the first time in Cuban history, every Monday a cultural supplement of eighteen, twenty, twenty-six pages slid under the door with the daily newspaper, dedicated to the best culture of the day. For the first time, contemporary graphic art was made known to the people. You could read a magazine dedicated to Borges, learn about a number of artists who were unknown in Cuba. Not only were they unknown but they were disowned because they expressed an artistic position that was so different in this traditionally prudish, inward-looking society. *Lunes* broke with all of that. As a result, I don't think that there has been a proper appreciation of it. Of course, there are political prejudices that belong to the story of *Lunes,* and not the aftermath of the journal per se, and the difference has to be brought out.

The closing down of Lunes coincides with the opening of publications by the Union of Writers and Artists (UNEAC). Did you then go to work for UNEAC? What was the significance of that organization in the early years of the revolution?

When *Lunes* closed, the Cuban government had already begun the process of institutionalization. In other words, that historic moment of forces that had been unleashed now started to be channeled and organized in various institutions. Behind that process one should also remember the Soviet influence, because I think that the July 26 Movement would never have thought of creating a Union of Writers. We had already published a special issue of *Lunes* on a technical and cultural exhibition at the Museum of Fine Arts that had been visited by thousands of people. That was the beginning of the evident Soviet influence. At that moment the prestige of some important Cuban intellectuals from the old Communist Party, the Partido Socialista Popular (PSP), like Carlos Rafael Rodríguez and Edith García Buchaca, exercised a fair amount of influence over leaders of the July 26 Movement. As you know, Marxist intellectuals are interested in culture and in directing it, as part of the struggle for power, and this has happened in all revolutions.

The old-time militants of the PSP always presented themselves as the leaders with a vision and a solution for any problem. And of course they had the tradition of the Soviet Union behind them. They also had an answer for every issue, every problem, that arose in Cuban culture and in life in general—when often the July 26 Movement had none. The foundation of their approach was to institutionalize and Sovietize the country.

For them, *Lunes* was a loose cannon, far too liberal in its outlook, and the opportunity to close down the magazine came as a result of the film *P.M.,* which to a certain degree seemed to criticize the incipient institutionalization of national cinema under the influence of ICAIC. That episode led to the end of *Lunes* and the creation of the Union of Writers. According to the Soviet model, it was necessary to unite all forces in a single institution and then hire a representative of that tendency, someone with prestige, to direct it. In the Cuban case, that person was Nicolás Guillén.

And so the closing down of *Lunes* was the consequence of the historical and political development of the country. It was not simply the decision of a bureaucrat or a political leader but the result of all the conditions that I have outlined. Pressure from the United States increased, and the relationship with the Soviet Union developed. The Soviets made several demands, one of which was that culture should pass into the hands of their representatives, like Edith García Buchaca. She had published a manual entitled *La superestructura* (The Superstructure) in which she provided an analysis of culture in a socialist society from the most elementary Marxist perspective. This manual provided some swift replies to a variety of problems, and those replies were interesting and provocative. Moreover, since there were no other alternatives put forward, her approach began to be implemented.

When Lunes closed down, did you go immediately to work on the journal Casa de las Américas?

No, I had already been working there. I founded that journal in 1960. I was happy to do so, as we did everything at that time. One day I was buying some old books on Monserrate Street when Fausto Massó came in. He was a very good friend of Haydée Santamaría, who was president of the Casa de las Américas cultural institute. They were both originally Catholics, connected to the revolutionary movement of García Bárcena, and Fausto had been invited to work at Casa shortly after. Fausto and I were also good friends, and the day we met, he asked me: "Why don't we set up a cultural journal at Casa de las Américas?" "Let's do it," I replied. That's the way it was in those days: An idea came to you, and it was immediately put into practice. We went to see Haydée and offered her the idea. She agreed and told us to do the journal.

You were one of the first writers to be censored in Cuba, because of your play Los siete contra Tebas. Why do you think that this work was censored, and why is it still censored more than thirty years later?

A small piece of the history needs to be understood. The play was going to be staged at Teatro Estudio by Armando Suárez del Villar, who asked me to do Esquilo's version of the work. I began to do so, but as I was working, it became something far more personal, until it ended up being my work with certain fragments from Esquilo—what today would be called "intertextuality." So then I gave the play to Armando, but Vicente Revuelta fell in love with my version and wanted to direct it. There then developed a major struggle in the group, since Armando wanted to retain it. Vicente even came to talk with me, but I refused to let him have it. It was at this time that I entered it in the UNEAC literary competition, where Raquel Revuelta, one of the members of the jury, began a campaign against the play.

She went to visit political and cultural leaders of the country and read them fragments that she thought were against the revolution. In general she created a rather negative environment. In the same literary competition there was also Heberto Padilla's collection of poetry, *Fuera del juego.* It was said by some that Padilla and I had agreed (in this country everything seems to have been agreed before things actually take place) that we would both enter the competition and then cause a political scandal. In reality there was no agreement between us, and it was only afterwards that we found out that we were competing.

This all takes place against the background of a major controversy raging between Lisandro Otero and Padilla, who had published an article in the journal *El Caimán Barbudo* in which he praised Guillermo Cabrera Infante and criticized Otero's novel *Pasión de Urbina.* There then followed a series of accusations and rebuttals. It's important to remember that at this time Lisandro was the private secretary of José Llanusa, the minister of education who was also in charge of the National Council for Culture, since the Ministry of Culture had not yet been founded.

I really can't explain what the important political matters facing the nation were that might have caused this to happen. These things are clearly small in a nation that is so eminently political as Cuba is, where political questions tend to decide things. So I think that behind this minor cultural battle there must have been some significant political factor that allowed culture to be used at a given moment in the political struggle for power. Similar developments have occurred on several occasions. Don't forget that in a socialist country like ours, culture is not an insignificant sector. Rather, it is an important part of the nation.

What has happened to the work since then?

The same as before. . . . It was not staged, it was published in a sham fashion, it was not sold, and it was kept hidden. Whenever a theater group seeks to stage it, something happens and it is not staged. And this hasn't happened with just one group. An actor once changed it into a sort of monologue, but it couldn't be put on then, either. Somebody wanted to write a graduate thesis on it for the Higher Institute of Art, until the professors recommended against it.

At this stage I still can't explain it completely. I do believe, however, that there are often minor or insignificant matters that can influence enormously the course of events. For instance, I can think of the moment when César Borgia planned a coup d'état, but decided against it because he had a cold. To develop this image, I think that somebody has a cold with my play.

And, of course, the significance of the cultural and political event in which all of this explodes, the Padilla affair, is important. What was the meaning of that affair?

It meant, and I believe that it still means, the first dramatic confrontation between literature and the dogmatism of certain bureaucrats involved in cultural matters and the Communist Party. It was the first time that certain individuals who were in charge of cultural matters found themselves faced with an issue that they didn't know how to resolve. They ignored the advice of wise observers like Alfredo Guevara, who suggested that they leave well enough alone, since in taking up the issue they were lending credence to writers and could turn them into important cultural figures. But they handled the matter crudely, with a definite lack of subtlety in understanding that literature is not a direct reflection of reality, and employed their Marxist orthodoxy. They created a situation that they could not handle, either with skill or with hypocrisy. After this incident, I believe that some of them have learned their lesson: situations which could have developed into other Padilla affairs have either been avoided or have been ignored in a silent form of censure. And above all, the bureaucrats have spoken with the writers and in general have had a far less contemptuous relationship with them than we encountered.

For example, in my case no leaders ever told me why they objected to my work. Instead, they broke all communication with Padilla and with me. There was never the slightest effort at conversation or negotiation. Not even the slightest lobbying. It was simply conveyed to us that we had committed an error and that they had to punish us, making an example of us as a warning to others. Yet that "punishment" brought an ideological scandal upon the revolution, when several writers and artists who supported the revolution, leftists and in some cases Marxists, openly opposed this approach to resolving problems.

As a result of this, you were marginalized. Did this come immediately after the UNEAC literary competition or after the Padilla affair?

No, it came later. After the prize was awarded to *Los siete contra Tebas,* I kept working at Teatro Estudio, and there was a general silence. It seemed as if everything was going to be worked out: They weren't going to talk with us, but nevertheless things were going to be resolved. From that point on, Padilla's conduct was not very intelligent. He was very angry about his treatment. He began to receive foreigners, to give interviews, and in general to create a situation that caused a great deal of concern and bother to the country's political leadership. At one point he was arrested and detained in Villa Marista for a month.

So, just when it looked as if things were going to be resolved, that suddenly changed dramatically. At that point the National Congress on Education was held. (Later it was amended to become the Congress of Education and Culture.) Originally it was to be a conference of school teachers, but it soon changed into a forum where directives were established that would rule the cultural and even moral life of the country for many years. Homosexuality was discussed there, for example. Measures were taken against several artists and writers, and an ostracism began that would last ten years.

How was it decided that you would work in a municipal library?

One day I was summoned to meet Luis Pavón Tamayo, who was president of the National Council of Culture. He did not meet with me, however, since to do so would be to recognize that I was important. A minor bureaucrat, Armando Quesada, received me and announced that I was to stop working at Teatro Estudio and transfer to the National Library. However, the director of the National Library thought that, given the problems that I had experienced, it would be scandalous of me to work in such a busy place, and he asked for a month to consider the appointment. Finally they phoned me to say that I had been assigned to work at the municipal library in Marianao, a suburb of Havana that is fairly distant. I went to the library, where I was received by the director, who sent me to work in the warehouse, tying up bundles of journals with twine.

I wasn't allowed to answer the telephone there or receive any visitors, much less write. One day Virgilio Piñera came to visit me, and shortly afterwards they read the riot act to me. I remember that I worked in a tiny department of the library, constantly watched over by the director. One day I got tired and took a break, leaving the library to walk around the building in order to get some fresh air. When I returned, the director called me and told me that I couldn't do that until I had finished my eight hours of work.

My stay there left a major impression on me. When I finished work, they checked the wastepaper basket to see if I had written anything. If anything ever went wrong in the library, I was automatically to blame. The library was on the official route from the airport, and so whenever an official foreign delegation came to visit Cuba, I was sent home, since I couldn't be in the library when they passed by.

On one occasion, some papers were burned in a small shed in the garden, and immediately I was accused of having burned them. The cleaning staff said that some kids had been playing with matches and had burned the old newspapers. And, besides, I was at home when this occurred. All of this was told to me later by the librarians. As time went by, I became good friends with them, and they paid no attention to the rule that they weren't to talk with me. They realized that I was completely inoffensive and that there was tremendous overkill in the manner in which I was treated. It was like using a powerful crane to lift up a single cigarette. In the end I was selected as an outstanding worker in the library and was given permission to study at the university. There I took courses in scientific information, studying in the afternoons and evenings.

Did they ever say why you were being marginalized in this way? And why did they decide to rehabilitate you?

I was never told why I was sent to spend nine years working at that library. There was no trial, no tribunal. No accusation, not even any incriminating documents. I was simply notified of decisions, often by phone. After I had spent nine years without any explanation, I wrote a letter to Fidel Castro. Twenty-two days later, I received a reply, signed by his secretary, in which I was told to go to the Ministry of Culture. That letter caused things to be turned upside down, and a few days later I was appointed to work for the journal *Revolución y Cultura*. I was to work there as an editor, but could not publish for one year. Then in 1981 my novel *La caja está cerrada* (The Chest Is Closed) was published. My rehabilitation had begun, and it has continued to this day.

How would you characterize the 1970s?

From the point of view of culture policy, it was an absolute disaster. They achieved none of their goals. They did not even create a tradition of children's literature! After the Congress they encouraged the development of children's literature, and Cuban writers were encouraged to write short stories for children. A number of freshly minted fictitious writers suddenly appeared. It was also the time when the genre of the detective novel developed, a form of literature that was written on the orders of the Ministry of the Interior. They thought that in this way they would be able to create a literature that would reflect Cuban reality and would displace earlier literature. This failed, too, because any literature ordered by the state is almost always a failure.

Which other writers were marginalized during those years?

There were many. Some that come to mind are Lezama Lima, Virgilio Piñera, Pablo Armando Fernández, Miguel Barnet, Reynaldo González, Abelardo Estorino, Eduardo Heras León, Norberto Fuentes, Padilla, Delfín Prats, Raúl Martínez, César López.

Were you ever offered any form of apology?

Here in Cuba, errors are rectified in silence. Without a doubt, the matter has been rectified. After the Ministry of Culture was founded, things improved under Armando Hart. Some matters became more flexible, more intelligent. I was slowly rehabilitated, I started to publish, they gave me several awards, and I was allowed to travel abroad again.

What toll did those years have upon Lezama Lima and Piñera?

Virgilio Piñera lived as a translator and worked at what used to be called the National Press, where he translated from the French original African novels. Lezama hardly left his house, because he was so overweight and walking produced dizziness. He received many people at his home, myself included. He talked a lot and slowly wrote *Oppiano Licario,* which he never finished. Piñera and I went out a lot, to the theater, to lectures, everywhere—even when we were completely marginalized. Something very strange happened at that time: Whenever I went to those events, people fled. Nobody would speak with me, apart from my most loyal friends. It was as if I had the plague, and it was one of the most amusing experiences of my life. After I was rehabilitated, those people who used to run away wanted to renew their friendship with me, but I refused to do so.

What evidence is there that things started to change in the 1980s?

Many writers and artists who had been excluded because they were homosexuals, which was considered a political aberration, were again allowed to develop their cultural pursuits. Of the two of us with major problems, Padilla and myself, he decided to go and I stayed. The letter I mentioned earlier stated that I would be allowed to participate in the literary life of my country. The 1980s were indeed a period of public rehabilitation. People started to give lectures, to publish, and especially to travel abroad again. One of the worst things was not being able to travel, something which has been forgotten because now Cubans travel so easily. Intellectuals also began to publish abroad, something which we do now very freely and without any consequences. Before, however, you could get into serious difficulties.

At that time you could only publish through official UNEAC channels and only if you were selected by the Union. And the articles were almost always published in the socialist countries. If anybody had published abroad, even if they weren't in a situation like mine, they would have been reprimanded and would have received a visit from a member of the Ministry of the Interior. As a result, it was virtually impossible for Cubans to publish abroad. Only major figures like Soler Puig or Carpentier, official representatives of Cuban culture, were allowed to publish with western publishing houses.

Is it possible to live in Cuba and publish abroad without restrictions?

This freedom which we enjoy now started with Cuban painters. They were the first to be allowed to travel and exhibit their works abroad and to have commercial relations with galleries in capitalist countries. Many had complained to the Ministry of Culture about their difficulties. An intelligent solution was then found, which allowed them—indeed, encouraged them—to exhibit their work wherever they liked and to live abroad if they so desired. Since then, everything has begun to be significantly liberalized, and now writers can do the same.

In this sense I believe that Abel Prieto has been a providential man for Cuban culture. He has been able to implement the cultural goals of the revolution with tremendous intelligence, but in a wise, subtle, and even spiritual way. When he was president of UNEAC, many things improved. Cultural life in Cuba was renovated, and it became possible to debate ideas, as a free space to express oneself returned. That and many more things are the result of his contribution. Now that he is minister of culture, he has intensified and developed his earlier work at UNEAC.

Have the harsh experiences of those years had any influence on your literature?

Once Salvador Redonet said something to me that left a profound impression: "You have created your own world." And I think that he is right, that I have created my own world, and that my literature (what I have been able to write, which is not that much) has been undertaken largely as a work of imagination. The relationship that it might possibly have with reality is so labyrinthine that at times even I have no idea what it might be!

Is it fair to say that now the levels of censorship and self-censorship in Cuban literature have decreased?

It is obvious that they have decreased. Now you find references to Cuban reality that would never have been allowed before. This form of conditioned freedom is something that has been won in recent years. There is no absolute freedom. It would be naive to think that there can be absolute freedom, whether it be in a socialist country or a capitalist one. But this form of conditioned freedom has been gaining space and is increasingly greater. In the cinema and theater, for example, which are a forum for popular concerns to be raised, we see themes treated which before could never have been expressed. A film like *Fresa y chocolate* (Strawberry and Chocolate) could never have been filmed in the 1960s or, for that matter, in the 1970s or 1980s. Self-censorship, which is the result of censorship, was such an unconscious reflex, so integrated into the consciousness of the artist, that these ideas would never even have occurred to them. We all worked with the assumptions that society had provided us with, and those same assumptions were so deeply embedded that we produced our work without thinking that there were other zones of reality or thought that we could deal with.

At the most difficult moments of this official shunning, did you ever consider leaving Cuba?

No. This is my country and always shall be. Here I have lived and will die. If by some chance I should die during one of my trips abroad, I would ask that my remains be brought back and buried in this land. I want to be close to the great Cuban writers who lie here, such as Lezama and Piñera. I ask for nothing more. I know that they will allow me to die here. Once Julio Cortázar said to me, "Look, Antón, what happens with me is that here they chew me up, but they don't swallow me." Something similar to that has happened with me. And now they are chewing me up and have started to swallow me. I think that for the first time this socialist society has realized that a man of letters can live here, a writer whose only goal is to write literature, nothing else, not even have a direct relationship with the surrounding reality. . . . I imagine that if my life can be of any use to others it is because I have created that space, one which others can also occupy.

Do you believe that one can talk about Cuban exile culture? For example, the literature of Cuban exiles that is produced abroad now, is that an independent phenomenon, or is it a part of Cuban literature?

I don't believe that there is a Cuban exile culture. One can only have a national culture in a particular land and within the limits of a country. There are Cuban writers and artists who express themselves through their work while living in exile, and some have produced fine work. Sooner or later, this work will be assimilated by the national culture and integrated into it, and in many cases this is already happening. As a result, it doesn't matter that it be independent from national culture, but rather that it be an expression of the situation which the same culture has created, and especially it is concerned with what has happened in Cuba. If, for example, Reynaldo Arenas writes his memoirs, that is a direct consequence of what occurred here in Cuba. It is a consequence, a rather adverse one at that, of all that happened to him, but at the end of the day it is a consequence. As a result, it is a work that expresses Cuban life and the influence that it can exercise upon the imagination of a writer.

Among recent Cuban literature, what genres, works, or figures seem most interesting to you?

I think that here in Cuba we are in the midst of some major developments, especially in the narrative. Although we have good poets, I think that we have excellent narrators. Many of them specialize in the short story, but there is also an initial movement toward the novel that will produce positive results.

I am working with some of these young writers. I have been trying to encourage them to see literature as a supreme treasure, an area in which they should create a work of their imagination, where art should not be a substitute for anything—be it religion, ideology, or science. Rather, it has to be seen for its intrinsic value. I find this interest in young writers nowadays, and I believe that it is also the consequence of the development of Cuban life.

There are many young people, ranging from fifteen to forty years, with great promise. Cuban literature, though, has always been full of such promise, and often this potential has not been realized. That may also be the consequence of the nature of living in a country that is underdeveloped in social and economic terms. You can also see the same phenomenon in major figures such as Lezama, Piñera, and Carpentier. All had a certain moment in their work when it appeared that a major work was about to appear, only to have this potential disappear. José Martí once made an extraordinary observation: "If the country doesn't grow, neither can I." Perhaps this position helps to explain why some young writers become frustrated with their work. Maybe, too, this is a rather naive claim, and something similar happens around the world. Sometimes people become wrapped up in their surrounding reality and as a result can see only that reality.

It is worth noting the current boom of Cuban literature in Spain and Mexico and what could also happen at any moment in the United States. I think that there is a good ten years to go for Cuban literature to awaken interest. In part it is the same interest that our country also provokes abroad. This country is extremely attractive for many reasons, as are its writers and artists.

Which sector of your work do you feel most satisfied with? Which works in particular do you consider the most pertinent, and of all your work, which book is your favorite?

Whenever I have published a book of poems, both the critics and my friends—who have been my worst critics—have stated that I am a better dramatist. Whenever I have staged a play, my friends the dramatists have told me that I am an excellent poet. In other words, I have received opposing views on my work. It seems to me that this intention to be a writer in a variety of genres will remain as my legacy. I have tried to write literature, and I say so with modesty.

Borges used to say that his was a vast and expansive literature, which I always found amusing, since he was a writer whose longest stories were never more than ten pages in length. I would never dare to claim that I had produced a vast literary legacy, although I do think that my work should be judged as a whole. In some cases I have tried to encourage the different genres of my work to help each other, to talk with each other and mix, in an attempt to wipe out limits and borders between them. That was my intention. It is possible, though, that such a mixture will not be well received in the history of literature.

I believe I have written some poems that will last, one or two works for the theater, among them *La zona cero* (Zero Zone), which is my favorite and which has never been staged. Perhaps one or two short stories and the same number of essays. Nothing else, really. In all, you could produce a useful anthology of my work of some two hundred pages. My favorite work is *¿Qué harás después de mí?* (What Will You Do after Me?), a collection of short stories. And finally, I would love to see *Los siete contra Tebas* staged at some point. I hope that this happens before my death. And if it happens after my death, I will also feel pleased.

In recent years, in addition to artistic respect, you have also received widespread recognition. Do you believe that this is a reward for your tenacity, for your resistance all these years?

Yes, they are a reward for resistance. Someone once said, "In this country it is the writer whose heart is still beating who is right." I believe that my heart has continued beating. Fortunately, the time has come when this respect can be shown and I can enjoy it while I am still alive.

3

Alicia Alonso

Living on the Tips of Her Toes

Because I feel nervous, I reach the offices of the Ballet Nacional de Cuba early. In many ways, an interview with Alicia Alonso is a meeting with a myth. She is far more than a dancer. She is the Prima Ballerina Assoluta, acclaimed by audiences throughout the world. She is the amiable yet tough-as-nails creator of this company, and for five decades she has nurtured it from its humble origins to its current status as one of the most respected ballet companies in the world.

To pass the time, I stroll through the courtyard of the beautiful Vedado building and spend some time watching a group of ballerinas rehearsing. The huge room in this mansion where they are practicing badly needs a coat of paint, and their outfits seem somewhat old and frayed. The overwhelming impression, however, is of the incredible grace and vitality of these young ballerinas, who are rehearsing a complex piece from an upcoming ballet.

When I am ushered into Alonso's office, I feel I have entered a museum, a sanctuary off-limits to all but the anointed. There is little light, and the colonial style of the immense room combines harmoniously with the souvenirs and artifacts of a career as long and as successful as that of Alicia Alonso. This office has something about it of a sacred place, an atmosphere that is complemented by the presence of this living legend. I notice immediately, however, that both sacred places and human myths are also affected by the implacable dictatorship of time. Then I see that the office also contains a modern hospital bed and some other equipment, made of shining steel, more appropriate for a physiotherapy department. Alicia Alonso has been virtually blind much of her life, she suffers from back problems, and she moves around in a wheelchair. But she continues to fight, just as she did throughout her adult dancing career, despite her blindness—and four major operations on her eyes. Alicia Alonso overcame these limitations, which would undoubtedly have terminated the career of another dancer, through her extraordinary willpower and determination. Instead she continued dancing, following some internal rhythm and sensitivity for ballet that virtually no other human being has ever possessed.

When they show me into her office, Alonso is sitting at her massive desk, rigid, shoulders straight, her gaze to the side. She reminds me of a Hollywood actress from the 1930s. One can see clearly her physical fragility, but one can also sense the strength of her battling spirit: the longest-living legend of the world of international ballet is putting on a show at which I am the only spectator.

Alicia Alonso received me with grace and refinement. While we spoke she never once left her role. The cordial, diplomatic tone was omnipresent—although it was not capable of hiding the earthy strength that still drives this 76-year-old woman, as hard as a rock and as fragile as a flower.

. . .

First of all, thank you for allowing me to interview you. I would like to begin with some information on your artistic training. When you first studied ballet, why did you not study Spanish dance, which was so popular in Cuba at that time?

Well, that is precisely what I did study first, and it started when I was seven years old and went to Spain with my father. He was an army veterinarian, commissioned to go to Spain and buy horses for breeding here. He bought a large number of Arabian horses. He took all his daughters to Spain with him. Altogether there were four of us, and I was the youngest. While we were there, my grandfather, who was Spanish, asked us to learn some local dances so that we could then teach them here in Cuba. So, as you can see, the first dances that I learned were Spanish, and I learned them in Spain.

When I returned to Cuba, I registered in a private club where they had opened a ballet school. It was there that I took my first ballet classes.

I can remember so clearly that first class. I was eight or nine years old at the time. I enjoyed dancing more than anything else in the world. The worst punishment that my parents could inflict was to take away my ballet class.

How was the profession of a ballerina seen at that time?

It was definitely not an appropriate position for a young lady. In "decent" families, as we used to say back then, in wealthy families, it was simply not considered acceptable. Neither ballet nor anything related to dance was deemed appropriate for people from that social class. We began this interest in ballet through the class given at that private club. Everything started with a simple exercise, an example of art, like someone learning the piano. They also opened an acting school, another in music, and we students were all members of the Sociedad Pro-Arte Musical, as it was called. There I learned everything. According to the teachers, I was very good in the acting classes, but I preferred ballet. I took classes in guitar, acting, and ballet.

Do you remember the first time that you put on your dancing slippers?

Of course! It was for the story of Cinderella. The problem was that there simply were no ballet slippers. As a result we had to learn ballet with running shoes. There were simply no ballet slippers of any kind. But there was the daughter of a diplomat here who did have these proper ballet slippers, which he had bought in Italy. When they left, she left the slippers for anybody who could use them. One day I arrived for a class and found all my classmates discussing them. Everybody had already tried them on, but they didn't fit anybody. So then a friend of mine said, "Alicia, these slippers are no use to any of us. We can't stand the pain. Why don't you try them on?" So I picked up the slippers, took out the cotton that they'd stuffed in, and put my feet in. I stood on my tip-toes and then ran out shouting, "Look, Mom, I can stand on my tip-toes." And I didn't take them off for quite some time.

What was the level of ballet here in the 1930s and 1940s? And why did you decide to study in the United States?

I continued studying here in Cuba for several years. But then I married very young [in her midteens], and it was at that time we went to the United States. It was in the United States that I studied with Alexandra Fedórova and an Italian teacher, Enrico Zanfretta. So it was there that I studied the two schools, the old Russian approach and the Italian. They were marvelous teachers, and I learned a great deal from them. Later, of course, one begins to add elements from one's own cultural tradition. But at that time I learned the method, the basic ingredients of ballet. Later I put together the dressing for this ballet salad, using strictly Cuban materials. That "salad dressing" which I added reflected my own culture, my traditions—of which I feel extremely proud.

How did you come to work in Broadway musicals? I read, for example, that in 1938 you had worked in Great Lady and then Stars in Your Eyes.

I danced on Broadway just at the beginning of my career in the United

States, because at that time there weren't any major professional ballet companies there. My husband [dancer Fernando Alonso] had to move there for health reasons, since the Cuban climate affected him badly. His doctors had recommended that he move to a colder climate, and as a result we went to the United States, where I continued to dance. And that's how I came to dance in the musicals there, since that was basically all there was for an aspiring dancer at that time.

You should also remember that there were many wonderful dancers in the United States who performed in musicals. They were colleagues of ours, and we all developed our talents together, while we were dancing on Broadway. From these origins there emerged the Ballet Theater, known today as the American Ballet Theater. It was the first professional ballet company in the United States, and we formed it while we were dancing on Broadway. It was an extremely important company, because it was practically the center of the corps de ballet at that time.

Is it true that the show business impresarios wanted you to change your name?

Absolutely. At that time Latin names like Alicia Alonso weren't considered flashy enough. Not at all. And as a result they wanted me to use something exotic like Alonsova, clearly a Russian name. But I refused. Then two or three years later they wanted me to change my name to Alice and to adopt a surname that sounded a little more American. I always rejected these overtures, though, because I am simply Alicia Alonso and nothing else.

Was there any racism against Latins who danced at that time?

At that time there was. It was impossible for many to imagine a Latin woman dancing classical ballet. They thought that Latins, and especially Cuban women, could only dance the rumba. But that was not the case, just in the United States. I remember, for example, that once when I went to England as the prima ballerina, a journalist came up to me and told me that I was very brave to dance the role of Giselle. I replied that he was mistaken, because it was not brave to do so. On the contrary, I told him, since the British appreciate ballet so much and have seen *Giselle* performed so many times, it was precisely in Britain that I had to dance this ballet and to allow the audience there to judge the quality of the various performances.

Did you ever consider the idea of staying in the United States and pursuing your career there?

Not at all. Never. And it was not as if there were opportunities to dance ballet here in Cuba, because here there was nothing, apart from some classes for children. I had many opportunities in the United States. For instance, I joined a small company called the American Ballet Caravan. Actually, rather than a ballet company, it consisted of groups that came together to dance in a particular venue. Today it has developed into the New York City Ballet. While I was a member of that company, the influence of the Russian ballet was very notable.

I remember that I had signed a contract once for a monthlong tour in the interior of the United States with the Ballet Caravan when I was approached by another company and asked to join them. I spoke with Lincoln, who was the director of the Ballet Caravan, and asked his advice. He told me, "This is not a regular ballet company. We are offering you the chance to join our company so that you can develop your professional career. However, if you want to change to be with the other company, I'll tear up your contract, if that is your wish." I thought that his gesture was a very noble one, and so I told him that I would stay with them. And when I returned from the tour, the Ballet Theater was already in the process of becoming established. I was then invited to become part of that company.

When did you first dance the role of Giselle, the role that made you famous?

That happened in 1943. I was dancing at the Metropolitan. All of the tickets for our performances had been sold, largely because it had been announced that Alicia Markova, a very famous ballerina, was to interpret the role of Giselle. She became ill, however, and none of the other ballerinas wanted to try and take on the role. I was then asked if I dared to attempt the role, and I replied that I would like to. By this time I had been dancing both in the corps de ballet and as a soloist. But getting ready for the lead role was extraordinarily difficult. I worked so hard and spent every day dancing and rehearsing at the Metropolitan studio. Every day, from morning to night. The only time I left the theater was at night, to go home to bed. After a week of this I finally felt comfortable with the role. And so, for the first time in my life, I danced the role of Giselle.

Since then I have danced the role on innumerable occasions. And you know what? Every time that I have danced this part I have found something new in it.

The role of Giselle is extremely important to me. I remember that, when I saw it for the first time, it made a lasting impression. I adored it! Its romantic style is particularly marked and therefore needs to be studied very carefully. And what a beautiful story! Since the very first time that I saw it, *Giselle* has always been a story that has moved me tremendously. When I entered the Ballet Theater to dance, I had already had one major operation because of problems with my sight. And Giselle was the first role that I had danced since the operation. And this was a leading role, in a major production. . . .

When I came back to dance after the operation, and after suffering for so long with my sight, it was like a magical dream for me. So, as you can see, the role of Giselle became something very important for me, in my history and in my life. As I already mentioned, it was the first time that I had danced as the principal ballerina and after a major operation and after the doctors had told me that I would never be able to dance again.

It was also a role that I had dreamed of dancing ever since the first time that I had seen it. And I had the chance to play it! I played the role in a production of the Ballet Nacional de Cuba in Paris, where it received the Grand Prix. As you can see, the ballet *Giselle* is a very important part in my life in historical and artistic terms. And it is also extremely important in the life of the Ballet Nacional de Cuba.

Would you describe the origins of ballet in Cuba? Let's go back to the 1930s and the ballet school set up by the Sociedad Pro-Arte Musical. What were its objectives?

Very simply, to construct a building where the young girls could learn to move elegantly and with grace.

It was over fifty years ago, in 1948, that the Ballet Alicia Alonso was formed in Cuba. When you returned to Havana from working in the United States, what did you find here in the way of ballet?

At that time there was no interest here in Cuba in developing the ballet. Period. You should also remember that, while I worked in the United States, I came back here to work whenever I had any free time. And then in 1948, I had to import dancers from the United States and Latin America to dance in my company. Why? Because there were no parents in Cuba who would allow their daughters to become professional dancers. I managed to find three or four and trained them so that they could participate in the company. So we created our first ballet company, which we called the Ballet Alicia Alonso, and then took the company touring that same year, 1948. And that is the beginning of the ballet in Cuba.

In North America and Europe, ballet has always been seen as an example of high culture. Was the same true for Cuba in the 1940s and 1950s?

What you have to bear in mind is that the Cuban people have always respected and liked dancing. We are a people who express our joy by means of the dance. We simply like dancing. And as a result, as soon as people here had the opportunity to see the ballet that we performed, it took off right away. Many years ago it was said—as is said throughout the world—that in order to appreciate ballet properly, it is necessary to have a strong cultural background. I disagree. What we have shown is that, for ballet to appeal and to be accepted, what is needed is for the audience to be human and to be sensitive to the dance. I believe that all human beings need art. And among the various arts, one of those that can be appreciated most quickly is dance.

In the 1950s, as you were establishing the company in Cuba, did you run into any prejudices against male dancers? Or black dancers?

Of course. You have to understand that to find black Cubans to dance was extremely difficult at that time. Many people thought that when women became ballerinas they lost their sense of decorum, their dignity. Indeed, when women learned to dance ballet, they were supposed to do so without sweating, since sweating was considered something dirty. . . .

And so the very first task that we faced was to raise the awareness of our people, to show them—men and women, white and black—that they all could participate in the ballet. That process only started after the revolutionary victory of 1959.

Could you comment on the interest in ballet that began to develop in 1959? How was contact established with the revolutionary government?

We were in constant communication with the revolutionary movement, and we supported it any way that we could. Our contact was my doctor, who went up to the Sierra Maestra to fight against Batista. When he went to the mountains, he took with him a detailed plan of the ballet project, including the kind of school that we needed and our plans once the Batista dictatorship had been overthrown. He handed all this over to Fidel. And after the revolutionary victory, one day they told me that he had come to visit me. At that time he asked me simply, "What do you need to form the company and develop the school?" And that's how it all began.

I have read that the Batista government tried to co-opt your ballet company, and eventually cut funding to it.

That is completely correct. He made a proposal to us. Whenever there were protests by the students against the government, or if there was a major public disturbance, he wanted me and the members of our company to give a performance to distract attention. It was a diversionary tactic, to get us to dance. In other words, he wanted us to entertain, to distract, and to cover up what was happening here in Cuba. They offered me money to do this, but I refused. They tried to buy off the ballet, and our response was to stop dancing. In fact, at one point I stated publicly that I would not dance in Cuba while Batista's troops were persecuting and assassinating people in the streets.

What were the first steps that you took in 1959?

The very first step was to go to various orphanages and select a number of young boys with the right physical and artistic qualities, move them to a residence, find teachers for them, and give them the complete classical education so that they could become the male dancers in the company. All of this, of course, took place with the support of the state. And after that, we began all the necessary work for the creation of our national school.

But how could you develop this sensitivity toward ballet among the people? Wasn't it a task that required a great deal of time?

It was not easy. But we have been extraordinarily successful. In 1998 we celebrated our fiftieth anniversary, fifty years precisely in that process of teaching people about ballet. I personally have spent some sixty years talking about the ballet and the need for a school to train people in its arts. In 1959 we started a series of tours around the island, continuously, talking about ballet. The revolution gave us many opportunities to visit many workplaces, to explain the nature of ballet, give demonstrations, speak about the life and training of a ballerina. As a result of this intense preparation, our people understand the ballet well. And today we have an excellent school where we have wonderful dancers, male as well as female.

How many male dancers are there in the Ballet Nacional de Cuba?

About forty.

And do you know what percentage of the Ballet's members are black?

Here we count our dancers not according to their ethnic roots but according to their artistic talents. But since you raise the question, it is important to emphasize how difficult this process of integrating dancers from different racial backgrounds was before 1959. It was inconceivable at that time that black people would participate in the ballet. We have changed that way of thinking. You will not find any professional company anywhere in the world that has the same number of black members as we do in our company.

How would you assess the evolution of relations during these past four decades between the Ballet Nacional de Cuba and the state? Have there been moments of friction?

We are always in a position of asking the government for more. And when the government can, it meets our requests; when they don't have the money, they can't. But they have not interfered in the management of the company. They have never placed limits on the number of dancers that we can have in the company. Never. Any talented dancers that I see, we hire for the ballet company. The state pays our expenses: the salaries, the maintenance of our facilities, the school's infrastructure. And they have been very supportive.

What have been the most difficult moments for the Ballet? In particular, what impact has the current economic crisis of the "Special Period" had for the company?

It has had a major impact, since maintaining a company of this size is not easy. Our ballerinas, for example, come to rehearsals on bicycles. However, government support has been constant, even at the worst moments of the crisis, and we have not had to reduce the number of people who work in the company.

One of the characteristics of Cuban culture during the last few years is that artists have had to look abroad for employment opportunities. Has the same been true of the Ballet Nacional de Cuba?

Yes, and it has happened in several cases. Some of our dancers now have major roles with various international companies: the Royal Ballet, the Ballet Theater, the Vienna Opera, and several others. I am proud that we are able to share this talent, because artists are like trees: they have their roots deep in their own soil, but their fruit is shared by everybody. That's the way it should be.

But doesn't it act as a negative influence among the ballerinas who remain here to work if they see colleagues working abroad part of the year who have greater financial resources?

Not at all. In fact, the reverse is true. There are several people who want to return here to work. And they do come back and dance in our company.

Given the new economic circumstances, what do you see as the most important challenges for the Ballet Nacional de Cuba to overcome in the future?

First of all, we need to dance better, because one should always strive for perfection. It is obvious that nobody can ever attain it, because perfection does not exist. However, the human condition is such that we always seek goals beyond our capability. We also need to develop our choreography. We always need to work on this. I think that the ballet world in general needs more choreographers, since there is a great scarcity of people with this talent.

Since your debut on December 29, 1931, at the Auditorio of Havana with your role in Sleeping Beauty, you have dedicated your life to the world of ballet, principally as a dancer but also as a choreographer and as director of the National Ballet of Cuba. When reviewing these diverse roles, which do you prefer?

Well, they are indeed different roles, but in the final analysis they are all closely linked. There is a clear connection between their functions, and they complement each other well. These diverse activities, which I have undertaken in my career, have provided me with a strength and have allowed for a continuous creativity in these diverse pursuits related to ballet.

Your leading role in the world of ballet in Cuba has resulted in your being seen internationally as one of the most important figures of contemporary Cuban culture. You have accepted this challenge for over four decades. Where does this obvious pride in being Cuban spring from?

Well, why shouldn't I have this deeply rooted patriotism?

But there are many others in the Cuban cultural world who do not feel the need to proclaim their pride in being Cuban, no?

I pity them.

There are many people who believe that, on a professional level, you would have developed more if you had remained to work in the United States or gone to live in Spain. Nevertheless, you have clearly chosen to remain here. Would you say that your art is a Cuban phenomenon?

Yes and no. I am proud to be Cuban, although it is also very true that art is an international phenomenon and belongs to all people.

That said, I think it fair to say that our effort to develop the art of ballet here in Cuba was indeed something important for this nation. As a result, since 1959 it has not been necessary for those dancers with talent to leave Cuba in order to pursue a professional career. Instead, they could do so here and develop their abilities. That is what we are seeking to do. We proudly show our skills abroad, but our home is here. This has been part of my dream throughout my life.

In an interview in 1988, you said that the most difficult thing for a ballerina to do was to look at herself in the mirror and see the truth of that image. If you look into that mirror nowadays, what can you tell us about Alicia Alonso?

That is very difficult. . . . I would say that Alicia Alonso has clearly had a life in which her positions have been consistently loyal, that she has shown great willpower throughout her life and tremendous love for dancing. I have been operated on four times, all to do with my sight. That has caused me a great deal of suffering, but I have always continued ahead. And that is called willpower.

And where does this obsession for dancing come from?

I don't really know. I simply know that, when I heard music, I felt the need to dance, to move. At first I had absolutely no idea about dancing ballet, no idea at all. I felt, though, that I had to move in harmony with the music. Why do I love ballet so much, and why did I take it up so passionately? I think that, of all the different types of dancing, it is the one that is most demanding for Cubans. And so in many ways it was a challenge for me. I think that helps to explain it. Besides, I am a perfectionist, and when I look at myself in the mirror, I always see my defects. Every time I go to a performance, I ask myself after the show, What worked well? What didn't work out? How can we improve upon it? That kind of self-analysis is usually done when we really like what we're doing. And when you like what you're doing so much, you feel capable of facing up to the truth.

There was a famous song recorded by the French singer Edith Piaf, "Je ne regrette rien." If you reflect upon your career, which has spanned so many decades, what do you think about your career, your life? What do you regret?

I regret absolutely nothing. Indeed, if I could start all over again, I would do exactly the same as I have done. Everything that I did was done because at that time it was the only thing which, in my view, I could do. If I could live my entire life again, I would continue doing exactly what I did. No question.

In which area of your career do you feel most fully realized?

I would say that in my work in ballet in general, both as a ballerina and as the director of the Ballet Nacional de Cuba, I feel fairly happy with my contribution. I believe at least that I have developed these positions and continue to do so to the best of my abilities.

By the time they have reached seventy-six years of age, most people have already retired. Yet you continue at the same breakneck speed. Have you thought about retiring or at least taking on a less demanding role?

Why should I? The day that I stop to think about that, I'll retire. Please don't bother me with such questions! And with all the work that I still have to do! At present I am creating two new ballets. I have to perform again *The Nutcracker.* And there's also a new ballet entitled *Tula,* which is about the life of a great writer of ours. And just yesterday I started to work with a group of our dancers to rehearse a scene from *Giselle.* Retirement? No, absolutely not, for while there's life, there will be dance.

4

Abelardo Estorino Lives and Writes in an Old House

There is a clear empathy between the house of Abelardo Estorino, in the Vedado district of Havana, and its inhabitant. Maybe this is because he has been living there for thirty years and has shared so many memories—of happiness and of repression—with his great companion and friend, the painter Raúl Martínez. Or maybe it is because this old house, with its tall supports and its large windows that open onto the peace of a neighboring convent, reflects in its own way the character of this dramatist. All here is luminous, fresh, and open but also modest and simple. It is in this house that Estorino has written almost all his works for the theater and become the most important Cuban dramatist in the past thirty years.

Although Estorino has received the prestigious National Prize for Literature, it is impossible for anybody who knows him to use the formal "Usted" form in addressing him. Seated in his old house, this man—himself old and venerable—manages to convey a feeling of intimacy to his visitors. One feels truly at home with him, as if he has been a lifelong friend.

Estorino has suffered repression. He has been marginalized, at times officially (and deliberately) forgotten, and often underestimated. Now, however, he has been deservedly recognized. Throughout his life, both in his work and in his words, he has remained true to himself, and he is one of the few people who deserve the term a "good human being." Thanks to this indestructible virtue (for at the risk of appearing melodramatic, this is the essential quality of Estorino), the dramatist has crossed through the most unlikely political and cultural quicksands. And, through all of it, he has emerged as few can—simply untouched by any of it.

. . .

How and when did you discover that there was such a cultural expression known as the "theater"?

It was when I was a child, although it wasn't really at a theater. It was at the circus. I remember that, way back then, in addition to having performing animals and trapeze artists, the Cuban circuses also used to have clowns: a mulatto woman, a black man, and a Spaniard, whose job was to make the crowd laugh. But there were also groups that toured the country, putting on wonderful melodramas. Some of them passed through my own town and acted in the same room where they also showed movies. It was when I saw those groups that I began to feel attracted to the theater, because later in my own home I used to play at acting out what I had seen in the show.

But I didn't have any real awareness of what the theater really could be until the 1950s, when I came to Havana to study dental surgery. I used to get together with a cousin of mine, who was very interested in the theater, and I used to go with him to the University Theater, where I met the actress Leonor Borrero, who was a very good friend of Vicente Revuelta. I began to attend their performances, and soon I was helping them with the lighting, the sets, and the staging. So, without completely realizing it, I entered the world of the theater slowly but surely.

And when did you become interested in the theater as a possible form of artistic expression?

When I was in high school, I loved to write short stories. I sent one of these to the magazine that the newspaper *El País* published on Sundays. To my great surprise, they actually printed it. But it was only much later that I began to think about writing for the theater.

If you liked literature so much, why did you decide to study dental surgery?

It was very simple. My father was a worker, and I wanted to rise in the social class and to leave my home town. I knew that if I had stayed there, I would have had to do exactly as my brothers had done—work in a local foundry or lathe operation. I felt rather strange in this environment. I was born in Unión de Reyes, a small town in the south of Matanzas Province. It was a typical small town found in any of our provinces: it had a local newspaper, a small group of people interested in the theater, and a small library. To study for my high school diploma I had to make several trips a day to the city of Matanzas. And so I decided to study something practical like dental surgery, which also had the attraction that it was a relatively short degree program and, according to my father, I could even get rich out of pursuing this career!

How would you describe the relationship with your family?

I think that mine was a very special family, one with tremendous amounts of love. My father adored my mother and watched over her even when they were both very old. He was even jealous when friends of my brothers hugged her! I don't know how I can claim that love is a fleeting emotion, when my parents loved each other so profoundly for over forty years. . . . Yes, I think that I belonged to an exceptional family. That's what we felt, in any event.

In a town that is as small as Unión de Reyes, we formed a kind of "royal family." An impoverished royal family, mind you. I remember that we used to refer to the Estorinos in the same way that we would refer to the Hapsburgs or the Bourbons. We had a rich uncle who owned some land nearby, and on holidays we used to go there and have a real feast, complete with the time-honored roast pig and beans and rice. How the Estorinos celebrated! I don't think that we had the monopoly on "blue blood," though, since people in the village also referred to the Gudes, Núrquez, and Martínez families!

But if I have done anything with my life, I owe it to the influence of my family: to my grandmother, who first put the Tarzan books in my hands, from which I acquired the vice of reading; to my mother, who recited "the flight of the turtledove" to me; and to my aunt, who took me to church, where I got to know the poetry of a truly indispensable book, the Bible. . . . Yes, I have to think that my family was special, all its members, because without them I would never have been able to write a single fragment of any of my works.

Tell us a little about those early years spent in Havana in the 1950s.

After I graduated, I worked for three years as a dentist and also as a graphic artist—until 1959 and the revolutionary victory. But since I was a student, I lived in a boarding house which the dramatist Rolando Ferrer had recommended to me. The owner of the boarding house was the mother of the painter Raúl Martínez, who painted scenery for local theaters. And that's how Raúl and I started a friendship that lasted an entire lifetime.

In 1952, after the coup d'état of Batista, Raúl left to study in Chicago, and when he returned he found a job in an advertising agency. And since I could draw reasonably well, I also worked there, not as a designer but as an assistant.

And what led you to start in the theater in 1959?

In 1954 I had written a piece about the attempted assassination of a politician by a group of thugs. It was a story that was somewhat inspired by Eduardo Chibás, the founder of the Orthodox Party. But it was basically an exercise in my apprenticeship, and I have always refused to publish it. Then, as I was saying, I started to become more connected with the theater, but without writing anything else. Shortly after the revolutionary victory, the National Theater was founded, and I decided to leave dental surgery and began to work there in the publicity department. I also wrote some short children's pieces that they asked me to do. While working there I wrote *El robo del cochino* (The Stolen Pig) and sent it to the Casa de las Américas literary competition. It received an honorable mention in the competition, and after that there was nothing else to do other than to live for the theater.

Which influences or models did you have in those early years?

The person to whom I owed the greatest debt of gratitude at that time was Rolando Ferrer, who was already a widely recognized dramatist with an overwhelming personality. I always remember him as a man of abundant grace and knowledge, learned and with good taste. Apart from that influence, my models were the North American dramatists, because I knew little of the European theater. And so when people said that my first works were influenced by Ibsen, they are only partly right, because whatever influence they may have of Ibsen came to me through the work of Tennessee Williams. It was not until later that I read the Europeans. Some people have also talked about the influence of the Cuban dramatist José Antonio Ramos, as seen in the social concerns of my work, but perhaps I owe more to the social vision of Arthur Miller than I owe to Ramos, whose work I hardly knew.

I was also influenced by the conventional treatment of dramatic structures in those North American writers, and this can be seen in my works *El robo del cochino* and *La casa vieja* (The Old House). It was not until after I had written *La casa vieja* that I began to search for my own form of expression, something which can be seen in the same theme of the struggle between two brothers that I developed in *Los mangos de Caín* (Caín's Mangos). Without a doubt, that play is a much more personal work.

I should also mention that I was fortunate enough to be a friend of important Cuban dramatists like Virgilio Piñera, Pepe Triana, and Antón Arrufat, and I had the privilege of reading them my works and receiving their critiques. Those terrific people gave me wonderful feedback—lots of irony, of course, but they were also demanding and very sharp. I am certain that contact with them made me far more exacting as a writer.

At times your theater moves in concentric circles, dealing with certain themes and concerns. Where do you find your inspiration?

Well, first of all, I think that I am difficult to inspire, because I almost always start from an abstract idea. For example, let's take the theme of hypocrisy, or the "double standard," as we say now. I start with that concept and not with any characters that live out this theme. Then I start to accumulate material and notes I've jotted down. These can come from anywhere: from a conversation with a friend who speaks as brilliantly as Oscar Wilde, from a poor novel that I'm reading, from Saturday night's movie, or from my own memories. Memories of my family, for example, or those resulting from the seventy-three years of my life. I don't write anything down until I have everything under control, with the appropriate characters and the story line set out. I have always thought that other writers lie when they claim that their characters take over the writing of their works. It must be my own lack of understanding about other ways of writing. I can't start to type a single line until I am certain that Oedipus will tear out his eyes at the end of the play. . . .

Actually, I'm lying a little, since at times the ending surprises even me. I love novels, and I enjoy very much the digressions of *Moby Dick* or the great book of Proust, but in the theater you can't allow yourself that luxury. Two hours maximum, sixty pages of text at the most; and the need to be absolutely inflexible with everything that has to be eliminated, even if it's the best sentence I've ever written. And then a second version, which again I have to cut down, and so on, indefinitely. . . . "My God, Villaverde, what torture!" says a character at the end of *Parece blanca* (She Seems White).

Let's move to the historical backdrop to much of your work. What did the revolutionary victory of 1959 mean for you?

I worked for an advertising agency where there was a great deal of support for the revolutionary struggle. I did what I could, supporting a strike or buying bonds to support the rebels, but nothing more. Like everybody else, I suffered through the Batista dictatorship, and often I felt afraid to be out late at night when I was working overtime. But the truth of the matter is that I knew very little about what was really going on. Shortly after the victory I remember writing a letter to Rolando Ferrer, who was in Canada, and telling him that a mythological animal was passing close by me, and that I had not recognized it. . . . And so the revolution was a major discovery for me. Suddenly it changed everything, and everything was full of hope.

On a personal level, my life also changed, because I stopped working for the advertising agency and began at the National Theater, where I formed part of a team of advisers for the theater groups. I provided them with information or analyzed other works. I worked doing this until *El robo del cochino* was staged, after which I entered the Teatro Estudio collective when we began to prepare *La casa vieja.*

It is significant that you have been awarded the National Literary Prize, since it recognizes both your own work and the value of the theater. What does it mean to you personally, since you are the only dramatist to receive this distinction?

Well, apart from inflating my vanity, I have always believed that such prizes are a question of luck, since they depend on the composition of the jury, their personal tastes, and a thousand other matters. Receiving that award did mean, however, that my plays would be considered as literature. That is why it surprised me so much to receive it, since I believe that here in Cuba there are prejudices against the literary value of the theater. There are also many writers who do not consider it really as literature. Because of this, in the past I have had heated discussions with the Union of Writers and Artists [UNEAC] when they attempted to move us from their union to the Dramatic Arts, since they didn't consider us to be writers. But that war we have clearly won.

Those who know your theater speak of stages in your work. How do you see the evolution of your work?

I think that ever since *Los mangos de Caín* I have found a more personal form of expressing myself. I also discovered that every central theme needed to be treated differently and that the excessive realism of my early works no longer satisfied me. This illusionary realism makes no sense to me: the theater is the theater, and the essence of the work represented there is that it is a representation. Its space for developing those ideas is the stage, and of course everybody knows that the actors are repeating a text that they have learned, and they need to perform as if they were in a medieval miniature. As a result, I began to look around for new forms, and since then I have felt the need to search for different methods. And if I don't do that, where is the adventure? Moreover, if I don't experiment, have I not changed in thirty years, and has nothing changed around me?

Perhaps an example of this process can be seen in the versions that I have done of two novels from different periods and at different stages of my life. In the 1960s, I took the story line of *Las impuras* (The Impure Women) by Miguel de Carrión and used the dialogues that the novelist had written, changing them a little so that it was easier to incorporate them into the play.

What exactly was the creative element that I added? Perhaps the selection of the chapters, the elimination of some unnecessary characters, and the reduction of the action to two or three locations. In essence, what I did was to provide my reading of the novel for a different medium.

By contrast, in the 1990s I was searching for a myth to develop into a play. I focused on the mulatta protagonist Cecilia Valdés, and then thought about Shakespeare, Brecht, and of course the Greek tragedies. I decided that all of this was basically just raw material and that I could do with it whatever I wanted. I then reflected on a variety of themes and events: the destiny of man, the role of history, the Punic Wars, Caesar conquering Gaul, the Napoleonic Wars, and World War I. I also thought about the way in which we humans kill each other for no reason at all, and about the novel *Cecilia Valdés,* where it is obvious that the characters are waiting for the conclusion with a crime that will inevitably take place. It occurred to me that this was the basic theme of the novel, and thus arose the inspiration for my play *Parece blanca.* I subtitled it *An Unfaithful Version of a Novel about Infidelity,* and when I read it for the first time in public somebody told me that in fact they thought it was the most faithful version that had been written—a comment which I greatly appreciated.

You have been linked to the theater for almost fifty years now.

That can't be! I only staged *El robo del cochino* in 1961, and that's less than forty years.

How would you evaluate plays written in Cuba between the 1950s and the 1990s?

Before the revolution there was no facility to undertake artistic theater, and very little Cuban theater was staged. Perhaps there would be a competition every now and then, won by people of talent like Carlos Felipe. What there always was, however, was a more commercial theater, full of double meanings and occasionally with fairly strong criticism of political events. But when people really make up their minds about doing something, they often realize those goals. As a result, despite enormous difficulties, a small theater movement was created here.

An important group was the Teatro Universitario, which presented classical works, while in smaller theaters that imitated Broadway or Paris there were groups that appeared and disappeared. Rubén Vigón had a small theater on La Rampa Street where he presented his "Tuesdays of Cuban Theater." This was done for a small group of professionals and others interested in culture so that playwrights had the opportunity to stage their works. It was, of course, important that, although we are talking about tiny spaces and very few people, significant works were staged: the classics, Chekhov, Strindberg. . . . And actors, technicians, and directors were all trained in this way. After the revolutionary victory, all of these professionals were able to work in a more systematic fashion.

And so we enter the 1960s.

I am not exaggerating when I say that the revolution put everything at the service of art. In the case of theater, for instance, groups were formed in every province, as well as teams of children's theater. There were competitions, art schools were opened, and there was no problem at all in staging works. As a result, major productions such as Brecht's *Caucasian Chalk Circle* were staged, along with a magnificent scenography and the large cast that it needs. A superb production of *Romeo and Juliet* was done, directed by an excellent, internationally recognized Czechoslovakian director, Otomar Krejcha. There was also a lot of Cuban theater staged, as was a lot of Virgil, and we saw several versions of *Electra Garrigó* and *Aire frío.*

This was a marvelous time for the Cuban theater—until 1966 when the new system of "approved parameters" was introduced. This was based on an official directive which insisted that all those who worked in the theater, education, or other fields where there was close contact with the public needed to obey certain "parameters." And it was shortly afterwards that they started to expel actors, directors, and others because they were homosexual or because of ideological matters, religious leanings, or other problems.

Did this take place before the Padilla case?

Yes. I remember that a commission was formed that called you for an interview, where they told you about all your problems: the unacceptable aspects of your personality, or your ideas, or even your personal life. You were told that, because of these "characteristics," you were not allowed to have contact with the public, "because we are going to create a perfect society, and you do not fit into it."

It is important to note, however, that there were laws in place which protected people against these abuses. And so all of those who had been expelled presented a legal claim. The law supported them, and so two years later the government had to reinstate them and pay them their salaries for the time that they had been off work. As is logical, this affected the theater very badly and halted the extraordinary impetus that we had witnessed until then. Not too long ago, I read the work of a sociologist who had provided a graph of the quality levels which our mise-en-scènes had achieved until this point. From the point of this rupture, the quality dropped, and although it rose again, I don't think that it ever achieved the same level, at least in artistic terms.

And how was it that this search for ideological and moral purity in Cuban society could reach such levels in repressing individuals?

What we witnessed was the idealization of reality and of what socialism should be. Many people thought that socialism could only be constructed by perfect individuals and that as a result we imperfect ones had no role in this process. What is curious, of course, is that in seeking to build a just society, those responsible were guilty of promoting discrimination and committing a series of injustices. And, although fortunately our legal system was able to ensure that they received financial compensation, on an individual basis there remained a feeling of pain that could never be removed.

After that traumatic experience, what happened in 1970?

The first thing was the Congress of Education and Culture in 1971, when it was clearly established that homosexuals could not work in the fields of education and culture. This was the beginning of a very harsh decade for the Cuban theater. Perhaps a sign of the times was the creation of what was called "new theater," which arose with the best of intentions. Here in Cuba we already knew about the experience of collective theater, based on public participation, which was being done in Latin America, especially in Colombia. As a result, some figures who were tired of working in small theaters and wanted to participate in a theater that was more connected with the people opted for that route.

With that in mind, Sergio Corrieri brought together a group of theater people. They then went to the Escambray Mountains, where they participated in an extremely important social project. I am not sure that they were as successful in artistic matters, largely because they were more concerned with the didactic and direct value of their theater than with purely artistic concerns. The good intentions of this project soon caused major problems for the theater in general, however. At the institutional level, for example, what was promoted and supported was theater resulting from collective participation. By contrast, traditional theater, performed in the normal manner, was seen as second-rate. We were not prohibited from performing traditional theater, although those works that were the result of collective creation were given almost all the economic support and were widely publicized.

And how did this 1971 Congress affect your work?

I have a play in which one of the characters notes that "to be too proper and morally upright is also a means of being rather distorted and deformed." Well, I am not sure if initially there were any specific guidelines, but as you know, the sense of smell is as important as any other. And soon the smell of danger and fear was in the air. I remember how I continued writing my works in the 1970s, although nobody ever staged them. I had no idea why this was the case until I was touring the country with *La discreta enamorada*, by Lope de Vega. We arrived at the Matahambre Mines in Pinar del Río, where I met the director of a local amateur theater group who had received an official document with a list of Cuban and foreign authors whose work he was not to stage. Among those names was mine, although it was in good company, since Ionesco and Beckett were also on the list.

At this point my group began to stage "recitals." I did one on Mayakovsky and the Russian poets as a sign of respect for the Russian Revolution, and then another to celebrate the attack on the Moncada barracks, together with Cuban poems and songs. I didn't do this because I had been advised to do so but because these were subjects that I admired.

Besides, this period was important to me because I had begun to do research on the poet José Jacinto Milanés, in order to write a play on him. The most enjoyable aspect of this play was the process of doing research in various libraries. I remember how I became a detective, following clues from book to book, without finding the guilty party. In that process I accumulated so much material that at one point I decided to give up looking and sit down to write.

Do you remember if Virgilio Piñera was among that list of prohibited authors?

I am almost certain that he was, although I can't remember now all the names on the list. But Virgilio is too important an author for his works not to have been staged during those years.

Can we continue into the 1980s?

After the difficult extremes of the 1970s, an attempt was made to put things on a more even keel, for the sake of art and the artists. The creation of the Ministry of Culture changed the situation completely. Once again traditional theater returned to the stage. Besides, I think that the Teatro Escambray had met its goals, as had similar groups who had taken its lead in factories, schools, and communities.

As a result, we started to develop a Cuban theater that asked questions about our reality, as we had done in the 1970s. And the public responded with great interest to this theatrical representation of their concerns. There was a fundamental problem, however. You will remember that before 1959 in one of those tiny theaters it was possible to see Cocteau or any other contemporary dramatist performed. But now people knew nothing about recent theater, vanguard theater. Nobody was familiar with the work of Jarry, or Strindberg, or Bernard Shaw, simply because nobody had staged them. And so that was the difficult situation when we entered the 1990s.

And the economic crisis. But sometimes crises bring benefits, no? For example, do you think that the material limitations that the Cuban theater suffers today have brought any benefits?

If we talk about benefits, I think that the most important is that we have gained significantly in imagination, which is one of the main characteristics of the Cuban theater in the 1990s. Today, for example, if somebody decided to stage a work from the eighteenth century, they would never dream of looking for costumes of the time. As a result they would have to invent something with the limited resources available, in order to create a believable atmosphere. I think, though, that we need many more real spaces in which to work, flexible spaces that will allow a certain renovation of our resources.

You have stated that you were never an optimist because they didn't give you the opportunity. . . . But I believe that you have been, above all else, an honest man—perhaps even a pure one. How do you see yourself?

Could it be that I have been astute? Well, it is a difficult question, and I am not completely sure how to respond to it. Maybe that's why I was a Presbyterian in my youth. . . . Look, I don't think that I am particularly virtuous. I have my envies and my problems, like everybody else. But I am not capable of speaking ill of a work just because I have had a personal problem with its author. I can separate one thing from the other. And when I love somebody, then I love them completely. And it is difficult for me to imagine myself being so virtuous, because it makes me feel like a Christian, and I am—unfortunately—no longer a Christian.

I would like you to speak a little about two people who have been extremely important in Cuban culture and in your own life. Tell me how you see Raúl Martínez and Virgilio Piñera.

My friendship with Virgilio has influenced me far more than I am capable of understanding, because he had an eternal youth. He was a person who never considered himself a classic, although he was very sure of his importance. But that did not make him vain or pedantic at all. As you know, he had the reputation of being a difficult person, somebody who spoke ill of other writers. In fact, he was a man who dedicated his life to literature, and when there was something that was poorly done, he said so in no uncertain terms. For example, it is known that he had problems with Lezama Lima and that they spent quite some time without speaking to one another. Later, however, he dedicated a poem to Lezama, and they renewed their friendship.

He and I were close, and I gave him my work to read. I came to understand the theater that he wrote, to enjoy the breadth of his cultural knowledge, even though nothing I wrote was anything like his work. I was lucky enough to receive his critiques, and so that you can appreciate the kind of humor he employed, he always used to say to me that I would be renowned in the history of Cuban letters because of *La Cucharita Martina,* a child's play that I wrote in the 1960s. It was typical of his sense of humor, and it always made me laugh.

I remember how, whenever he felt ill or a little depressed, he would come and see me. He loved to cook spaghetti and thought that he made the best spaghetti in the world (which was not true). He came to the house ever since Raúl Martínez was working at *Lunes de Revolución.* Whenever supper was late, he used to protest and say that at his age he couldn't eat late, and so he would ask for coffee while he was waiting.

He also had a wonderful interest in the artistic talents of the young. And so if anybody approached him and said that they were thinking about writing, he would listen to them, question them about their writing, read their story, and tell them honestly what he thought of their work. As a result I believe that his reputation was not deserved and arose from people who did not know him well, because when you spent time with him you immediately saw that good nature which he hid behind his barbs.

With Raúl the situation was completely different. He transformed my life and helped me enormously, because we spent an entire life together. Because of him I left behind the forceps and grabbed an Olivetti typewriter. Thanks to him I learned to appreciate contemporary painting and other artistic expressions. Raúl always demanded a lot from art, from himself, from me, and from everybody else, too. I always used to read him what I'd written as I was writing, and that helped me. However, when I would say something about one of his works in progress, he always told me that nothing on the canvas was definitive. He was also an extremely generous man. I remember how he used to help struggling artists, and if somebody just starting out was organizing a collective exhibition and asked him to participate, Raúl was extremely generous and gave his paintings, with as much happiness as if it were for the best international gallery.

Returning to your own work, can you tell us why you have continued to both write and direct?

In the Cuban theater, especially among the young directors, it is quite common for them to use the text as an excuse to say what they want to say and not what the original author did. There is a particular case, that of Julio César Ramírez, who directed a completely free version of *La casa vieja* without consulting me at all. Nevertheless, it is a version of which I feel a part. But I don't like directors taking my work to express other ideas.

The other problem is that when I direct my plays I feel that I take away from them, because another director, with different ideas, would surely add to them and enrich them. When I am creating a scene, often the actors will make suggestions to me, and they discover things that I had not considered or that in fact I had thought about but did not know how to express. And that is why I would prefer other directors to stage my works. . . . There is a final facet worth noting, too. Since I earn my salary as a director, I need to come up with plays to direct. But if nobody ever asks to direct my works, then I am happy to direct them myself.

Which actors have you most frequently worked with?

People say that I have worked a lot with Adria Santana. The fact of the matter is that I like intelligent actors. That's all. I believe that there are actors with intuition, capable of creating marvelous characters. I have been lucky in working with a group of sensible, intelligent people, and I can honestly say that my mise-en-scènes have often almost been done by the actors themselves. I did not participate in the trend of collective creation that I mentioned earlier, but it is definitely true that I depend greatly on the actors, and to a large degree the staging of my work depends on the participation of all of us.

Do you see yourself as a playwright who defends the value of words?

I would say rather that I am a believer in the power of words, because I continue to believe in words. My latest work consists of long monologues, "Words, words, words," and when I stage it I will try to offer the appropriate scenic format, but without disregarding the value of words.

How does a director and playwright like yourself receive payment?

I am paid my salary as a theater director, and in fact I could earn the same whether I directed or not. As an author I am also paid my royalties, according to Cuban law. I believe the law stipulates that, after a fixed time, if somebody stages a play of mine again, I am to be paid again. It doesn't happen often, though, that my work is staged again right away.

The system for directors is somewhat anarchic. I receive my salary in a group where we are four directors. But with the economic conditions in Cuba being what they are, you can't stage more than four works in a year, which means that each of us directs only one per year. There was a period before when we used to work more, since there were shows from Monday to Sunday and two shows on Sunday, but now they are only on the weekends.

Who chooses the plays to be staged?

The directors. They look for works that they like, or that interest them, and then they go to the general director of the group for his approval. In this sense there is no censor as such, somebody who says which plays can and cannot be staged. At the same time, the director always knows which plays can be shown without political difficulties. That is clear.

In your work, have you been pressured by anybody either to deal with a certain topic or to avoid dealing with one?

I have always written what I wanted and in the way that I wanted to write it. I know that I could write about other issues, but I am not personally interested in those. The ideas that I write about in my plays are the ones that really matter to me, and they're the ones that I want to express.

In recent years you have been traveling fairly frequently to the United States. From your experience over the last few years, have you witnessed an evolution in the Cuban exile community?

The first time I went after the revolution, I was invited by Repertorio Español, a theater group that stages its plays in Spanish. They had been in Cuba, where they saw *Vagos rumores* (Vague Rumors), and they invited me to stage it in New York. Before this, as you know, Rosita Fornés had been in Miami, where she was greeted by threats and protests. New York, however, is completely different from Miami.

Nevertheless, several people here [in Cuba] were skeptical about my play. They knew that I lived in Cuba and that the play was about Cuba, and as a result they believed that it would be a piece of political propaganda. Some friends of the theater company said that they were not interested in that kind of thing, but those who did go found that it was very different from what they had expected. They appreciated its artistic qualities, and it was well received. As a result they invited us to stage *Vagos rumores* and *Parece blanca.*

Miami, however, is different. Some people claim that after the recent problems with the Latin music festival, things have improved, but after speaking with some people about Miami, I understood that it was difficult to establish any close relationship there. There are many others in Miami who think differently, of course, and even the theater director Sarraín has staged works of Alberto Pedro and Abilio Estévez.

And in conclusion, a question about the future. How long do you plan to continue writing for the theater?

Whenever I finish one of my dramas, I believe that I no longer have anything else to say. Later, however, I usually surprise myself by jotting down notes, ideas, sketches—and once again I feel the need to write. But now that we are concluding, let me add one thing, and it really doesn't bother me if it sounds pedantic. . . . I have always proposed to myself a work that is beyond my capabilities, something that is so grandiose that it is simply beyond my ability. As a result, I never reach my goal, and it always seems to me that I've fallen short of it. That is my healthiest ambition, one that I have never achieved. And that's because I believe that I will never be able to resign myself to what I've done, thinking that somehow I have achieved perfection. Of course, the truth is that it would be marvelous to achieve these goals. But don't you think that's terribly vain?

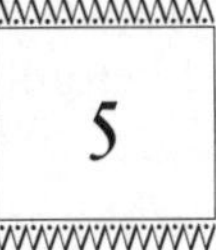

Chucho Valdés

Traditional Rhythm and Jazz in Search of a Grammy

Jesús "Chucho" Valdés is an extraordinary pianist, composer, and musical director. He has composed six "classics of Latin jazz," won two Grammy Awards, and received an honorary doctorate from the University of Victoria in Canada. In 1999, Cuba awarded him and his colleague, Leo Brouwer, the National Music Prize.

To speak with Chucho Valdés is a great privilege as well as a tremendous feat. He is busy composing and touring, so he does not like to spend the little time left replying to questionnaires. However, he did consent to an interview in January 1999. We met him at his Havana home, where he started the conversation by announcing that he and his band, Irakere, had just been nominated for two more Grammy Awards.

. . .

Can you tell us something about your early life and in particular what musical influences you can remember?

My earliest memories are of music being played all around me. I began to play the piano when I was only three years old, playing by ear pieces that I had heard on the radio. And playing with two hands! I was born surrounded by musicians, next to a piano, and hearing music all the time. My father is Bebo Valdés, one of the most famous musicians and directors of Cuba. My mother used to play the piano, too, and sang very well. Living in that musical environment was as natural to me as breathing.

When did you begin to study the piano?

I was born in 1941 in Quivicán, a small town in the interior of Havana Province, where my father had also been born some twenty-three years earlier. Soon afterwards we moved to the capital, where we lived in the Santa Amalia district. It was there, when I was five years old, that I had my first piano teacher, a private teacher named Boufartique, who taught sol-fa and composition. Then, when I was nine years old, I registered in the conservatory. My studies went well and very quickly, since I started out in the fourth year of the program and finished before I was fifteen. It was then that I began studying to be a teacher.

I continued all this time taking private classes, and by 1957—before I was sixteen years old—I was already recording with my father's orchestra, the Sabor de Cuba. Shortly afterwards, in 1958, I joined the orchestra as a pianist, along with the singers Fernando Álvarez, Rolando Laserie, Pío Leyva, Cascarita, and Miguelito Cuni, who at that time had left Chapotín's orchestra.

When you started to play at home with your parents, were you mainly interested in popular music?

Yes, because that was the type of music I liked, and it was also what my father played. I was then, and remain today, the greatest fan of the music of Bebo Valdés, and I thank him for all the lessons he taught me. The years that I played for him in the Tropicana Orchestra and in the Sabor de Cuba were for me a great musical lesson, since it allowed me to learn about the big bands. It also prepared me to work with any kind of orchestra and for all sorts of orchestra directors. I have performed in a symphony orchestra with Manuel Duchesne Cuzán, González Matinci, Félix Guerrero, Rodrigo Pratts, Gonzalo Roig, and Rafael Somavilla. Somavilla was the best all-round Cuban director of all time as well as one of the most intelligent musicians that I've ever met.

In short, it was this great experience that, even though it might sound presumptuous to say so, allowed me to become a great musical director. And as a result I have been able to work since then with all sorts of musical groups—from large symphony orchestras to small jazz bands. It also helps to explain why, when I formed my own band, I was able to play any kind of music.

How long was it that you were unable to play with your father?

He left Cuba in 1960, and we didn't play together until 1995. But that session was really memorable, and several Cuban musicians who live in the United States also joined in. Fortunately, we recorded it.

What can you remember of the musical environment in Cuba in the 1950s?

It was an era of tremendous atmosphere, with a lot of movement. My father had a leading role in the music scene of the time, and of course I was influenced by it all. The very first Cuban orchestra to use batá drums was founded in 1952, and it was directed by Bebo Valdés and his Batanga Rhythm. At that time Benny Moré had returned from Mexico, but he was totally unknown here in Cuba, and in fact it was my father who invited him to sing. My father's Batanga orchestra disbanded afterwards because it had some twenty-five musicians and the radio stations couldn't pay so many people. Nevertheless, it left an important musical legacy in Cuba.

How did you become interested in jazz?

That too started when I was still in my cradle. . . . I learned various kinds of music at the same time, because the orchestra from the Tropicana nightclub played them all in their different shows. You would get a tremendous variety—a Brazilian samba, the Spanish classics, North American jazz, and the music of Nat King Cole—all of this just as easily as Cuban rhythms. I saw all of this on a regular basis, and then I practiced it, while I saw people like Sarah Vaughan, Dizzy Gillespie, or Jimmy and Tommy Dorsey perform. And I learned jazz in their practices, in jam sessions, since my father frequently took part.

When did you organize your first group, which I believe was called Jesús Valdés and His Combo?

Well, even before that, several very important things had happened to me. . . . At the beginning of the 1960s, even though I was very young, I felt pretty satisfied with what I had achieved. As a pianist I had played in several important hotels in Havana, such as the Deauville and the Saint John. I had also played in the orchestra of the Teatro Martí, and was working at the time in the Elegante Bar of the Riviera Hotel with Rolando Estrella's group.

Well, one day a young guy comes in, more or less my own age, and since at that time there was nobody there, I was playing a Mozart piece that I really liked. He came over, bought me a drink, and said, "Hey, you're too good to be playing in a hotel bar." I replied that this was not just any hotel—it was the respectable Riviera Hotel. He insisted, however, and told me that I should do something else. He mentioned that he had just returned from the United States, where he had studied guitar at the famous Juilliard Conservatory, and just as he was leaving he told me his name, Leo Brouwer.

From that moment on, Leo and I have been very good friends. Two years later, he invited me to play in the orchestra of the Teatro Musical of Havana, where he was the conductor. Under his guidance, I met exceptional young musicians—Paquito D'Rivera and Carlos Emilio, for example—and with Leo's help I continued to develop, learning composition, harmony, counterpoint, and orchestration. This was because I had to prepare the numbers that we were going to record.

For me it was simply a fabulous era, one in which we participated in an important cultural project, since in 1963 we were the founders of the Teatro Musical of Havana. Leo revealed to me a musical world that was very different from the one that I had worked in until then. I had as my teachers Tony Taño and Federico Smith. I also worked with Alberto Alonso and composed music for the ballet. With the experience that I had acquired there, and with some of the musicians I had met, I founded my first group—all the time with Leo's guidance. I called that group Jesús Valdés and His Combo, and personalities of Cuban music like Paquito D'Rivera, Carlos Emilio Morales, the older Oscar Valdés, Kike Hernández, and Emilio del Monte played with us.

Wasn't it at that time that you participated in the founding of the Cuban Orchestra of Modern Music?

The project started out with the idea of forming an "all-star" orchestra, with the best musicians for each instrument. I was interested because they talked about the possibility of playing jazz, which was a form of music that I was particularly interested in. We all joined the new orchestra in 1967, but things didn't turn out as we had expected, since most of the time we either played music of other composers or accompanied singers in various festivals.

Around that time I had changed the personnel in my own group and formed the Modern Music Quintet, which worked parallel to the orchestra. It was made up of younger members of the orchestra—Paquito, Carlos Emilio, Cachaíto, Enrique Pla, and myself. A little later Jorge Varona joined us, and at that time I talked to them about the possibility of separating from the orchestra so that we could develop our own project. I was very keen to do new things, to free up my approach to music, and to put into practice all that I'd learned from my father, from Leo, and from all the great teachers I'd had.

Toward the end of the 1960s, Cuban music had become fairly stagnant, and all you could hear were the same musical sounds. At the same time, in international circles a great enthusiasm for African-inspired music had arisen, one that extended as far as rock, as you can see in the music of Carlos Santana. Moreover, there were also African groups having great success in Europe and the United States. Yet curiously we Cubans were clearly outside this musical loop, although the very center for that Latin and African musical tradition was here in Cuba.

So we decided consciously to work on that kind of music. We started with a very serious research project, building the drums that we needed, including electronic instruments to develop a more contemporary sound, and we even learned some of the African languages such as Yoruba, Lucumí, and Arará. The most important ingredients were already here, and the musicians who worked with me on the project were undoubtedly the best in Cuba.

As a first test I composed a piece called the "Black Mass," a very spiritual composition but one that also had elements of jazz, Cuban music, and a clear African influence. We recorded it in 1969, still with the quintet. Other musicians had done this type of experiment—for example, Mario Bauz and Machito in New York in the 1940s. Two decades later, however, this form of music would be baptized as Latin jazz or Afro-Cuban jazz. But way back then it became too commercial with the boogaloo of Mongo Santamaría, and as a result it ran out of steam.

The following year we had the opportunity to appear as Irakere at the Jazz Jambore festival in Warsaw. Since Afro-Cuban music wasn't very well known, they put us next to last on the program, which was long, about four hours. Right after us was Dave Brubeck, the star everybody was waiting for. But first we came out. To end our performance we played "Black Mass," and to tell you the truth I got rather scared. We were overwhelmed by the applause, which ended up as a kind of stampede. They gave us a standing ovation, and although we tried to leave the stage to make room for Brubeck, it was impossible, since they kept on calling us back onstage.

We did so finally, and at the end of the show Brubeck came up to us and congratulated us on our performance. He said it was the most novel approach he'd ever heard to Afro-Cuban jazz, and he encouraged us to continue experimenting with that material. "Never stop!" I remember him telling us. I was particularly impressed when he said that the most extraordinary aspect of the group was the pianist and the composer, because I was both of those things!

Brubeck's enthusiasm was so great that he took the recordings of the concert and recommended to some festival organizers in the United States that they should invite us. Unfortunately, the information arrived too late, and so we couldn't attend. I was soon amazed, however, to discover that *Playboy* had included me in a list of the world's greatest jazz pianists, behind people of the quality of Bill Evans, Herbie Hancock, and Oscar Peterson. They even placed me above Chick Corea!

After all of this, it became even more important to separate from the orchestra. We also decided that we needed to expand the group and make our music easier to dance to. In this way we wanted to make people more familiar with the group, to get them to appreciate better Afro-Cuban jazz. So that's how our group, Irakere, developed as one that also played popular music. We wrote several numbers for our repertory, among them "Bacalao con pan" (Cod with Bread), which became a big hit and helped to make our work widely known. That was in 1973.

What was the importance, both for you and for the other members who later joined Irakere, of your experience with the Cuban Orchestra of Modern Music?

At one point the orchestra became a nightmare for us, because it wouldn't allow us the freedom to continue working as Irakere. There were so many rehearsals, so much work, that we felt asphyxiated. And so we had to rehearse our own work, the material which we really wanted to play, afterwards, at midnight. And no matter how often we asked to be allowed to leave and play with our own group, they always denied us the opportunity to do so. It was understandable, of course, because if we all left—Paquito, Arturo Sandoval, Enrique Pla, Carlos Puerto, Jorge Varona, Carlos Emilio, and me—who was left to play in the orchestra?

In reality, Irakere was already an established group and widely recognized in Cuba, despite the fact that we didn't belong to any particular musical organization and as a result had no official support. After a major struggle we did manage to leave the orchestra in 1975. Don't get me wrong: That orchestra had been a real school for us all. Indeed, any musician who didn't have the opportunity to play in it missed out on a tremendous experience. It served us very well until we reached the point when the need to make our own music became too great.

Is it fair to say that Irakere really arrived, was first really accepted, in a particular concert?

By 1978, when the group was well known and sufficiently popular, we decided to return to play Latin jazz. To do so and see if we could retain our musical influence among the public, we decided to try a major test, one in which once again my friend and teacher Leo Brouwer participated. We organized a concert with him, one in which there were no borders between classical and popular music. This is important for me, because there are only two kinds of music, good and bad.

And so we played the *Concierto de Aranjuez,* the Preludes of Villa-Lobos, as well as "Black Mass" and "Cod with Bread." This was very important because followers of classical music don't normally like popular music, and vice versa. Yet that concert packed the largest theater in Havana and ended up pleasing everybody. Those who had never heard Leo play came away convinced that they had seen a great guitarist perform, while those who knew far more about Leo than about Irakere admitted that "Cod with Bread" had a pretty catchy rhythm. From that moment on I think that Irakere was a mature musical project, capable of taking on any challenges.

In this work of rescuing Cuban jazz you have had a major role in organizing the Jazz Plaza Festivals. Do you think that the success of those festivals is due to the influence of Irakere?

We started to organize the Jazz Plaza Festivals after 1980, and they were extremely well attended. I think that the greatest contribution of Irakere was to give its concerts at the festival, since that attracted people with all sorts of musical tastes. We, of course, continued playing the type of music that we had been working on. The first festival that we organized was for national groups, but by the time we were working on the third it had taken on an international character. And today the festival is so large, with thousands of people attending, that we need various locations to please the public.

After you had won the hearts and minds of the Cuban public, how did you develop the international profile of the group?

Our international career began after 1978, when we received a contract to record an album for Columbia Broadcasting. That same year we participated in the Newport Jazz Festival, and it was the first time that a Cuban group had played in the United States since 1959. We then gave a concert in Carnegie Hall, and our recital on that occasion was also recorded. With that album, called simply "Irakere," we won a Grammy Award. That too was unusual, since it was the first time that a Cuban group had won. The success of that record, the promotional work by the record company, and the concerts that we gave in the United States prepared the way for the development of our career. Afterwards, Irakere became a famous group on the international stage, and we were swamped by invitations to participate in festivals around the world.

How did Irakere manage to combine jazz with popular Cuban music?

It all comes down to a mixture of our own background and our interest in jazz. We had all started out by playing Cuban music, but we also knew jazz pretty well. I have already mentioned how in my house playing traditional Cuban music was a daily occurrence; it was something that I'd played personally since I was a child. Besides, I grew up surrounded by the distinctive rhythms of *santería* played on the drums all around our district of Santa Amalia.

And remember that I'd also had the experience of seeing my dad playing with so many superb artists, from Celia Cruz, Arsenio Rodríguez, Peruchín López, the Romeu family, Antonio María, Armando, and Zeneida Romeu to others who played romantic music of the "feeling" style. People like this came by the house every day. And there would also be composers like Ernesto Lecuona, whom I met and saw play in my living room. Somebody else who used to drop by frequently was Bola de Nieve, and we used to visit him in his home in Casa Blanca, where we used to eat lunch with him on Sundays.

In other words, I was lucky enough to be born into a family that lived totally immersed in music and at a time when Cuban music possessed an enormous richness. I was able to digest some of great variety, and out of it there sprang a kind of collage which I have tried to express ever since in my music. It is therefore no surprise that the journal *Latin Jazz* should consider me the most complete Latin jazz pianist, basically because I don't limit myself to one class of music or one style. Besides, I am fortunate enough to be able to play either a Mozart concerto or dance music, and that flexibility is something that pleases me a lot.

How important is it to be popular?

It is relatively important. My major concern has always been to continue studying. I'm constantly buying books, I assimilate a lot of information, and I hear a lot of music. And I am particularly interested in the quality of music that I play. I know that popularity is important, but I am not interested in being popular if in order to be so I have to sacrifice my work. I don't want to be popular without having work that is of good quality, because once things cool down, you're simply dead if your work is poor.

When did you write your first composition?

It was a *danzón* piece that I wrote for the piano when I was eleven years old. That particular piece was recorded on an album made in 1950, *Roses of Fall*. My father helped me a great deal with all of this. He always told me that I had a great talent for writing melodies and that I could be a good composer. That was important. Some of my teachers had told me that I would need to decide between interpreting music or composing it. It was clear to them all that I had a great future as a pianist, but I wanted to develop my twin passions, both playing and creating. And that's why I always wanted to have my own musical group.

Do you prefer interpreting music or composing?

I think that I prefer to play, although when I am composing I do feel some sort of ecstasy. For me they are totally different exercises, and I could never give up one in favor of the other. They complement each other very well, and they compensate different aspects of my musical needs.

What do you think of the musical contribution of great Cuban musical figures like Mario Bauzá, Machito, and Chano Pozo, who settled in the United States?

The first thing I have to do is recognize Mario Bauzá, because if Latin jazz has a "father," it is him. Moreover, Frank Grillo, Machito, is the "godfather." I don't think people can really say that they composed their work in the United States. It is true that they recorded it there, because there were better conditions to record and promote their musical work. There was also a public there for their work.

That said, the origin of all that they did can be traced back to its Cuban roots and the areas of Havana where they grew up. There is no doubt that they assimilated elements of North American music, thanks to figures like Dizzy Gillespie, and you can see the American big band sound in much of their work. In other words, they participated in an exercise of cultural feedback, because in turn they added Cuban rhythmic elements, even in North American jazz. In the end they brought about a fusion of musical elements from two major cultural powers, Cuba and the United States, and in this way contributed to a work that is of universal value.

Has it ever been inappropriate, or even politically incorrect, here in Cuba to play jazz?

It's a complex matter. The problem is that often there has been a confusion around jazz that is completely alien to the music itself. For example, there were times here when it was not appropriate to play Cuban music in the United States, because if it came from Cuba then it had to be "Communist music." But music is never socialist or capitalist. It is simply music, a form of art that belongs to humanity.

There were also moments of confusion in Cuba, which fortunately were cleared up fairly quickly. One of the projects that helped to overcome those prejudices was the Cuban Orchestra of Modern Music. After their major contribution, toward the end of the 1960s, it became possible to perform jazz. Around the same time, other mistaken opinions were corrected. A good example is the official attitude toward the Beatles' music, which at one point was considered politically harmful for young people and which also changed about this time. All of these feelings of suspicion were overcome with time, and now we jazz players have every reason to feel comfortable.

We have, for instance, an international jazz festival that is supported by the Institute of Music, a festival to which some of the most prominent figures of universal jazz come. There are also several programs of jazz (I have mine on Radio Rebelde every Sunday). North American musicians are highly respected and loved, and their performances are widely advertised. We saw this with the recent visit of Max Roach, one of the greatest drummers in history. And when we have given concerts in cities like New York, we have been well received by North Americans and Cuban Americans.

Perhaps a good example of the real meaning of music would be a work like "Yesterday" by the Beatles. It's a song that is known throughout the world, regardless of different cultures and languages. That song is patrimony of the entire world because music is the only true universal language. Music, then, knows no political boundaries.

Which jazz pianists have most influenced you?

There are millions of them, to tell you the truth. Perhaps the first was my father, and then people like Art Tatum, Bud Powell, Duke Ellington, more recent figures such as Bill Evans or Keith Jarret, and young pianists like Danilo Pérez, Gonzalo Rubalcalba, Emiliano Salvador, Hernán López Nussa. . . . Yes, lots of them.

And outside jazz, who would be the most notable influences on your work?

There are also many of them. I should recognize first of all the influence of the so-called classical music: Bach, Beethoven, and Chopin, whose work I studied very closely. And the impressionists, as well as the masters of the twentieth century, especially Stravinsky. I was also influenced by Spanish popular music, from the *jota* and the *paso doble* to *flamenco.*

If Cuban jazz musicians are to succeed, do they need to do so in the United States?

Not at all. Why should that be the case? Of course, the Mecca of jazz is there, as is the possibility of universal recognition, because there is such a great market. And a jazz musician has to prove his quality there. The same thing would happen here in Cuba for percussionists, because specialists in conga music would have to prove themselves here. Or if we were talking about samba music, they would have to do well in Brazil.

What does it mean to you to have won two Grammy Awards?

Nowadays the Grammy is the greatest possible recognition granted by the music industry to a musician. And it doesn't just depend on popularity or on record sales. What decides Grammy winners is quality. To have won a Grammy is proof of that quality. I feel particularly proud to have won it twice, and I am pleased to have been nominated on other occasions, especially now that I am nominated in two categories.

Do you believe that in recent years the reception given Cuban music in the United States has changed?

I know nothing about the political aspects of how our music is received, first because I am not interested in that, and second because when we go on tour to the United States, I never have time to think about it. We play one day in a particular city, and the next day we head off somewhere else. What does interest me is the reaction of people to our music, and I can tell you that North Americans—like people around the world—are increasingly interested in Cuban music. That is extremely important, because we are representatives of that culture, and we feel very proud to represent the country where we live.

Have you thought about eventually living outside Cuba?

I've never thought about it until now, because here is where I live, and it's from here that I have been able to carry out my work. At the same time I don't criticize anybody who decides to live abroad, because at times it is absolutely necessary to be able to move to other places, to obtain visas easily. Perhaps tomorrow I'll also have to live somewhere else, besides Cuba, to make my professional work a little easier. Perhaps one day I ought to do so, as Gonzalo Rubalcalba and many television actors have done, but until now it has not been necessary.

In your opinion, what conditions have contributed to the impressive developments in Cuban music and its international influence for the past two centuries?

I think that the cultural roots which joined in the formation of our identity are the key factor in determining our musical prowess. Unlike Brazil, we don't have the contribution that results from indigenous music, because our natives were exterminated within a short period, and as a result we don't have the indigenous influence that can still be seen in the work of contemporary musicians there. In our case, the African influence is particularly strong, not just because of the rich culture that African slaves brought with them, but also because of the Spanish influence, which itself had been influenced by eight centuries of Muslim presence on the Iberian peninsula.

You can imagine, then, the fusion of the Spanish culture and African influences from several parts of the continent. The only thing that could logically result was a rhythmic fusion, a creole blend of rhythms. And that is why Cuban music is so varied. Any country with such cultural origins naturally will create its own environment for the development of musicians. And if those musicians are given the opportunity to develop those innate skills, the end result has to be tremendously favorable for the music they produce.

To understand why Cuban music is recognized internationally nowadays, it is important to remember that, although many great musicians left the country in the early 1960s, a cultural renaissance took place, with many art schools being opened in Cuba. In addition, great European professors came to Cuba, bringing with them the technical depth that it had not enjoyed until then. It is from this new cultural experience that great musicians emerge: Paquito D'Rivera, Arturo Sandoval, Emiliano Salvador, Juan Pablo Torres, and many others who began to play at that time. And so, by the end of the 1960s, there were once again a number of fine musicians, all with great technical development. The proof of that can be seen in the quality of the work undertaken by the Cuban Orchestra of Modern Music.

There then arose a problem because a number of rigid concepts were imposed upon people in the cultural realm. We tried to overcome them, and eventually did so. . . . And try and imagine now in this new period the potential that has been developed in Cuba. We always were a major power with our natural rhythms, but now for the first time we had percussionists who had graduated from specialized schools.

Despite the recognized quality of Cuban musicians the world over, is it difficult for them to penetrate the world market?

The question of the market is entirely another matter. What's at play there is the work of some of the major businesses and their capacity to move musical products. One way or another, Cuban musicians have entered that market, but still in a rather indirect fashion. The case of salsa is different, because salsa itself offers a great international market. Indeed, because of the commercial work of Fania and other companies, Cuban music has become known more through the salsa label than for any understanding of the *son* or other Cuban rhythms. Still, however, our contemporary music has not entered that market of international businesses in a massive way. Despite that, at this particular moment our music is stronger and better than ever, starting with traditional Cuban music, which has produced a phenomenon like that of Compay Segundo and that of the Afro-Cuban All-Stars. To a large extent it's because this music is easy to dance to and has a purer sound. And, of course, there's no music with a better beat to dance to than the *son*. Salsa or the so-called Cuban timba, a variation on this, is a more localized phenomenon. It is directed at those who know how to dance Cuban music, and on the one hand it is based on a complex series of rhythms, and on the other it depends on slang or current phrases. These rhythmic and linguistic elements are only understood fully by a very limited public, the Cuban people.

In sum, Cuba has produced a form of music that is hardly commercial at all. I think that music has to follow a certain logic, and when I talk about commercial values, I am not talking about a cheap product. Instead, the music has to be of such a quality that it can be easily accessed by all and understood. That is all. Sometimes music is too complicated, even for the Cuban ear, since spaces for silence are hardly employed at all. And silence is golden in music.

6

Pablo Armando Fernández

Clearly Onside

Pablo Armando Fernández has exceptionally blue eyes. Not in the least bit Latin, and indeed rather strange for a Cuban. Several years ago his hair turned completely white, and Pablo now has a long, straight mane that he sweeps back with some frequency. He also speaks English fluently and with a perceptive knowledge of the language, probably because it is the language in which he began his studies, which he employed every day during his many years in New York, and in which he wrote his first poems.

Nevertheless, despite this combination of rare qualities, Pablo Armando Fernández—like very few Cuban intellectuals—knows intimately the peaks and valleys of the Cuban cultural process these past fifty years. In fact, a study of his personal involvement in the national literary scene reveals that he has gone through almost all the possible permutations for writers during that time: from exile to success, from being marginalized because of his views to being received with revolutionary fervor, from accusations of counterrevolutionary sympathies to official acceptance.

He is both a novelist and a poet. He has won several prestigious awards, including Cuba's 1996 National Prize for Literature. Today, the author of *Los niños se despiden* (The Children Bid Farewell) could be described as an "official" cultural personality on the island, yet that has not always been the case. For almost three decades he was one of the black sheep of the Cuban cultural fold. He was savagely attacked by the cultural commissars, who forced him to work for nine years in a printing press. Then they refused to publish his work for fourteen years and would not allow him to leave the island for another thirteen years. Like a tiger, Pablo Armando Fernández bears on his skin the marks of his passage through the stormy process of the cultural life of this revolution. Moreover, he is also a privileged witness of all that has transpired during these years because, like few others, he has been one of the main protagonists.

Pablo, I would like to start by asking about your early life in Delicias. I read an interview in which you stated, "I have never stopped living in Delicias." It is very clear from a reading of your work that this period of your life had a lasting impression on you. This town may also be compared to the Macondo of García Márquez. Or am I wrong?

No, you are right. My maternal grandfather was a landlord who participated in the second war for independence alongside Mario García Menocal. García Menocal built a sugar mill, the Central Chaparra, and my grandfather became the first sugar planter there. In 1909 my father, then a young man from a Spanish family—and with the same color of eyes as mine—set out with his father, Elpidio Fernández, to look for work because the war had reduced them to poverty. He then met my mother and they married. Later, after the Delicias sugar mill had been established, an uncle of my father was appointed to a high position there, and my father went to work with him. My father's job was to cut down all those beautiful forests so that sugar cane could be sowed. And that's where I was born in 1930, in a family that already had eight children. All my family, on both sides, comes from Holguín.

I went to the company school in Delicias and began to study English when I was six years old, mainly because it was an American school. Then it was closed down and I went to public school, where I stayed until sixth grade. But during this time I continued to study English. It is curious, but my ties with the English language are extremely remote, and I have no idea when they originated. I think it must have been in a former incarnation. . . . I do believe in reincarnation, by the way, since otherwise my life doesn't have any meaning.

And are your ties with literature as remote as well?

I'm not exaggerating if I say that it was Emily Brontë who made me into a writer. What is more curious, perhaps, is that it wasn't through reading her work but rather through hearing it on the radio. I was a child when a version of her novel, *Wuthering Heights,* was broadcast on Cuban radio. And ever since I heard that first chapter, I realized just how powerful a medium it is to write.

How did the major jump from Delicias to New York come about?

In 1944 I convinced some members of my sister's family who were living in the United States to let me go and live with them there. I left in 1945, when I was fifteen years old, with five hundred pesos that my family gave me in my pocket. When I arrived there, I lied, telling people that I was sixteen so that I could work. Then in 1952 I returned to Cuba, where I took a job back at the Delicias mill.

And was it in the United States that you began to write?

Exactly. And my first work was in English. One of the first poems that I wrote was in English (I was seventeen years old at the time), and I called it "Al Hudson" (To the River Hudson). However, what changed my life as a writer occurred in an extremely strange and mysterious way one night in New York. I was with a Puerto Rican friend, Fajardo by name, and we were at a house there to hear the reading of a text entitled *A Member of the Wedding.* It was read by a tall, slim lady whose name was Carson McCullers. After the reading, she and I went to the kitchen for some potato salad. I took advantage of that moment to tell her that I also did some writing, and a week later I took her some things that I had written in English. She read them and then said, "So you write poetry." I told her that she was mistaken. "But this is poetry," she answered. Then she picked up a pencil and began to divide up one of my texts. "This is *your* poetry," she told me. "It is your breath, your voice."

I listened to her, but I wasn't in the least convinced, because poetry was something quite different. It had to have a certain rhythm, cadence, a proper structure, verses, etc. And I wasn't trying to do anything like that. In the end, however, I heeded her advice, and those "poems" were published in journals over there. All of that bothered me a lot. It even hurt me, because I definitely didn't want to be a poet. I even told her that I was a writer, not a poet. I looked up information on the lives of some poets, and I wasn't impressed.

And when did you begin to write in Spanish?

I had to go through a long apprenticeship in order to recover my Spanish. At first I used a lot of terms from Spain, words that weren't used in Cuba. For example, in one poem I used the term *platicar,* to talk, which is a Mexican word that people in Cuba simply don't use. I also used the word for supper used in Spain, *la cena,* which again is not used in Cuba. In my first poems written in Spanish there are therefore a lot of words that I found in a dictionary or that I took from a poem of Góngora, whose work I read a lot at the time. I became fairly obsessed with the Spanish language while going through this literary apprenticeship.

It was at that time that I met the poet Emilio Ballagas. I was already writing with a greater awareness of literature, and I put together a collection of my early poems, which is called *Cuadernos de Manila Hartman* (Notebooks of Manila Hartman). It is fair to say that it is always women who have had the greatest influence in my life—Emily Brontë, Carson McCullers, and Manila Hartman.

And when I returned to Cuba in 1952, I already had two collections of poetry, *Al Hudson* and *Distancia y otros poemas semejantes* (Distance and Other Similar Poems). Both of these were written in Spanish. It was at this time that Ballagas introduced me to Cuban poets like Fina García Marruz, Lezama Lima, and Cintio Vitier, who published another book of mine, *Salterio y lamentación* (Psalter and Sorrow).

So did you remain in Cuba or return to New York?

Look, at that time I was crazy. I kept on coming here and returning there, and so on. The only thing that I wanted to do was to live here in Cuba, because this is where Ballagas, Lezama, Cintio Vitier, Guillermito Cabrera Infante, Heberto Padilla, and other friends lived. But I also ended up returning to New York. And it was on one of those trips that I met my wife, Maruja, whom I married in 1955. We stayed in New York until 1959, when I returned to live in Cuba. Let me confess something to you: I still feel very tied to New York. Without my years spent there, I would be nobody.

In Learning to Die, the collection of your poetry edited by John Brotherton, he refers to the way in which you taunt yourself repeatedly for your "critical absence during the insurrection" against Batista. How do you react to this observation?

I agree with his observation and have expressed this in several poems. I did write several poems for the July 26 Movement at that time. I also wrote *Las armas son de hierro* (The Arms Are of Iron) at that time, a drama about the insurrection. After many difficulties we managed to have it staged in New York. I remember that at that time many friends would come to our house on the weekends, and we would talk about the latest developments in Cuba. Among them were Humberto Arenal, Miriam Acevedo, Oscar Hurtado, Edmundo Desnoes, Néstor Almendros, and Calvert Casey. It is curious how we all returned to the island after 1959.

How would you define yourself, in political terms, at the time that Batista was overthrown?

I was not a Marxist-Leninist, although I was a member of the July 26

Movement. In New York I had met Haydée Santamaría and José Llanusa and had spoken a lot with them about the revolution's goals. And so, when I came back to Cuba, I immediately got in touch with Haydée and with Carlos Franqui, who asked me to write something about Abel, Haydée's brother. Because I had studied his life very closely for many years and had a deep personal respect for Abel Santamaría, it was easy for me to write about him. In fact, I almost finished a book on Abel. . . . In political terms, to return to your question, I had no firm ideological convictions. I was simply a Cuban.

Did you consider yourself a revolutionary?

I don't know how to reply to that question, because the term has been used so much that it has lost a fair amount of its value. The same thing has happened with the word *socialism,* which has lost a lot of value, too, since it was never applied properly anywhere.

I was in the Soviet Union in 1960, and what I saw there really scared me. And because I criticized the Soviet Union here, I was publicly chastised. In good Cuban, they told me not to say such crap. I was also in China that same year when Mao Tse-Tung gave a speech in which he noted that Cuba was one more star in the socialist constellation. I then repeated that phrase in a toast, only to be told by the head of our delegation not to drink any more, since Cuba definitely was not socialist. . . . In fairness, I don't think that I could define myself as being anything in particular.

What did you do when you returned to Cuba? How did you start working with the cultural supplement Lunes de Revolución?

I arrived in Havana on January 16, 1959. The very first person I saw was my old friend Carlos Franqui, who had lived with me in New York on more than one occasion and who was then directing *Lunes.* Later I saw Guillermo Cabrera Infante, but after about a month in Cuba I returned to the United States. They came to visit me in New York in April 1959, and Guillermo convinced me to return to Cuba. So I came back in May, and my first job was with Manuel Urrutia, at that time president of Cuba. A month later, he was thrown out of office and I left the palace (which at the time was surrounded) in the same way that I had arrived, like an invisible person. . . .

And so I decided to move back to the United States. I went first to Delicias to say good-bye to my parents, and while I was there Guillermo called to ask me to visit him when I got back to Havana. When I arrived there, he was in the middle of a meeting with some thirteen members of *Lunes de Revolución.* Shortly afterwards, a controversial article by Baragaño was published in issue number 19 of 1959 (which is dedicated to the July 26 Movement and the Agrarian Reform), and some of the members of *Lunes* resigned.

I remember that it was not easy to publish *Lunes*. At that time there were two basic groups in this country: the July 26 Movement and the Partido Socialista Popular, who had their own newspaper, *Hoy Domingo*. Every week it appeared, there was friction between the two groups, and as a result there were always problems, with controversies raging on the pages of their two newspapers and cultural supplements, *Hoy Domingo* and *Lunes de Revolución*. In addition, some members of the PSP were keen to join the two supplements together. We couldn't accept that, because we knew that we would be taken over by them.

That's roughly how things were at the start of 1960. At the end of that year, Guillermo and Carlos Franqui were invited to the USSR and China, and when we returned from that trip there was no longer any interest in joining the two cultural supplements. Instead, we were faced with another project, the founding of the Union of Writers and Artists of Cuba (UNEAC). At that time it was a terribly sad organization, since it had been created with the objective of controlling the creative spirit of Cuba and directing every act of artistic creation.

In the midst of all of this, Sabá Cabrera and Orlandito Jiménes made a film called *P.M.,* which was about night life in Havana. I had a television program at that time, *Lunes en la Televisión,* and I showed the film on it. There was no problem when I showed it. Afterwards there arose some problems between Néstor Almendros and ICAIC [the Cuban Film Institute], and as a result of these problems Guillermo was pushed out of ICAIC. A serious problem then arose between the newspaper *Revolución* and ICAIC.

Around that time a major Congress on Culture had been organized, but in view of what had just happened, those of us who worked at *Lunes* decided not to attend. If anybody wants to follow up and see precisely what happened, I've got all the documents, signed by the participants. The Congress was suspended, and this led to three major conversations with Fidel Castro at the National Library. This ended with the concepts formulated by Fidel: "Within the revolution, everything is possible; outside, nothing is." This was how Fidel responded when Mario Parajón asked him what a Catholic intellectual should do in this revolutionary process.

Remember that we're still in 1961. . . . During this conversation it was decided that the literary supplements of all newspapers would disappear, and they would be replaced by a literary journal to be published by the Writers' Union and another publication, *La Gaceta de Cuba,* in essence the continuation of what Nicolás Guillén had done in the 1950s.

Lunes de Revolución was closed down on November 6, 1961. I was left without any work until I joined the team of the journal *Casa de las Américas,* and Guillermo survived a year giving lectures every Friday on North American cinema. I think this was the worst year of my life, because Haydée Santamaría was absent from work (she was pregnant at the time), and so the journal was directed by a Paraguayan poet, Romero, who made life absolutely impossible for us.

The best evidence of just how impossible life had become for us can be seen in issue number 8 of *Casa de las Américas,* which has nothing to do with the real format of *Casa.* The journal had been set up following the format of *Orígenes* by Fausto Massó and Antón Arrufat. But if you look at issue 8, you'll see that it looks more like *Sputnik* or *Reader's Digest*—and all because of Romero's ideas. By the next issue it had gone back to its traditional format. I've always said that the day they award me a major international prize I'll redo issue number 8, in the way it should have been done.

Given your position "in the eye of the storm," I wonder if you would explain your views on the most controversial event of these forty years of cultural policy in Cuba: the Padilla affair.

I could lie to you about this, but I'm not interested in doing so. What has happened with the Padilla affair is that the whole affair is so dirty that there is no longer any such thing as a "true" account of it. My interpretation will be contradicted by Heberto Padilla, Lisandro Otero, Guillermo Cabrera Infante, and others. And since they are living abroad, for many people they have greater credibility. Nevertheless, I'll try to be as fair as I can.

Toward the end of 1962, Guillermo and I left Cuba as cultural attachés in Brussels and London, respectively. Heberto Padilla was already working for *Novedades de Moscú* in Moscow. Then in 1965 we all returned to Cuba, for reasons that have nothing to do with politics: Guillermo's mother died, the ambassador in London decided to leave his post, Carlos Franqui had returned from Europe, and Padilla (who had been in Czechoslovakia) was offered a job here in Cuba. So we were all back in Cuba. When Padilla came back, he brought with him a number of poems that were published in several Cuban journals such as *Casa de las Américas, Unión,* and *Pueblo y Cultura.* Again, there had been no critical comments on this work.

I was unemployed until 1966. My life was rather normal, however, since the Ministry of Foreign Relations continued to pay me a rather strange salary—since I was not doing anything. It was at this point that I received a letter from Graham Greene, notifying me that he had been invited to visit Cuba, but that he wasn't coming because he didn't want to create an embarrassing situation for me. I gave this letter to Carlos Franqui, who handed it to Haydée Santamaría. She in turn called Raúl Roa, the minister of foreign relations, and in the end they gave me a small job in the Cuban commission of UNESCO. Then in 1967 I was invited to a meeting of the PEN Club in London. But this invitation caused friction between the National Council on Culture, which didn't want me to attend, and the Communist Party, which did want me to participate. Finally the Party had its way, and I went to London.

When I returned, I found myself unemployed once again, and it really offended me. I took advantage of the time on my hands and finished an old novel that I had started in 1952, *Los niños se despiden* (The Children Bid Farewell). This novel won the Casa de las Américas literary prize for best novel. The plot thickens, however. . . . Finally Graham Greene came, but that in turn caused a series of misunderstandings between Heberto Padilla and Lisandro Otero when in an interview Padilla (in my opinion, unjustly) stated that Otero's *Pasión de Urbina* was a bad novel. And so Padilla attacked Lisandro Otero while at the same time defending Guillermo Cabrera Infante. All of this was very clear; details of this episode have been published, and there are no secrets. As you know, we often have bad intentions and bad journalism, as well as bad fiction in literature. Far more dramatic, though, and far more moving is reality itself.

You also have to remember the international context in which all of this was happening. In 1967, at the PEN Club meeting in London, the famous dramatist Arthur Miller (who at the time was president of PEN Club International) proposed holding a writers' conference in Cuba. His plan was to have a regional conference of the PEN Club, and he promised to bring a group of important North American writers. It was really an attractive concept, and it was supported by both Graham Greene and David Carver, the secretary of the PEN Club. Unfortunately, when I presented it in Havana, it was seen as a very dangerous idea, something like a form of foreign intervention, basically because the idea hadn't come from here in the first place. In some ways it resembled Track II of the U.S. Torricelli bill, as they saw it back in 1967. In reality, however, it was a delightful idea of Arthur Miller, who was full of good intentions.

To try and overcome this idea, which some intellectual circles were discussing, it was decided to hold a Cultural Congress here in Havana in 1968. We were invited at the last moment, precisely the day before it was to start, at the request of some of the foreign participants. Until that point we had been excluded from the Congress. I knew about all this through Carlos Franqui, who came here to the house to let me know that several bureaucrats were ferociously opposed to my participating. All of this gives you an idea of the intellectual atmosphere of Cuba in 1968.

But things got even more complicated. . . . Among the people whom I had suggested for the 1968 Congress was Jorge Edwards, a young Chilean diplomat and a good friend of Pablo Neruda, whom I had met in Paris. Edwards participated in the 1968 Congress and then stayed afterwards as a member of the jury for the Casa de las Américas literary prizes. Apparently he convinced the jury to award the prize for the best novel to Norberto Fuentes for *Condenados del Condado* (The Condemned of the County), a decision that was received very poorly, since Norberto's book was not considered to be in the least revolutionary. To make matters worse, the theater prize had been won by Virgilio Piñera, a person detested by the Cuban bureaucracy, while I had won the prize in the novel section with *Los niños se despiden*. I was told the very night of the awards ceremony that my novel was a counterrevolutionary work. As you can see, the cultural questions were really heating up.

In 1968, the problems between Lisandro and Heberto got worse. Heberto had rejected a post that they had offered him in Paris, which seemed very strange to people. And then in 1968 he sent his collection of poetry *Fuera del juego* (Offside) to be considered for the competition organized by the Union of Writers. The poems in this particular collection had already been published and had received no negative public commentary. But by this time Heberto had run afoul of the cultural bureaucracy. In addition to his critical poetry, he had also denounced in *El Caimán Barbudo* the "anonymous policeman" who dragged Guillermo off the plane when he was returning to Belgium. In sum, Heberto already had too many enemies among the bureaucrats and government officials, and he had just sent in this book to the [very official] Union of Writers.

At the same time Antón Arrufat had written a play, *Los siete contra Tebas* (The Seven against Thebas), which had been read here in this house for a group of friends. There had not been any negative response in official terms, and the play was being rehearsed at the Teatro de Estudio.

But the background political situation in Cuba was tense. Between 1967 and 1968 we had here what was known as the "revolutionary offensive." And then in 1968 we witnessed the purging of what the government called the "microfaction." There had also been a number of critical studies published: for example, *Guerrillas in Power* of K. S. Karol, another book by Bettleheim, one by René Dumont, and an article by Magnus Enzenburger. It was also significant that Che Guevara had been killed in Bolivia. As a result, it was widely believed here that there was some sort of conspiracy against Cuba.

Things improved in 1969, and we all went off to try and reach the 10 million ton sugar harvest. By July 1970, after the harvest was over, we were all back here in Havana, happy and unconcerned.

In December of that year, with Salvador Allende in power in Chile, Pablo Neruda suggested that Jorge Edwards should come here to open the Chilean embassy. When he arrived, however, he was already a persona non grata, since Edwards had very few friends indeed among Cuban officials.

Meanwhile, Padilla had been writing a novel. His book of poetry, *Fuera del juego,* had been published, as well as Arrufat's play, both of which were accompanied by prologues which stated that they were considered counterrevolutionary works. Padilla, however, was becoming increasingly popular abroad in international circles. And when the official prologues were read, a host of intellectuals from Julio Cortázar to Jean-Paul Sartre all expressed their strong disagreement with the claims made in them.

As a result of that prologue in his poetry collection, Padilla became quite a personality. And in 1969–70, when internationally recognized intellectuals visited Cuba, they came to see Padilla. Padilla really liked that game, since he finally had a leading role.

In 1970 a man named David Bussi, now living in the United States, told people that Padilla was circulating a counterrevolutionary novel and that it was to be published by Jorge Edwards. It was at this point that Padilla's house was searched, and they found the novel—just where Bussi told them that it was hidden. And Padilla was detained.

When Padilla was released some thirty-seven days later, he gave an extremely long speech at the Union of Writers. It was a pathetic speech, in which he accused several of us of being counterrevolutionaries. And by the next day, based solely on Heberto's accusations, we were seen as counterrevolutionaries. Absolutely nobody wanted to have anything to do with us. He condemned several of us: himself and his wife, Belkis Cuza, Pablo Armando Fernández, Norberto Fuentes, César López, and Manuel Díaz Martínez. Later his speech was published in *Casa de las Américas* and *Unión* and was translated into several languages.

As a result of all of this, I was sent to work at a printing press, where I spent nine years. Padilla was given a fairly decent job as a translator. He translated the poetry of the English Romantic period as well as some books. And César was sent as a translator to the Academy of Sciences. In 1980, Heberto left for the United States.

I think that I lived as nobody did the so-called Padilla affair because this house where we are today was the center of the whole matter. Heberto practically lived here, and day by day afterwards I suffered the impact of the affair—before, during, and after.

You spent nine years working at the Academy of Sciences printing press, fourteen without publishing a book in Cuba, and thirteen without leaving the country. But in the 1980s you once again published: collections of poetry such as Aprendiendo a morir (Learning to Die, 1983), Campo de amor y batalla (Fields of Love and of War, 1984), El sueño, la razón (Dreams and Reason, 1989), and the novel El vientre del pez (The Stomach of the Fish, 1989). How did this normalization process come about?

You are right. In the 1980s things worked out well. I went to the United States in 1980 and to Mexico in 1983. In 1981 I was awarded the National Prize for Culture, and in 1985 the Critics' Prize for *Campo de amor y batalla.* I later received several more awards, including the National Literature Prize.

Clearly this was an extremely brusque transformation. Who changed: you or cultural policy in Cuba?

After all that I've been through, I think I have the right to publish a book entitled "The Book of Infamy." It would not be fair to do so, however, because these events have nothing to do with the revolution per se. Let me give you a concrete example of the infamies to which I have been subjected. . . . A neighbor of mine stabbed me here in the back, and I required surgery. But what happened to him? He was detained just an hour! The villain of the piece was me, since Padilla lived here in this house, and therefore I had to be a counterrevolutionary! All of this is true, I assure you. But let me return to your question: I honestly believe that I have not changed. Moreover, I haven't written a single line in my work that I should be ashamed of.

Things have changed a lot here. For example, Cuba is now publishing books that would have been unthinkable in the 1960s and 1970s. I think that several people who were really concerned about literature and art, and who wanted an ideological confrontation, are no longer here. There are two or three left, perhaps, but they have no power. Yet they still try to do some pretty ugly things.

Things have improved a lot. I no longer see the sinister, indeed evil, examples of twisted policy that we witnessed in earlier periods, such as the persecution of homosexuals. This reached a ridiculous point when young people were pulled out of universities because somebody had accused them of being homosexuals.

What did they say when they awarded you the National Prize for Literature?

Without being in the least vain, let me tell you that they should have awarded that prize to me much earlier. They hadn't done so because there had always been certain individuals who opposed my receiving it. But look, I have three novels, a book of essays, another of short stories, a play that I staged in New York in 1958, and sixteen collections of poetry, translated into twenty-two languages. . . . Not bad at all.

So would it be fair to say that, in awarding you the prize, they were paying off a literary debt to you?

I don't think so. I think that indeed some pretty criminal things were done against literature, and several texts were used to justify this. For example, closing down the theater because they said the actors were homosexuals. And so the theater virtually disappeared. In 1966 Havana was an international center for theater—until they started their campaign against several actors and actresses. I think the same is true about literature in general. Don't forget that the poems of Padilla with which they took issue had all been published here in Cuba, in the journals edited by Nicolás Guillén, Roberto Fernández, and Lisandro Otero.

And the censorship that we saw so clearly in Padilla's time, is it still as strong, or has it fallen off? And what about self-censorship?

This aspect of self-censorship is difficult to comment on, because I have no idea what other writers do. Censorship doesn't exist anymore. If it did, the recent book by Garrandés wouldn't have been published. Nor would *Estatua de sal* (Statue of Salt) by Mirta Yáñez and Marilyn Bobes. Nor would many of the books published by the Union of Writers or the Letras Cubanas publishing house. They have never censored any of my work. Never.

Some critics believe that the only writers who have remained in Cuba follow the official line, defending the government, while those writers who live abroad are enemies of the revolution. What do you think of this interpretation?

Well, first of all, it is too simplistic and does Cuban literature a great disservice. Here in Cuba nowadays we are publishing excellent literature, literature which definitely does not toe any official line. Let me go further: I wouldn't change any of the texts that we publish for the works of writers in exile that have received prizes abroad. It is very easy for exiled writers to win those prizes, since many of the editorials have hidden political motives. The prizes are not given just for literary merits. I distrust that type of "literature of exile." I doubt the value of any literature that seeks to turn itself into merchandise, some form of commodity. In this particular case, its value as a commodity is the fact that it is literature opposed to the current Cuban system. It hurts me to see literature used for that end. I also believe that all of that literature will be forgotten. When that fashion disappears, as indeed has already begun, people will come here to study what happened in Cuban literature between 1959 and 2000, and they will find some pretty interesting things.

And what do you think of the quality of literature that is currently being produced in Cuba?

I think that current Cuban poetry is splendid, and the same could be said for the short story and the novel. There are also some interesting new genres: the detective novel, the testimony work that bears witness to a particular reality. The whole idea of magic realism, which was more popular in Venezuela, Colombia, or Argentina, for example, has also been revitalized. I think that we have here a wonderful quality of literature and one that is intelligent and decent.

Some months ago, Julio Quiveiro wrote in the Nuevo Heraldo of Miami that the ideas Fidel Castro expressed in 1961 ("Within the revolution, everything is possible; outside, nothing") are as pertinent today as back then. He ends his article, "If you want to write literature, get away from the revolution, since only then can you write." How do you react to these views?

That they're a bunch of crap. Let's think one moment about Heberto Padilla, who was an extraordinary poet. What has he written in the past eighteen years? Padilla is a serious poet, a very cultured man. He is no fool. But he has never written as he did in Cuba. And where is the work of Antonio Benítez Rojo? Or that of the poet Armando Alvarez Bravo? Where is the theater of Pepe Triana? Why did Edmundo Desnoes never write another novel? What literature are they writing? Guillermo Cabrera Infante is still repeating the same story. I imagine that the journalist you mention is referring to Zoe Valdés or Daina Chaviano. But that isn't literature. That is writing in order to earn money.

As I hear you talk about these writers living abroad, the question still remains. Since you had such terrible treatment at the hands of the government, why didn't you go, too?

That is an interesting question since, as you know, I came back to Cuba largely because Guillermo Cabrera Infante asked me to in 1959. Yet he left in 1965 and I remained. I have a letter here that accuses me of being disloyal, since I refused to follow him into exile. I very much regret his perspective, but in the last analysis I decided to stay here because this is my country, my home.

Of course, I have wonderful memories of my life in New York. I met some wonderful people there. I remember the city so well: the East River, Central Park, the Village. Ah, New York, New York, what a wonderful town. . . . But how could I leave Cuba to live there? No, I could never do that. I had assumed the revolution as an act of grace. Participating in our revolution was like sharing an act of love with your neighbor. Look, for example, at the concept of guaranteeing education to everybody. Absolutely magnificent! I think it's extraordinary that in this country everybody—even the physically challenged—has a teacher. There are schools all over the country! I was born in a place where there was school for the children only up to sixth grade. Then I had to go to the United States. I could never receive the same education as my children. And now my tiny little town has a high school, and high schools are all over the country. There are even universities in Tunas and Holguín. Can you begin to imagine what that means?

Despite everything that happened to me, I always felt that I lived in a state of grace here in Cuba. And I had near me people whom I loved—like Heberto Padilla, a person with whom I had shared everything. I love him without reservation, and he loves me in the same way. If anybody loves me in this world, it is Heberto Padilla. And here too I had so many other friends: my brother César López, Miguelito Barnet, Manet and his wife, Olga, Pepito Rodríguez Feo, and Virgilio Piñera, who lived here in this house. After he had been arrested, he lived here with us until he found an apartment in the Vedado. Ah, Virgilio, what a man! A real character. . . .

So, quite simply, I could never leave here. . . . I never even thought about returning to live in the United States. I really was living in a state of grace here. My family was all here, Maruja, my friends. There was always food. I had a ridiculous salary, 226 pesos, which is not to be found on any official books anywhere. I worked from seven in the morning until four in the afternoon, and I started to learn German. All that has happened is the result of our destiny. And mine was to stay and work here.

Speaking about destiny, you are now seventy years old. What ambitions do you still hold?

I would very much like to travel to Egypt as well as to Guatemala, Brazil, and Germany. Nothing more. I would like to see Munich and Berlin, to walk through the streets. I would go to Guatemala because a friend of mine used to speak to me about it all the time, and when we were adolescents he said that some day we would go there. Egypt—why not? And I'd love to go to Brazil because I've always been in love with Carmen Miranda.

Leo Brouwer

Passion Has Six Strings

Since Leo Brouwer usually gets up early, we had arranged to begin this interview at 8 A.M. Unfortunately, he could only allow one hour because he had a rehearsal here in Havana at 9 A.M. with the National Symphonic Orchestra. What is worse, however, was that he was just passing through Havana, and as a result we had only that one hour—or none at all. And this for a conversation with one of the most important artists that the island of Cuba has ever produced.

My technique therefore had to change. I proposed the following scenario to Brouwer: I would ask questions and he would answer until 8:55 A.M. Then I would leave a list of the remaining questions, along with my tape recorder so that—if and when he had some spare time—he could dictate his replies onto the recorder. Brouwer accepted, and I started firing questions at him.

While he responded, I gazed at his hands. It seemed strange that there was nothing special about them, since with those same ten fingers this man had brought out the most extraordinary sounds from the guitar. I gazed at his face and again saw nothing that would indicate what a musical genius this man is. What did surprise me was the lack of wrinkles on this sixty-year-old man. I was pleased to see him enter with some confidence into problematic and potentially touchy areas, as if he were accustomed to thinking about these concerns. What impressed me most, however, was the absolute simplicity of this man who has received international recognition for so many years. Since his youth he has been considered a true guitar maestro, as a composer and a player. Moreover, in Cuba he is regarded as a cultural icon, and in 1999, he and his collaborator, jazz pianist Chucho Valdés, were awarded the highest cultural award in their field, the National Music Prize.

As I sat before Brouwer in his Vedado house, I experienced the strange sensation of having fallen into a different dimension, both of space and of time. But as I think about it again, I am comforted to recognize that this artistic genius is, in fact, my contemporary. He has lived in the same city that I do, and has allowed me to place this tape recorder in front of him, so that he can speak about the guitar, his life, and his work.

. . .

Maestro, you come from a line of distinguished piano players, and yet you chose to pursue a career with the guitar. How did this decision come about?

My relation with the guitar started out of a personal fascination. I would even say that it was a strange fascination, because at home there were always pianos. Moreover, my family has long been part of the national piano tradition in Cuba. Don't forget that my grandmother was Ernestina Lecuona and that her brother was Ernesto Lecuona, one of the most important piano virtuosos of Cuba and a tremendous composer. Because of this, because I had seen and heard him for so long, the piano was something that was absolutely natural. In my home it had a daily, visible presence and always seemed so familiar. The guitar, however, was somewhat different. I still remember, therefore, when my father—who was a doctor but a great admirer of the guitar—used to sit down and play it. It had an immediate spellbinding effect on me. I think that was the beginning of it all.

At that time I used to live in Santos Suárez, and after my parents divorced, I moved to the corner of Infanta and Carlos III, in the center of Havana. It was about then that I decided to study the guitar. It was already rather late for me to start to learn an instrument, but for me playing the guitar responded to some sort of natural impulse that I simply couldn't refuse.

The years I spent learning the guitar were very harsh. For four or five years, I studied every day without ever going to the movies or anywhere else. You can see what kind of spell had been cast upon me, since this kid of twelve years of age took it upon himself to pursue a ten-year musical program and to finish it in just four. It is true. It was a form of enchantment that I never awoke from, not even after my final examinations. And so, at sixteen, I began to play in concerts; soon after that, I even began to compose music.

Tell us about your first guitar. Where did you first play it?

At that time I used to get twenty-five cents each day, which was to pay my bus fare and also buy a snack. What I used to do, however, was to walk six kilometers and go without eating. Some eight months later, with the money that I'd saved, I bought my first guitar. As you can imagine, it was of very poor quality, and instead of proper strings it had nylon fishing line. For me, however, it was a real treasure.

This took place in the last years of the Batista dictatorship. A group of young people used to get together at a local hangout, the Cine-Club Visión, in Santos Suárez. Several talented people used to attend, including film directors Julio García Espinosa and Manolo Pérez, the painter Servando Cabrera Moreno, the Revuelta family and others from the theater, and all sorts of people from Cuban cultural life. They were my first audience.

Was there anybody in particular, or any particular event, that helped to define your interests and tastes at that time? What music did you like to listen to?

If anything helped me to define my interests, and myself, it was my relationship with Professor Isaac Nicola. He played for me works from the Renaissance and from the Baroque period, and in so doing he awoke in me a taste that I had not had before, since I had no particular tastes or any profound understanding of the history of guitar music. After I heard those pieces from the Renaissance and Baroque eras, no other guitar music could startle me so much. In general musical terms, however, I was amazed by Bartok. His quartets and Stravinsky's "Rite of Spring" were my musical models, and I preferred Stravinsky to Brahms, and Bartok to Beethoven—for reasons I still don't completely understand.

When did you give your first concert? And when did you first compose?

I gave my first concert in 1955, and it was in that same year that I began composing. The first decent compositions were written the following year, however, and they have been edited and recorded around the world. Now that is a matter of real luck and perhaps even a miracle.

At that time, didn't it seem rather bizarre in Cuba to pursue a career as a concert guitarist?

I never intended to pursue that career, nor did I ever intend to become a composer. You have to understand that the guitar for me was a form of passion. I still don't think that I have pursued any kind of career, even though I clearly have. Instead, I think that it all comes down to destiny and to a passion that ultimately became my profession.

During those years of your apprenticeship, which side of your artistic talents came out on top: those of the composer or those of the guitar virtuoso?

I think that both aspects benefited tremendously from the experience, in essence because the playing and the composing complemented each other so well in the creative process. Of course, I started by writing some pieces for the guitar, and afterwards moved on quickly to compose for the orchestra, because that was what I most enjoyed. My love for the guitar sprang from a sensual reaction, whereas my devotion to music was more an intellectual pursuit, although it, too, always possessed certain sensual qualities. My communication with music has always begun through that sense of feeling.

Where did you give your first concerts?

I gave my first concert at the Lyceum Lawn Tennis Club. It was a middle-class club where they organized the best art exhibits that you could imagine at that time. The last great collection of Eduardo Abela was shown there, as well as the best exhibits of Portocarrero or Raúl Milián. There were also excellent chamber orchestra performances given there. It was there, too, that the younger musicians did something with the Sociedad Nuestro Tiempo, although I could never afford the one or two pesos a month that it cost to join that society.

It is often said that the 1940s and 1950s were periods of a cultural vacuum in Cuba, yet what you say would indicate something quite different.

In my opinion there was indeed that vacuum, despite everything that was done. What happened during those years was that there was a far greater interest in universal culture, and as a result local cultural pursuits were largely ignored. For example, we had the Philharmonic Orchestra of Havana, which was one of the best three orchestras in Latin America, directed by the greatest musicians of the world who always came as guest conductors to Cuba. But if you examine their repertory and their projects, it was very much an elitist orchestra. It had a standard classical program, and you would never find the work of any Cuban composer being played.

As a reaction to all of this, in the 1940s José Ardévol—one of the most important figures of Cuban culture—initiated the Movement of Musical Renovation, together with his students Harold Gramatges, Julián Orbón, Edgardo Martín, and Argeliers León. Despite their efforts, they only managed to create a minor cultural refuge, which later joined with left-wing political activity in the Sociedad Nuestro Tiempo.

Musical Renovation is the best example of those responses (so important in artistic terms, even if they had only a modest impact) taken by proponents of a progressive culture when faced by those of a class-based one. The cultural activities of the élite were important, of course, and they were well presented by the most powerful institutions like Pro-Arte Musical. The necessary Cuban cultural element therefore made itself felt more as an act of resistance than as a natural presence, and so there was that relative, but real, vacuum.

Is it true that one of the reasons you composed music was because you were dissatisfied with the works that you were conducting?

Yes. There were indeed repertoires which, for reasons of aesthetic fashion, never lived up to their potential or a level that one hoped they could reach. I thought that Beethoven had developed the sonata form well. There were also sonatas for the guitar which did not have his magnificence or genius in regard to formal development. At the time when I began to compose, no matter how minor the pieces, I fell into a sort of trance, and I received a vision of the world through an absolute conceptual rigor that caused me to see reality in morphological and compositional terms.

It really was a very strange phenomenon that I still don't fully understand and can't explain to myself. Suddenly the world that surrounded me seemed to consist of modules of composition, and I could apply the framework to everything—from the form of a chair to any vertical structure or to the tensions of any shape. I used this revelation of intuition and confirmed its relevance when I studied major works. I realized then that my vocation was not mistaken. As a result I was able to "read" my teacher Paul Klee, one of the great painters in history. He and Kandinsky were my professors of composition. They taught me as nobody could that lines are part of both the culture and the structure of mankind.

Do you think that any particular stylistic definition can be applied to your musical work?

In 1967 I wrote an orchestral piece that was performed for the first time in 1969. The title was significant: "Traditions can be broken, but it takes a lot of work." It was a work influenced by a fortuitous series of events, at a moment when a furious vanguard of talent was in the process of blooming, one that played a major role in the development of our music.

Fifteen years later, the work produced at that time had been baptized "postmodern," although in fact it had been written when "postmodernism" didn't exist. Indeed, the "modernist" stage hadn't finished yet! And although all of this appears rather absurd, I think that if we undertake a proper analysis of what is considered musical postmodernism, it's fair to say that I consider myself a postmodern writer. It goes without saying that for me postmodernism doesn't mean throwing everything into a large bag, stirring it up, and then seeing what comes out. Rather, for me it is the symbol of this epoch, in terms of lived experience, materials that artists can employ, ideas, concepts, forms, cultures, contacts, and experiences that often appear contradictory. Because of that open approach, I consider both myself and my work to be postmodernist.

In 1959 you went to the United States and studied at the Juilliard Conservatory and Harvard University. How important was that academic experience for you?

It was extremely important because it represented an open window on materials and information that were impossible for me as an individual to obtain. Besides, in all of Cuba much of that information was not to be found. You could find everything in the Juilliard archives: they even had some scores of mine, some small pieces for piano and guitar that Argeliers León had edited in small, rather modest editions of the National Library. The fact that they even had some of my work shows how extensive their holdings were at that time.

They had lots of material on the history of music around the world: western music (even before the Middle Ages), as well as ancient religious pieces from India, Japanese kabuki music. . . . Everything was there. There was also an exceptional professor, Vincent Persichetti, who gave a lecture that I heard seated next to Leonard Bernstein, Lucas Foss, and Paul Hindemith, who at that time was teaching at Yale. I also took classes with a professor as talented as Stephan Wolpe. . . . With musical experiences like that, it was not difficult to become inspired.

Despite the tremendous opportunities that you had there, and the extraordinary intellectual talent all around, you decided to return to Cuba. Did you do so out of cultural necessity or because of a political decision?

At that time I was faced with the opportunity to finish my degree at the University of Hartford and take up a post there as professor of guitar. I was also offered the opportunity to tour the United States, sponsored by Columbia Management. In other words, I could have stayed there and had my professional career well developed. My decision to return was, however, totally political—although the scholarship that I had was scarcely enough for me to pay for a roof over my head and eat a couple of times a week. . . . I also made my decision at a time when relations were broken between the United States and Cuba, which of course complicated any decision. Let me point out, though, that I never regretted my decision, and I don't regret it now.

To what extent did the political and cultural environment of the 1960s influence you?

I have always said that period was one of unforgettable catharsis. Until that moment, artists involved in cultural pursuits had been struggling to reaffirm a nationality that Batista had denied, a deeply rooted nationality led by figures like Carpentier, Fidelio Ponce, Abelia, Amelia Peláez. When the revolution took place, this need to define ourselves and to defend ourselves took on a new meaning, and it now became one of collective spirit, of love, of pledging ourselves to build something new. I have a small composition for guitar called "Tres apuntes" (Three Notes), which I wrote on January 1, 2, and 3, 1959—those three crucial days of the revolution led by Fidel Castro after the flight of the dictator. I signed that work and put "1959, Free." The revolution was a sort of utopia in which I have believed ever since.

Although people now refer to it as "postmodern," back in the 1960s it was called music of the "vanguard." Did that "vanguard" imply breaking with the past, or continuity?

It was a breaking with the past, despite the fact that we had a form of universality and very solid roots that we did not need to deny in absolute terms. But the handful of us who began the initiative back then, and those who subsequently joined the movement which was called "the vanguard," did so with an enormous sense of identity. Even those of us who had some points of contact with the language of the previous vanguard now used in our work a language that was somewhat broken and disarticulated. As a result it was very close to the serialism and the fortuitous nature of culture, and this showed that we had come a long way from what had been achieved until then.

You have already stated that your relationship with the cinema started in the 1950s. But how did you come to link your creative talents to the cinema? And how did you become the director of the Group of Sound Experimentation at the Cuban Film Institute (ICAIC)?

When the ICAIC was created, a group of those who had founded it—Alfredo Guevara, Tomás Gutiérrez Alea, Santiago Alvarez, and Saúl Yelín—called me, and I joined the group that created the department of music. There I brought together composers, and I sat musicians down with filmmakers in a kind of café where we didn't even have chairs to sit down on! And so began the relationship between the musicians and the nascent Cuban film industry. This gradually evolved, with some composers who simply couldn't fit in with what we were trying to do and so stopped composing for the cinema and others who were able to understand the project and who stayed to work with ICAIC.

I was among the latter group, and for many years afterwards I wrote the music for almost a hundred films, some of which were never even finished. The cinema is one of the most complete art forms, and it challenges the composer, because it is not just a case of creating for yourself but rather doing so to support the dialogue of a film, the image on the screen, the script.

And how did the Group of Sound Experimentation come about?

I conceived of the idea, but the initiative was founded by Alfredo Guevara. It was all related to a crisis in song writing that he had noted. Alfredo is one of the most important figures in Cuban culture, with a very special character, somewhat severe. Whenever a crisis arose—whether it be over film posters, or poetry, or music—he left no stone unturned until he found a proper solution. And so, after he had requested cooperation, we decided to work together in order to improve the state of song writing in Cuba. The very first thing that we did was to bring together a dozen or so exceptionally talented singers and song writers who were scattered all over the place. They represented the roots of the Group of Sound Experimentation, which soon came to function as a source of music for the films.

A fundamental error in interpretation was made by those who claimed that I was part of the New Troubadour movement. The fact is that the New Troubadour movement didn't exist at that time: it only came to exist after the boom produced by the Group of Sound Experimentation. That movement was due to the genius of individuals like Pablo Milanés, Silvio Rodríguez, Noel Nicola, Sara González, Emiliano Salvador, and Sergio Vitier—most of whom were banned from state radio and television, as I was, because we were considered dangerous. We liked to perform a different type of music, we developed an art form of commitment that was unusual, and we had long hair.

We fought against this as a group and gave numerous concerts in high schools, universities, and camps in the country. Because of this constant work, and then the success of the Group of Sound Experimentation, there was no way that they couldn't put the songs of Silvio and Pablo on the radio and then others by the group. It was then that people began to speak about the New Troubadour movement in Cuba.

Can you remember when and where you first conducted a symphony orchestra?

Since I had studied at Juilliard, upon my return to Cuba I believed that I would be able to direct the chamber orchestra. I found, however, that the directors in this genre had already established themselves, and there was no room for me. Fortunately, José Ardévol, who was the director of music for the Ministry of Education and Culture, commissioned me to conduct some concerts of chamber music that had just been completed. These served as a form of training for me. But it was only much later that I began to conduct my own works with orchestras from France, Italy, Canada, and Spain.

And when did you begin to be recognized as an important musician, both in Cuba and abroad?

I don't know exactly, but in 1968 several musicians who came to Cuba to attend the Cultural Congress asked for me, because they knew my work. You may remember that the Congress was organized by former minister Llanusa (for whom I was a persona non grata, and because of that I wasn't invited to participate). Then composers like Luigi Nono, Hans Werner Henze, and Peter Schat spoke about several of us—Fariñas, Juan Blanco, myself, and others of our generation. And everything started to move after that. In 1970 Benjamin Britten invited me to the Aldeburgh Festival, after which I was invited to give recitals in several European countries. As a result of those concerts, the largest recording label, Deutsche Grammophon, with whom the Philharmonic Orchestras of Hamburg and Vienna record, invited me to record with them. I made three records with them, and then three with Erato. Afterwards I started to tour every year, and my path was pretty clear by then.

Was it about that time that the Ford Foundation offered you a scholarship, which you refused?

Yes, it was in 1971. But those are small matters within the realm of artistic matters. The Germans also offered to make me a major musical figure if I moved to Germany, but I turned them down. I truly don't think that this was so important, since the possibility to become a "major musical figure" was all completely hypothetical. By contrast, what is real is that we humans live just once, and I believe that what we always need to do is what is asked of us by our culture, our training, and our environment.

You have been intimately connected with the world of music since your childhood. How does that music provide you with inspiration? How has it formed you in cultural terms?

You have to separate things clearly here, since Cuban popular music has many facets and genres. My connection with that music is rigorously directed toward models that are today universal but that exist also as "local" music. Specifically, the roots and the very essence are the result of Afro-Cuban musical rituals. It is that musical tradition, more than any other, which has nourished me as a composer. I am not exaggerating when I tell you that I have been marked all my life by an experience I had when I was just twelve years old. I went to a santería ceremony in Guanabacoa and by chance attended the funeral of one of that religion's great priests. At that time I heard the music of ritual drums played in its purest state.

Three years earlier, in another ceremony on Línea Street in the middle of the Vedado district of Havana, I remember stopping in front of another Afro-Cuban religious celebration. One of the matrons, an eighty-year-old woman dressed completely in white, invited me in, not just to that particular ceremony but into that entire world. And anybody who witnesses or lives through one of those authentic ceremonies has to feel an extraordinary emotion. And it doesn't matter whether they are a believer or an atheist (as I am), and nine or sixty years old.

Another way in which you have linked your own work with popular music is through the work of the Beatles. How did that admiration for their music come about?

The music of the Beatles reveals an extraordinary artistic genius. But in their music (which, by the way, is undoubtedly universal) they managed to combine so many influences—black North American song, Celtic music, and that of the Isabelline era in England—all gathered together and synthesized in a marvelous fashion. That kind of synthesis is extremely important and can only be achieved by truly great talents. And I personally respect that ability to bring diverse cultural influences together and to synthesize them in an inclusive style. And because of that, I have always felt great empathy with their work.

When did you stop performing the guitar in recitals, and why? What did that decision mean for you?

I had an accident in 1980, and it prevented me from playing as perfectly as I wanted. I could still play, using some skills to make up for the missing qualities, but I decided that if I couldn't play the guitar perfectly—which was always my intention—then it was better not to play at all. And that is precisely what I did. From time to time I feel very nostalgic for the pieces that I used to play, for the music itself. I don't miss the act of playing. When you play, you communicate with your public, and I have been able to preserve this ability to an astounding degree when I conduct orchestras. And so giving up playing was not particularly traumatic.

Which aspect of your work do you prefer: interpreting music, composing, directing an orchestra, or teaching?

I can't answer that question in rational terms, because each of the four choices that you have indicated implies a sensual decision rather than an intellectual one. In many ways it resembles the taste of a gourmet, who tries one dish today and another one tomorrow. If we eat the same dish all the time, it is terribly limiting.

It is sometimes said that there is a Cuban style of playing the guitar. Do we have a particular style or school? And if this is the case, what is it based upon?

This is rather complicated. In principle, if there were a Cuban school of guitar, this would not have any strong tradition or history. As a result, if there is one, it is extremely young and exists because of individuals who for years now have developed it by teaching this approach. Since the days of Nicola, this Cuban school has passed along this tradition to our guitarists. These teachers, though, should not be placed alongside our great teacher, the maestro Isaac Nicola. It is he who, since the teachings of the Pujols school (which, by the way, is different from the Cuban model), has developed the Cuban school. In historical terms, then, Nicola would be the founder of this Cuban school, although not in the case of technique.

On a secondary level, I would place those of us who have been working on this for the past forty years, especially the younger players. It is these people who make up the Cuban school, one which can only be defined by one fundamental characteristic—imagination. The isolation suffered by Cuba has made me work in my own individual manner and has caused other guitar players here, either by accident or deliberately, to react in the same fashion. Given the little information we have received, our imaginations have been extremely important. And, since we have received so little music, we have composed our own. We have had so few references that we have imagined them, and this has contributed to our composing our own music. At present there is more information available, but I think that the leap in quality that we see here has been given because of the imagination of Cuban guitarists. Our talented guitarists are less the result of having been trained by certain professors than they are of their own imagination, since they have created music from almost nothing. Another characteristic of this Cuban school is the search for perfection, which has become increasingly refined until reaching admirable artistic levels.

Of the hundreds, and perhaps thousands, of guitarists whom you have seen and heard, who do you most admire? Have you envied any of them?

It is curious that one of the most outstanding figures, and one with whom we had major problems, is Andrés Segovia. Today it seems to me that, if I have to envy anybody, it is Segovia. He was a magician, both in the sound that he produced and in the way that he interpreted music. It is true that he was totally anarchistic in the way he played and respected no historic styles, but he was still a genius. And although nowadays people play in a different manner, as did my own generation, it is nevertheless true that the bewitching beauty of the sound he produced was his most important contribution to the history of the guitar.

There have been few figures of his magnitude, even though there have indeed been many other exceptional figures like Barrios Mangoré, a Paraguayan native who influenced many guitarists, almost in an anonymous fashion, since he played in so few major concert halls, possibly because of European jealousy. There have been great guitarists like John Williams and Julian Bream, two pillars of the guitar who are so different in character, form, and style. And among the new generation, there are many people with great talent, among them several Cubans and Latin Americans, such as Manuel Barruecos, Pierri, and the Cuban Rey Guerra.

And among guitarists who play popular music?

I would mention Paco de Lucía, Gismonti, John MacLaughlin, Vicente Amigo, Joe Satriani, Pat Metheny, and Stanley Jordan. These are names that I automatically think of, although there are also many others of great musical quality.

Why did you decide to leave Cuba and go to work in Córdoba?

The basic reason was for family reasons, since I went at a time when I needed to be by myself for a while. Then too because I felt the need to do something new, something which has always been true of my nature. Perhaps that is why I created the music department of ICAIC and introduced a new manner of teaching contemporary harmony in the curriculum of Cuban conservatories. For the same reason, this desire to assume new challenges, I formed the Group of Sound Experimentation, and then re-created a different approach for the National Symphony Orchestra. And now I have founded the Symphony Orchestra of Córdoba in Spain.

To carry out this goal, I searched for musicians who had never played in symphony orchestras. I worked with them, together with six Cuban musicians who accompanied me to work there. The end result, some five years later, is that in Córdoba we now have one of the best of some thirty symphony orchestras in Spain. Soon the orchestra will be able to makes its own way, as occurred with the Group of Sound Experimentation, and I'll move on to see if there's something new that I can create.

In your view, what is or should be the responsibility of artists in Cuba?

For some time now we have heard talk about artists as people with political interests. I have always understood this political role, and I still accept that challenge. That fundamental principle does not mean, however, that artists have to depend upon any particular ideology. Rather, they have a historic responsibility, namely, to participate fully in the society that surrounds them. If this does not occur, then their art has no political value, no matter how they seek to explain themselves with demagoguery and shows of dissidence, real or pretended. If they do not have the influence of society, historically and politically assumed and inserted in their work (and vice versa), they are guilty of demagoguery.

You are now sixty years old. Looking back on your life, how do you see the Leo Brouwer in 1959, when he was just twenty years old? Or in 1979, when you were forty? And what can you say about the Leo Brouwer of today? Moreover, if your youth had not witnessed the romantic 1960s, but instead the discouraging 1990s, what kind of artist would you be?

Now that I am sixty, I see myself when I was twenty years old as a young man with tremendous immaturity but at the same time very open to the surrounding world. I remember myself as a frightened child facing a colossus, and yet at the same time like a sponge soaking up all sorts of influences. By the age of forty, I was not surprised at anything because, as Rossini used to say, when I am twenty ideas pursue me; when I am forty I grab at ideas; and at sixty I pursue ideas, since they are already beginning to disappear. . . .

And it is very true: the idealists of the 1960s gave me a touch of optimism that the 1990s do not have to offer. I think that if I had been twenty years old in the 1990s, I would have dedicated myself to pop music and tried to earn as much money as I could. Probably this cynicism is a defensive attitude, because I would like to think that, even without the direction of the romantic 1960s, I would have become the same person that I have been all my life—a position based upon the society and circumstances that surrounded me.

In your opinion, what have been both the errors and the successes of the cultural policy of the Cuban Revolution?

The errors and successes of Cuban cultural policy are infinite. Among the errors, I think we should indicate the general support, so badly directed, that we all gave to the amateur cultural movement in the 1960s. That movement should have been directed into a movement for lovers of art and music. We should have developed people into "aficionados," teaching them to love music, and not to try and make a living from it—which is what happened in the end.

And so, even if we can talk about a particular work of cinema or literature being censored, or the manner in which we were repressed in the 1960s because we had long hair, I always think of global errors like the one that I have just mentioned. Or perhaps, too, the lack of communication and understanding of art and culture that has often existed because political figures, people with power, warriors, often don't understand those of us who live by thinking, through cultural expression. And they forget that in the Roman Empire it was when Caesar disregarded the philosophers that the real decadence started.

What do you think about the current boom of salsa, both in Cuba and abroad? How much of this boom is due to business promotion, and how much is due to real artistic expression? What do you think about the image of Cuban salsa singers?

Despite the fact that there is a very clear commercial element, I think that salsa today also reflects the surrounding culture, and as a result salsa will continue to exist with money or without it. Of course, it is better if it continues with money for the salsa singers, so that they can live as they deserve. In recent years their image has become highly respected, as salsa has become so popular. I am fortunate to know some of the major figures of salsa. Some of them live here in Cuba, and that is no coincidence. One of them is Juan Formell, who will go down in Cuban cultural history because of his role as a composer and performer and because of his efforts in promoting music for so many years with his orchestra.

Because there are such fine figures as Formell, it is a pity that salsa should be seen just as a business. It is also a pity that there are indeed many musicians who do perform salsa purely to earn money, and this can be seen in the lyrics of their songs and in their style. Whenever a certain style becomes successful, competitors rush to imitate it. This can be seen, for example, in the manner in which some writers use local slang terms in their music—and they do so without achieving the refinement that it needs if it is to be treated artistically. I am not suggesting that our writers should seek to develop some sublime or extraordinary turn of the phrase (as, by contrast, the genius of the members of the New Troubadour movement did). Rather, I am suggesting that language be assumed appropriately and processed aesthetically. In this way its contribution will not be limited to a slang phrase from the street which is then forgotten when another piece of slang takes its place.

In sum, I believe that all cultural artists should take care of the image of their product, whatever it is, because salsa is an important expression of popular art and will not disappear, although of course it is preferable that its splendor be lived out in better artistic conditions.

8

Nancy Morejón

"A Black Woman from Cuba, That's All"

Nancy Morejón, one of Cuba's best poets, considers her defining qualities to be her race, her gender, and her nationality. This conjugation of factors at a particularly interesting point in Cuban history—the Cuban Revolution—has made for a particularly fortuitous body of poetry.

Morejón is a writer who is extremely comfortable with her race and her reality, her gender and her political views. She has dedicated a significant part of her work to reaffirm the Cuban revolutionary process with enthusiasm and a profound sense of responsibility, even though she suffered a form of official literary ostracism for several years. Because of this understanding of the complex reality of Cuba and her commitment to its revolutionary essence, she is indeed the poetess of the revolution. Without a doubt, she is the poetic heir of Nicolás Guillén, recognized as the poet of the revolutionary process. Morejón is gifted with an exceptional lyricism. She is also an intellectual who has participated in many facets of Cuban cultural life, from the plastic arts to theater. (She is currently working as an adviser at the National Theater.) Her academic research into the larger Caribbean context, on which she is an internationally recognized specialist, has allowed her to connect Cuban culture with the broader geographical and cultural area to which it naturally belongs. Her poetry, meanwhile, has allowed her to focus on her own historical context, the contemporary reality of Cuba.

Finally, she is a passionate supporter of Havana, the city which for decades has inspired her poetry.

. . .

Who is Nancy Morejón?

It is very hard for me to read my true nature. I believe that I am a black woman from Cuba, that's all.

Could you speak a little about your childhood? Tell us about your family environment, the district in which you grew up, the influence of your parents.

It is curious that you should start with the issue of my parents, because this is the first interview that I have given since the death of both of my parents. My father died in 1987, and my mother in 1997. They are an essential part of my life and of my work, because they passed to me a legacy that has profoundly affected both my life and my work. They never opposed my vocation as a writer; indeed, they understood it well and supported me. This was somewhat strange among people of such humble origin.

The issue of social justice was very important at home. My parents were both workers—my father was a stevedore and my mother was a seamstress—and they both belonged to unions. They both defended the rights of working people. Perhaps the most important feature of my early development was that I acquired the habit of reading. Every day my father would sit down to read, because we had subscriptions to most journals and the best newspapers. I first discovered the poetry of Nicolás Guillén in my father's library. Actually his library was a small bookcase with some books. Reading was thus an important part of daily life at home.

I also consider myself a creature of the revolution in the sense that all the efforts that my parents made to support me actually came to fruition when I went to college. This was significant because after 1959 the university opened its doors to all social sectors in the country.

Besides Guillén, which other writers did you discover at your home?

I used to read many textbooks, which included the work of great Cuban poets such as Gertrudis Gómez de Avalleneda. It was a memorable experience for me at the time to read her sonnet "Al partir" (Upon Parting). I also read José Martí a lot, naturally, although at that time it was not that popular to study his work, and when his work was studied it was not done properly.

That was the atmosphere in which I grew up, with lots of encouragement for me to get a good education and to improve myself. That is why I began to study English when I was nine years old. My parents also showed a great respect for good manners. This is important, especially nowadays, since in recent times (which have been so hard for people) some rather strange ideas have been circulating. There is a fair amount of ideological confusion these days, and some people think that socialism means full equality for all, in the worst sense of the term *equality*. In other words, things simply have to be ugly, and as a result we are expected to fight against beauty. My parents were great admirers of beauty, however. For them, culture could never be simply a means of consumption. Rather, culture possessed a civilizing objective in the positive sense of the term. And I inherited that notion from Felipe Morejón.

It is often claimed that North American influence was particularly strong in the 1940s and 1950s. How did you take in this culture?

Before he was a stevedore, my father had been a sailor and often sailed to the United States. One day he told me of a trip that he had made to Louisiana, where he went to see Louis Armstrong play. At my home we often listened to black musicians from the United States, and my father particularly liked the music of Nat King Cole, because he had been to some of his concerts in New York.

At that time the problem of racial segregation was very noticeable in the United States. Rosa Parks had not yet taken her stand against racial segregation, and my father used to tell me about his own experiences in the South, when he had to sit at the back of the buses he rode on. "Back to your seat!" he was told. All of this linked me with North American culture, created an awareness of its power, and helped me enjoy popular music from the United States. I particularly liked jazz, undoubtedly because there is a cultural connection between North American and Cuban culture, a connection that comes from the African component.

When did you first realize that you had the vocation to become a writer?

When I was a student at the Havana Institute, I had a teacher who often gave us writing assignments. One day she asked me if I liked literature. I told her that I did. "Do you write poetry?" she asked me. "No, I don't, although I do keep a diary." She asked me to bring it in so that she could look at it. The next day she took me to one side and told me: "I want you to know that this is not a diary. No, what you have here are poems. You write poetry." This occurred when I was about twelve or thirteen years old.

I had an excellent literary preparation during my years at high school, with a first-rate appreciation of literary texts. And so, little by little, I entered the world of literature. Afterwards I was lucky because the revolution took place when I was fourteen years old. At that time many doors opened up, especially to places where, given my father's poor socioeconomic status, I probably wouldn't have been able to study. At the time of the revolution we experienced here an explosion of justice and progress for the most humble sectors of our society. This proved a marvelous opportunity for me, and I could do all that I wanted to and study what I wanted.

In what year did you publish your first book?

I entered the university and published my first book in 1962. Everything fitted together wonderfully. That first book was a collection of those poems that I had taken to show my teacher in the last year of high school.

My university years, 1962 to 1966, coincided with a period of tremendous cultural excitement. In my own case, for example, the very first time that I set foot in a theater was after the revolution. It was a time when the state provided grants to a variety of cultural groups, the arts in general were there to be enjoyed by all Cubans, and a fascinating music was produced. All the ingredients connected to this new form of culture appeared in the 1960s. In addition, many foreign intellectuals came to visit Cuba, and we followed with great interest the debate on the role of culture in socialist society. We young people were thoroughly swept away by this tremendous wealth of culture that we had just met.

In your poem "Amor, ciudad atribuida" (Love, Attributed City), you use the following metaphor to describe the impact that poetry had upon you: "Poetry arrived here with a wonderful lance and pierced my breast." Does poetry still have this effect on you?

I believe that poetry has to have this profound impact, although of course I do not think that it has to be a form of suffering. Rather, it allows us to see so much, to enjoy so many different sensations. It is a tool designed to help us raise questions, evaluate experiences.

Do you believe in inspiration? Is writing a vocation for you?

I personally believe in inspiration. I don't know what causes it, but yes, it does exist. At the same time, one cannot leave everything to inspiration. There's so much to read, so much to study. As my grandmother used to say, "If inspiration comes, then please let it find me working hard." I also believe in the concept of a literary vocation. At this stage of my life I have reached this conclusion. It seemed very clear to me when my mother was very ill, and I had to look after her. It was a time when I abandoned my profession, leaving behind the world of reflection. It was a very useful experience, since it allowed me to understand the importance of this particular vocation.

I believe that, in addition to spontaneity, it is also necessary to have a great deal of rigor. In my own case this vocation has developed in an unusual form during the years of the "Special Period" here in Cuba. And it's all been due to the blackouts, when the electricity has disappeared. In recent years we've spent as many as six hours without electricity, and at times I felt desperate. And when the light finally came on again, I felt very much like writing and so picked up a pen and paper—only to find that I couldn't write. And on one of those occasions, while I was wondering when the lights would come back on, much to my surprise I started to draw. And for a while I didn't write at all. I simply sat down in front of the paper and started to draw. It was also good therapy, since it took away lots of worries I had, and so this new form of expression is due to our blackouts.

What do you believe are the responsibilities of writers? In particular, what do you see as your obligations? And what are your rights?

I believe that I possess every right, naturally, and in addition I run all sorts of risks. I was educated between 1962 and 1966, which is when I was really formed as a writer. Living in Cuba at that time was like living in the midst of a constantly evolving social laboratory. A revolutionary process is a workshop, a phenomenon that helps to enrich you as a person, both giving and taking away. I was brought up with the idea that I belonged to the intellectual model of small countries. And for me it has always been important to share. Sometimes it is simply impossible to specialize in what you want to. Somebody may want to be a novelist, but instead has to work as a chemist, because that is what society needs at that time. I also possess a profound sentiment of the need to contribute, to give back—speaking in intellectual terms—the benefits that were given to me. And that is why I have published my works and participated in many other projects, supporting and developing our culture in thousands of ways.

I think that we have lost certain aspects of this concept. Now young writers seek only to achieve success. I want success, too, but not as the only goal. I believe, for example, that there are many ways of being successful. It is also important to me to be useful.

What problems do you see in the publication and diffusion of literature in Cuba?

I believe that we have to return to what Che Guevara called moral incentives. Let me give you an example. I have a book that was awarded the Critics' Prize. For me as a writer to receive this award was one of the most moving events in my life. That book is sold in bookstores around the country, yet nobody knows that it received this award. Why don't the bookstores in Havana have a special stand to promote books that receive prizes like this? I received a considerable amount of pesos as a prize for that work. I am very pleased to have received it, but I believe that we need to promote our culture far more.

Literature here has gone through a very difficult period because of the lack of paper. But we also need to think about reprinting many works, because there are people who have just started reading and have no idea of the cultural wealth of the 1960s. Basically because there are no more copies of works produced at that time. Soon we'll be referring to "the past century," and yet students don't have the material to appreciate what this really means. Nor do they have a solid vision of the key authors of this century. It is ironic because there are many specialists in Cuban literature who live outside the island, while here—due to so many limitations that we face here—those works are hardly known at all.

You have referred to the years 1962 to 1966 as being a key period in your development. As you look back on your work, can you see clearly defined periods?

There is an initial period between 1962 and 1969, and then another from 1969 to 1979, which is when I wrote a lot of essays and other types of literary work, since I wasn't allowed to publish poetry at that time. Some horrible lies were invented, and I was on a kind of blacklist. As a result, my poetry wasn't published. I returned to writing poetry in 1979, and there is then a period that goes until 1985. And then another from 1985 to 1995. And now my most recent work.

The first stage revolved around the publication of a book full of literary stuttering, with several different styles, largely because I wrote with tremendous freedom. At that time I believed in expression for expression's sake, without any formal limitations—in sum, a period of great spontaneity. Then I began to focus on the city of Havana and to analyze the reality of this country. I began to enter the debate on the problems of the individual and of the artist in society. I also initiated the search for the Cuban essence by means of the social changes that resulted from the Cuban Revolution. Then my poetry ventured into some controversial terrain, and I experienced a great number of confrontations. Later, I became somewhat more aware of gender issues, starting with "Mujer negra" (Black Woman), which I wrote in 1975.

Your profound love of Havana is clearly visible in much of your work. Is it fair to say that you live a life that has been invaded by this city?

I adore Havana. It is something very strange, quite bizarre. Despite the degree to which it has deteriorated, its abandoned state due to the way in which the country has had to reorient its economy in recent years, I still think that it is an exceptional place. There are many things that could be done to alleviate its problems, because what is needed has less to do with a lack of financial resources than with willpower. First of all, we have to take stock of the problems. Then we have to demand answers: Why do they not sweep the streets? Why does so much garbage simply pile up? What is the government doing about these problems? We pay taxes now and are well aware that is a duty which we all have. Yet we should be demanding more. Of course, the impact of the U.S. blockade is an important factor, yet despite this we should be asking for more. We see here so much neglect, and it's not all due to our neighbors across the Straits of Florida.

What, precisely, is the importance of this city for your work?

It provides me with tremendous inspiration. I stroll by places that are just exquisite. I adore the colonial area, the bar district, the diversity of it all, and the architectural wealth of it all, the commercial zone, the Malecón coastal road, the port. . . . And because of that love, I am concerned at the way in which many people are abusing the city at present. Many people migrate here from other areas of the country, but once they arrive they don't respect the customs here. These people just don't fit in and don't settle down, because they see the city as a Mecca to make money and consume whatever they find. This is an attitude that we must change. They have to learn to respect our traditions, because what they are doing is an affront to those of us who were born and bred here. This city is very beautiful indeed, and it has inspired my work for many years. But we also need to love it, because even if there are lots of resources, if we don't love it, we won't be able to save the city.

There are several poems of yours, such as "Abril" (April), "Renacimiento" (Rebirth), "Una rosa" (A rose), "Mitologías" (Mythologies), and "La noche del Moncada" (The Night of the Attack on the Moncada), in which your full identification with the Cuban Revolution can be seen. Do you think that the label that several people have given you, as the "poetess of the revolution," is fair?

I think that they are exaggerating, because the revolution is something that clearly surpasses my talents. I have many defects and feel incapable of deserving such a title. Besides, in my opinion there is only one poet of the revolution, and that is Nicolás Guillén, largely because he lived through the entire process. I developed as a writer at a later stage, and that label far exceeds my abilities. At the same time, I would like to be seen as a person who works for her country and does things to contribute to its development.

Does the fact that you are a poet and a black poet mean that you have more responsibilities than a white woman?

I am always fearful of stereotypes. Of course, the very notion of being a white writer in Cuba is an exceptionally abstract concept. To a large degree my analysis is based on the fact that every Cuban is a person of mixed cultures and diverse racial origins. Every Cuban is a true cultural blend. I have read many books on feminist philosophy, and I think that we have to proceed with great caution when analyzing any stereotypes. At the same time I believe that, as a black woman, yes, indeed, I do have things of value to say. Because of those origins I come from a history of suffering, and I always have to be alert, to share that history, to have it felt by others. At the same time, I don't have to exaggerate.

Is there still racial prejudice in Cuba?

Yes, because eradicating it is an extremely slow process. For me, racial discrimination is the exercise of those racial prejudices. To stop that, I believe that making people aware of their conduct, developing an ideological understanding of the problem, is far more effective than resolving the abuses solely through legal means. This does not mean that there should not be laws against discrimination—only that we also need to channel the true spirit of the revolution to all sectors.

Some people here say, "Don't talk to me about the race question." But we do have to examine this again, because it is an important matter here in Cuba.

At times people have been afraid to talk openly about it and have not known how to deal with it as they should. And that is why there are such gaps in our understanding, gaps which we hear more about all the time. That is why we need to reconsider so many facets of our revolutionary traditions, because this problem of racism is a universal problem, one affecting all humanity, and not just Cuba. For example, if we analyze what has happened since 1989 in the former socialist community, we can see how the question of ethnic identity has been revisited. The proof of this can be seen in Bosnia-Herzegovina or in Chechnya. If we don't address this factor, if we do not study it and seek to resolve it, we may ultimately face unwelcome surprises. And so I think that we should examine in more detail the question of race relations.

Do you, as a black woman, feel any responsibility to help in this process?

Yes, I do, and also from my perspective as a writer. But it has to be by means of a high-quality artistic expression, because no matter how good the message may be, it will be useless unless it is done well. But I also need to speak with others in the cultural milieu. I have already spoken with film directors and have suggested the need to make a film about this very issue. We cannot simply forget the racial question. We also need to see black characters somewhere other than in films about slavery. We badly need something more contemporary and more pertinent.

A question on the concept of Utopia, which you describe well in your poem "Divertimento" (Amusement). In it you refer to Cuba in the following manner: "Between the sword and the carnation / I love Utopias / I love an island which lies piercing the throat of Goliath / like a palm tree in the center of the Gulf / I love David / I love everlasting freedom." How do your feelings of evident nationalism react to the "pact with the devil" that the Cuban government has undertaken in order to survive? How do you feel when you are faced by the new realities of tourism, prostitution, search for the dollar, and foreign investment?

It is a reality that in many ways is upsetting, in part because it was so unexpected. We need to be audacious if we are to function properly in this new context. We are convinced about what we need in order to survive. We also know well that the process cannot be stopped, since otherwise Cuba would remain completely isolated. In essence we have witnessed several developments over which we had no control, and as a result we had to reconsider many things. Now that tourism has returned to play such a major role in the economy, we have the opportunity to receive a fair amount of income for the national economy. At the same time we have to be careful about the type of tourism that we seek to develop. We can't develop the form that they have in Barbados, for example. We can have, for instance, a positive kind of tourism, one that does not need to use the bodies of our women as a hook to bring in male visitors.

It is fair to say that we have been surprised by the kind of tourism that has sprung up in certain sectors. It has been painful for us in many ways. At the same time I don't believe that this situation will be resolved by repression. Rather, we need to reflect upon the whole issue of tourism, in order to see how it can be useful for our country and also what we need to confront in a vigorous fashion. We have discovered a very serious phenomenon, but again it seems to me that this cannot be resolved through repressive means.

Have you written anything about this new reality of Cuba?

No. And that's not because I haven't wanted to, because I have thought a lot about this new reality (which in many ways I dislike). Rather, I haven't written anything because I don't want any of my comments to be misinterpreted. At times if you say something controversial, people think that you want to become some kind of famous dissident. And that is definitely not my case. I believe that I have had many opportunities to play the role of dissident, but I'm not the slightest bit interested in that game.

At the same time, I do believe that it is necessary to have a space where you can air concerns. We have to encourage people to study this reality and to be honest when facing the problems that we have. If that's not the case, we are in trouble.

In your opinion, what have been the major cultural successes of the Cuban Revolution? And what have been the failures?

Often we see errors, but we don't realize just how serious they are until later. And we regret that they were made in the first place. But let's start with the positive elements. One can note there the tremendous potential which we came to see in ourselves. The revolution opened doors for us and allowed an enormous social mobility. Many walls that blocked communication were demolished, and taboos were cast out. At the same time there came a certain point when the idea of massive numbers of people pursuing cultural interests became a priority of the government, often above everything else. They forgot that, in order to appreciate art, people have to have some basic ideas about the need to recover the essence of beauty. It is very true that liberating social sectors as well as progress and social mobility clearly need not be limited to the individual. Just the opposite: They have to reaffirm it. The problem was that often, closely connected with this emphasis on such a massive approach to culture, there came the accompanying practice of justifying mediocrity, often in the name of a supposed form of equality. As a result, we have often protected mediocre cultural expressions, and I believe that we should be more rigorous.

Looking back on the stormy periods of cultural development in Cuba, which errors do you think have been committed in the past that now need to be recognized?

The Padilla affair is a particular case, complex and unusual. He was a poet with a terrific work, an excellent person, and a kind, pleasant man. I admired him a great deal. But he lacked the maturity to understand the role of the intellectual in Cuba. I emphasize that you need to understand the context in which developments occurred. At that particular time, his poetry was less important than the intellectual trajectory of Padilla, particularly when judged in the light of a series of economic factors, literary factors, indeed, all kinds of factors. I believe that a very serious error was committed here in the way in which the whole issue was handled, just as I believe that he also committed serious errors. Later he made many mistakes, and he allowed himself to be manipulated. All of that provided us with a history that left a series of experiences in its wake, on which we have to reflect—and learn from.

In every society there are absolute and limited freedoms. How would you describe the freedom that currently exists in the Cuban cultural forum?

I think it's important to take into account our reality. We are a country that is still under siege and one that has never been alone. We must always remember the hostility to which we have been subjected. There are other limitations that need to be considered. In this Special Period, we have had limited paper and, of course, all sorts of limitations on cultural resources. This country has a very high level of education, and much of the money that we could have used for cultural purposes has instead been used to buy textbooks. We simply don't have the resources to do both. Very often people abroad see us talking about our free education as some sort of empty political slogan, but in fact it is a reality and a priority. This element, in the midst of the Special Period, has limited literary life enormously, and as a result there are fewer journals, literary competitions, publications, etc. We need to recover all the lost terrain in this matter.

I feel that Cuban writers today are demanding things that simply cannot be conceded in a period like this, since we are facing difficulties as critical as the Bay of Pigs invasion or the Missile Crisis. This country has to survive. Moreover, "freedom" has many facets, and many people think that they have to make demands on the state for their freedom. I think that there are, in fact, several "freedoms" and not just "freedom" in absolute terms.

And freedom here has to be conditioned, or affected, by the hostility that we have encountered in the last forty years. Now it is practically a psychological phenomenon. We are all subjected to the same tensions. I personally believe that a writer has to feel a major responsibility resulting from the nation's identity, as well as a major ethical responsibility in regards to the community. As a result of those twin factors, one needs to know that there are things that can and cannot be done, because the revolution has the right and the duty to exist.

Of course, there have been many errors here, basically because we all have limited conceptions of what the revolution should be. To give you an idea, my parents had a utopian idea of the revolution. They would argue, for example, that a revolutionary shouldn't drink Amaretto liqueur. . . . As you can see, we have come to accept many stereotypes, and we badly need to struggle against that. We need to respect differences and diversity, and precisely because of that fact I am certain that there were errors in cultural matters. Che, too, was a declared enemy of socialist realism, and I believe that we should respect his honesty. By all means we should have the freedom to criticize dogmas and stereotypes, but we must always bear in mind the reality of our history.

9

Roberto Fernández Retamar and Literary Commitment

Roberto Fernández Retamar is a proponent of "engaged" or "committed" literature. From his earliest poems and essays, he has demonstrated his commitment to the revolutionary process. As director of the internationally recognized Casa de las Américas cultural institution and the Center for Martí Studies, he has continued this trend. Moreover, in numerous international and national fora, this Havana intellectual has been a solid and consistently faithful spokesperson for the revolutionary government's cultural policy. He has also been elected a deputy to the National Assembly of People's Power (the Cuban parliament) and has served on the Council of State of Cuba.

Fernández Retamar possesses a profound awareness of the work of José Martí, Cuba's national poet and independence leader. He has also written some outstanding essays on Cuban and Latin American identity. And he is an exceptional poet, comfortable in a variety of styles from the epic to lyrical poetry, from intimate love themes to openly social and political matters. His body of work has been widely praised, and he has received the National Prize for Literature in Cuba as well as other literary distinctions. His work, however, has generally been viewed through the prism of his political commitment to the revolutionary process since his youth.

He is considered an official cultural personality in revolutionary Cuba. His views are therefore extremely important, for they reveal both unswerving loyalty to the revolutionary process and the change of mentality toward cultural matters in recent years.

. . .

Can you share with us some thoughts on your childhood here in Havana?

I was born in 1930 in a district of Havana known as La Víbora. My father was an accountant and a professor, and my mother worked in an office until she married, as was the custom at that time. I came from a family of professionals of petit bourgeois origin. But my parents were very rebellious and totally opposed to the dictatorships of Machado and Batista in prerevolutionary times. They were also avid readers, and I was pleased to receive a clear legacy of these ideals. As a result, they cultivated in me a love for letters and for my country. They were extremely important in my life, and so I never went through the normal process of rebelling against parental influence.

The importance of that relationship with your parents can be seen in a poem like "¿Y Fernández?" Did your father write poetry?

No, although he recited poetry and liked to act. He had a literary vocation that was never realized. He was a man of letters who did not write and an amateur actor. These qualities helped me when I developed my own interest in writing, since both he and my mother always supported my literary inclinations.

And your education?

I studied the first three grades with the nuns, because they ran a school just fifty meters from where I lived. I have very happy memories of the years that I spent with them. The mother superior was Mother Guadalupe. Many years later I learned that they were Mexican nuns who had been expelled from their country at the time when Plutarco Elías Calles was president of Mexico. My family was not particularly religious, and after third grade I went to study in a lay school whose philosophy was more in agreement with that of my family. It was a private school called the Instituto Edison, where I had very good teachers.

My high school education was at the Instituto de La Víbora, which was a public school, because my parents did not have sufficient money to send all three of their children to private schools. You often hear people talk about how good German and French schools are, but I too had a secondary education that was of very high quality. My principal academic interest was mathematics, and at one point I even thought that I would become a mathematician. But then I had an excellent literature teacher who helped me to change my options and to develop my interest in literature.

I started to write at a fairly young age. I was fifteen years old. However, it was impossible for me to choose between arts and sciences, as I was supposed to do when I reached the fifth year in high school. I refused to choose, and instead took both of them, characteristically I suppose. As a result, when I finished my secondary education, I registered in the Faculty of Architecture, since in this way I hoped to be able to blend my vocation as a mathematician with my artistic interests. But I was an absolute disaster. So I switched to philosophy and letters the following year. That was about fifty years ago now.

How did your first writing come about?

I was very young at the time, just fifteen years old, as I mentioned. I used to write poetry, very bad poetry at that, which was influenced by the style of writing of the great Cuban poet Julián del Casal. There was also the influence mixed in of the Spanish poets, the modernists, the romantics, and of course José Martí. At the same time I used to write reviews in *Ideas,* a journal put out by the Instituto de La Víbora. That would be in 1945. In 1947 I began contributing to a journal for young people, *Alba.* I eventually became head of information at that journal. I remember that, when I was seventeen years old, I interviewed Hemingway.

How did the interview with him go?

Unfortunately, it went very badly. I didn't have sufficient background information to do it properly, although Hemingway was extremely polite. I had read some of his narrative, but I didn't know his work well enough to do the interview properly. Besides, I preferred poetry—difficult, obscure poetry at that. Quite frankly, at that time I believed that Hemingway was a superficial writer. I didn't understand then that his apparent simplicity was the result of his maturity as a writer. And as a result I didn't have sufficient preparation to do a proper interview with him. And that's the truth. I have read over the interview on several occasions to see if I could rescue it, but it's full of the pedantic remarks of an adolescent who simply didn't appreciate Hemingway's work.

In "Elegía como un himno" (Elegy like a Hymn), one can see very clearly your political concerns at the time. This was published in 1950, and I wonder how you defined yourself in political terms at that time.

That booklet, because it can't really be called a book, was published when I was twenty years old. It had a very limited edition, some two hundred copies in all. At that time there really weren't any real publishers that specialized in literature. I have always been proud of the way in which that booklet was published. A friend of mine, who was studying law, had a small press in his house that belonged to his father. That friend was the great film director Tomás Gutiérrez Alea, known affectionately as Titón.

The booklet, of course, had little impact, obviously because of its limited edition. I was fortunate, however, because some established writers, such as Emilio Ballagas and Mirta Aguirre, published reviews of it. Indeed, because of its publication I began a long correspondence, as well as a friendship that I very much appreciated, with José Antonio Portuondo. Indeed, just recently the University of Havana published the correspondence between José Antonio and myself between 1950 and 1959. In those letters you can see an adolescent engaged in dialogue with a true master.

When I wrote that booklet, I considered myself a socialist. You have to remember that the 1940s—when I came of age—were marked in political terms by the confrontation between fascism and antifascism. I remember clearly the influence of several books, especially George Bernard Shaw's 1944 book, *Everybody's Political What's What*, a title that is practically impossible to translate. It is a large book that he published when he was eighty-eight years old. It was his last book and perhaps his definitive political testimony as a romantic socialist, which is precisely what I think I have been all my life.

You have to remember the context of those years, the general atmosphere. It was a moment when the Left was growing in importance and influence. At present we are living in a period when the Right is very strong in the world, and it is difficult to imagine just what it was like back then. But when I was between fifteen and twenty years of age, the presence of left-wing thought was very strong. And that booklet, "Elegía como un himno," was published in the midst of that period.

The person to whom it was dedicated, Rubén Martínez Villena, was a notable Cuban poet in the 1920s who later became a political leader and died very young. One of my uncles attended primary school with him, and his name was mentioned often at home, since my family was opposed to the dictatorship. At home we talked often about figures like Martínez Villena, Mella, and Guiteras, and they were highly regarded by us.

Much of your work is concerned with themes connected with key moments of the revolutionary process. Can you explain what inspired some of the poems you wrote at the beginning of the revolution, such as "El otro" (The Other Person), "Mi miliciana" (My Militia Woman), and "Con las mismas manos" (With the Same Hands)?

Those poems are, in fact, from a later period and are connected with my personal experiences with the revolution's victories. "El otro" is part of a booklet entitled *Cuenta de la antigua esperanza* (Reckoning of the Ancient Hope), which was published in 1959. It was supposed to have been published underground, since at that time I was collaborating with the underground press. But then, fortunately, the government of Batista was overthrown, the revolution was victorious, and so it was published in the early months of 1959.

After "El otro" I wrote the poems that you mentioned. Those poems never formed part of a separate book, but I did publish them in 1962 in an anthology of my poetry that is called *Con las mismas manos*. It was just about to be printed when the 1962 Missile Crisis took place, and so when it was published I was able to include some poems inspired by the Missile Crisis.

How do you feel when you read those same poems some forty years later?

Well, fortunately I have never regretted anything that I have written. All of my poems are an integral part of my very being. In my interview with Hemingway, I asked him which of his books was his personal favorite, and I remember his reply: "I do the best job that I possibly can when I write my books. But then I don't make them compete with each other like in a horse race." I was very impressed with his reply, since I, too, refuse to have my texts compete with each other. Each was born out of a specific context, and each represents the best that I could do at that particular time. And so it doesn't really make much sense for me to give my opinions so many years later. Besides, somebody else should make that judgment.

You mentioned the poem "El otro." I wrote it on January 1, 1959, when I was very moved by the fall of Batista and the revolutionary victory. I was also thinking about the many Cubans who had been killed to make this revolution possible. The other poems that you mention, and many others that I have written, are all related to my interpretation of the development of the revolution. This revolutionary process has always been for me a profoundly romantic event, and I use the term *romantic* in its noblest sense. And it has been an enormous privilege for me to have participated in this project.

In your poem "Sería bueno merecer ese epitafio" (It Would Be Fine to Deserve That Epitaph), you make a clear reference to your absence from Cuba at the time of the struggle against Batista. When did you return to Cuba? Do you feel any sense of guilt, since you were living in the United States at that time?

No, I don't feel any sense of guilt. I think that for the past forty years I have given my entire life to this revolution. Besides, each one of us is different and contributes what he or she can. You must also remember that I am not a man of action. I am a man of letters, an intellectual. I had been a professor at the University of Havana and then at Yale University, a position which I remember with great satisfaction. In the spring of 1958 I returned to Havana, and shortly afterwards I accepted an invitation to teach at Columbia University in New York.

I was supposed to begin teaching in April 1959. But when the revolution took place, I resigned the position at Columbia and remained here in Cuba. That was the only thing that I could do. In 1959 I decided my life when I decided that I was going to stay and support the revolution, knowing full well what the risks and difficulties would be. I mention all this so that you will understand that, if I am not a man of action, I have been consistent in my work. Since I was fifteen, I have been a writer, and what I have always sought to do is to turn my intellectual work into something that is both useful and of high quality.

For many years you have had a leading role in the Casa de las Américas cultural institute. Can you speak a little as to how this has evolved? And what do you see as the major challenges facing Casa in the future?

Here we undertake a permanent mission of circulating cultural material and seeking truth. Our role in this mission is, I hope, both useful and relevant. At Casa de las Américas we have also sought to debate themes and issues that are pertinent, some of which are now extremely important, like the issue of women's role in society. The issue of ethnic identity is also extremely important in our continent. I mention these two issues to give you some idea of matters that we seek to discuss. Casa de las Américas has many years of experience and a network of well-established contacts throughout the Americas, and cannot abstain from participating in these discussions.

Our role has also evolved. It is not merely to promote art or literature, since this process has already advanced substantially. The role of Casa de las Américas is not limited to a purely cultural phenomenon, and indeed it has evolved to mirror the challenges facing the continent. I think that if you read our journal, *Casa de las Américas,* you will see clearly how we have confronted various challenges as they have emerged. And, of course, these challenges will always be there.

With regard to these challenges that you mentioned, I would appreciate your thoughts on the polemical, but very important, issue of cultural freedom. Can you give me a definition of this concept? What cultural freedoms exist, and do not exist, in Cuba?

The word *freedom* (whether in cultural or general terms) is beautiful, in much the same way that the word *democracy* is. I don't see how anybody can be against these concepts. That doesn't mean, however, that those who proclaim the importance of these concepts, often with great fanfare, are the ones who practice them. . . .

You have asked me to comment on the case of Cuba, a country which is an atypical case, since it has been blockaded for some four decades. Indeed, it is the victim not only of a blockade but also of a brutal economic war waged by the United States. As the old Mexican refrain goes, "So far from God, and so close to the United States." Well, perhaps we're not so far from God, although we clearly are very close to the United States. Given these conditions, it doesn't make much sense to speak about freedom in an abstract sense.

Besides, what freedom does a homeless person have in the United States? I understand well the freedom that a millionaire enjoys in the United States, but I'm more interested in finding out about the freedom that the poor have, as well as black Americans and the indigenous population. What is their freedom? If you tell me that the United States is the country that best illustrates this concept of freedom, I don't know whether I would laugh or cry.

Here we are fighting to obtain the most freedom that we can, even under such adverse circumstances. Within the current conditions, we wish to enjoy the greatest freedom possible. But we need to remember that this concept of freedom is always a relative idea, based on the context in which we find ourselves, the possibilities at hand. And that is why one of the fiercest wars that we have waged as a nation, and at Casa de las Américas in particular, is to obtain the greatest possible freedom that we can, even in the difficult situation that we find ourselves in.

We also need to remember how the United States had to limit many aspects of these freedoms during World War II, essentially because they were at war with the Nazis. Well, should we not be allowed to do something similar if the United States has declared an economic war on us? We have done nothing in this vein to them. For instance, we have not invaded the United States—something which they have done to our country. Nor have we declared an economic war on them. The fact of the matter is that we are in a difficult situation. The leaders of the United States see us as enemies, and they are just ninety miles away from our country.

That said, it is only natural that mistakes have been made, especially in a process like the Cuban Revolution, which has lasted some four decades. It would be completely normal for these mistakes to occur, especially given the adverse circumstances facing Cuba, as you have explained. If you could correct any of these mis-

takes in the cultural sphere, which would they be? For instance, I remember how a dictionary of Cuban literature was published several years ago, and the name of novelist Cabrera Infante was omitted. Don't you think this is an immature gesture, both in political and literary terms?

I agree completely with your argument. I say that not out of politeness but because you are right. Naturally, over a period of forty years we have committed many errors. Those errors should be recognized—and rectified. I understand that many already have been rectified, but others need to be as well. You have referred to an absurd example. That writers should have been excluded from a dictionary of Cuban literature for nonliterary reasons is simply an error. Indeed, if you were to publish a dictionary of Cuban astronomers, you couldn't exclude good astronomers simply because they were opposed to the Cuban Revolution. It makes no sense; it is absurd. But let's go back to the example that you raised. . . .

I think that, in the case of those writers who are hostile to the revolution, they should be included, and indeed a note should be added to their biographies saying that they are opposed to our process. That is part of their biography and not necessarily of their literary work. It is, of course, possible that their literary work will be contaminated by their political rancor. That is another story. That said, if their work has literary value, they should be included in a dictionary of Cuban literature.

There are often moments of great passion that normally correspond to initial moments of major changes. And in these moments of passion, injustices such as those we are discussing are committed. You have to recognize that we often act passionately in life, for better or for worse. Where this gets out of hand is when passion is transformed into a mechanical process, as would occur with the exclusion of writers, as we have been discussing. This cannot be justified, and Cuba has committed many errors like this. I cannot defend those errors. I have been, am, and always will be opposed to such acts.

What other limitations have been imposed on Cuban writers?

Well, at certain periods some writers did not have their work published. In this case the same criteria were used as in the issue of the dictionary of Cuban writers that you mentioned. And this was because they were hostile to the revolution or because they were thought to be, which is far worse. All of these approaches are definite errors. I understand, by the way, that they are publishing a new edition of the dictionary that you mentioned, and I sincerely hope that they don't make any such foolish blunders again. I also understand that it will soon be impossible to stop publishing a writer because of nonliterary reasons. Of course, it is important to remember that we don't live in the best of worlds, we don't live in a paradise, and there will always be certain limitations. There are also some writers whose opinions can cause a great deal of irritation because of their fierce opposition and their lies about Cuba. It will be more difficult to publish their work than that of other writers. That is only natural.

While we are discussing errors, I also believe that it was a great error—and this does not affect intellectuals exclusively—to have implemented the policy toward homosexuals that we did. Of course, this hostility to homosexuals was not invented by the revolution. Unfortunately, human society is very backward in many matters and is still very slow to recognize many areas of difference, such as the question of sexual orientation. This seed of inflexibility fell in a land where machismo has deep roots, and it prospered because of Cuban machismo. I understand that our society has struggled against many elements of this machismo. A great deal of ignorance has been weeded out, but there still remains a lot to do. And, of course, there are many other areas that we could mention, too. During these forty years, the revolution has committed many errors, and not just in cultural matters. It needs to rectify them and always will need to rectify its errors.

Two aspects of the cultural area are often seen as being particularly controversial, and I would appreciate your comments on them. I am referring to the case of the cultural supplement, Lunes de Revolución, and to what has been called the Padilla affair. Can one say that the revolution went overboard in these cases? Or, given the context in those years, do you believe that the approach adopted by the government can be justified?

They are two very different matters that are often quoted by enemies of the revolution. Let's look at them separately. First of all, you need to remember exactly what *Lunes de Revolución* was: It was the cultural supplement of the newspaper *Revolución,* which was the publication of the July 26 Movement. In other words, it was not a publication of what we would now call "civil society." On the contrary, if there was an official publication in Cuba at that time, it was *Revolución.* And so *Lunes* was the cultural supplement of the official newspaper par excellence in Cuba at the time.

The cultural supplement published important materials and some extremely pertinent issues dedicated exclusively to particular questions. Unfortunately, however, it was in the hands of a person who, despite literary ability, was profoundly disturbed. He was also a professional liar, as can be seen in his nonliterary texts. And, together with several others, he poisoned the cultural environment of the country by taking advantage of the privilege of controlling an edition of hundreds of thousands of copies (paid for by the Cuban people) of *Lunes*. There then came a moment when there were profound contradictions in the newspaper, which was, I repeat, the official newspaper of the July 26 Movement. The decision was then made to close down the cultural supplement.

There had been savage attacks, very unjust, against Cuban writers such as Lezama Lima, Cintio Vitier, and others. The people leading the attack gave the impression of being strong supporters of the revolution, but their attacks stemmed from their resentment, since they had not been published in *Orígenes,* Lezama's magazine. Unfortunately, among those who attacked the *Orígenes* group so rudely was the poet Heberto Padilla. And here we see the possible connection between the closing of *Lunes de Revolución,* which clearly was the right of the July 26 Movement to do, and the so-called Padilla affair.

This was a very different matter. Moreover, when I look back at it with the advantage of hindsight, I feel very sorry, because I believe that it could have been avoided. Padilla and I were good friends. I would have preferred it if he had not taken up the positions that he did, and I would also have preferred it if things had not unfolded as they did. I believe that it affected his life very much. Heberto left Cuba and never developed as the writer that he could—and should—have been and as I personally would have liked to see him develop.

As we know, a gigantic "show" then resulted, and details were circulated around the world. The overkill was extraordinary. It was rumored that he had been horribly tortured, that he had been executed—about fifteen times, if one were to believe all that was published abroad. Fortunately, he was not tortured, nor was he shot. Fortunately, both for him and for everybody else involved, it didn't happen like that. What did happen, however, was the resulting malaise that damaged both Padilla and the revolution. As a result, it was an episode that I observe with great sadness. If the whole issue had been handled with more tact, we would have been able to avoid the damage that affected everybody.

It is important, however, to understand that both matters are very different. Of course, the ideal situation would have been for *Lunes de Revolución* to have undertaken a positive approach and not to have adopted the negative style that it did. If that had happened, it would not have been necessary to close down the supplement. And it would have been better for all concerned if the Padilla affair had never occurred. That would have been the best solution. But now we're not talking about what would have been best but rather about what happened.

If we turn to your cultural legacy, I wonder if it could be summed up in the same way that you did for your own father. I am referring to the poem "¿Y Fernández?" in which you define him in the following manner: "Rebellious, picturesque, as rhetorical as a count, or rather better than a musketeer. I don't know. He lived literature as he did ideas and words. With a startling authenticity." Could this definition also be applied to you?

No. That is how my father was, and it does describe him well. I consider myself to be a passionate person, but he was far more vehement, and I don't believe that I deserve those words. At the same time I do hope that my work has been useful and that I have helped to bring more clarity than confusion to matters. And I hope that my literary work will be appreciated as that of an artist who refused to turn his back on justice and who tried to be an artist concerned with what the great nineteenth-century Cuban philosopher Luz y Caballero termed "that son of the moral world."

You are now entering a new phase in your life, following your election to the National Assembly. How did this come about? Many people think about retiring when they reach sixty-five, but at sixty-seven you are assuming new responsibilities. Why are you getting involved in these matters now?

I'm not getting involved in anything. The Union of Cultural Workers and the Federation of University Students both nominated me to the National Assembly. My position is merely the result of those nominations. I didn't nominate myself, but I did accept this honor and this duty. And so I took up my position on February 24, 1998. We'll see how it all turns out. Hopefully, if all goes well, it will be with continuous passion and effort. We'll have to wait and see.

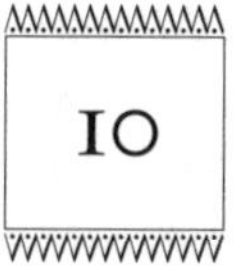

The Exceptional Art of Roberto Fabelo

Roberto Fabelo is bordering on his fiftieth year. He has a tireless need to pursue formal and conceptual models and a reputation both at home and abroad as one of Cuba's most accomplished artists. He is one of the most extraordinary designers ever produced on the island, and one of the most important artists of the twentieth century in Cuba.

Fabelo has created many types of work and shown his efficiency in a variety of pictorial techniques, but he has always been an artist who remains distant from all fashions and tendencies. Faithful to his own discoveries, although in constant albeit measured evolution, his work has always sought to establish a dialogue with everyday life. At the same time, his expressive and formal resources refuse to make the slightest concession to mundane local manners, much less to decorative and superficial tastes.

Perhaps because of that the head is the representation that best sums up the pictorial art of Roberto Fabelo. Around this nucleus of the human body the artist has for many years developed the most diverse variations in his work, always seeking to depict histories, emotions, and human beliefs. The heads of Fabelo are never simply photographic; rather they are a form of narrative, and in his drawings of human heads there is always an expression that goes beyond the mere reproduction of characteristics. In this way he enters the deepest recesses of the psychology of the characters that he creates.

Fabelo is best known for his pictures of heads. Heads covered with cats, dogs, and birds, lizards who squeeze the human brain, and ideas. Heads that remain hidden behind masks that are used to change sex, expression, and feelings, or simply hide them, allowing other features and emotions to be glimpsed. Heads decorated with hats or flowers, with various types of adornment, or sometimes with grotesque objects. Black heads alongside multicolored ones. Heads of men, women, old people, or young people who look old—like the famous characters of Velázquez. Deformed, repulsive heads that injure the senses and yet are profoundly attractive.

Every head bears its own story. Or two, or perhaps even a thousand. A story that Fabelo imagines and then represents by means of this head presented on the canvas. A thousand stories that are created by those who observe his drawings, paintings, sculptures, watercolors, and sketches. Each story is connected to a character, and each character to a situation that always reflects upon the surrounding contemporary reality: heads that provide a chronicle of this moment, although there are a variety of potential interpretations and readings of the work. This complex simplicity is typical of the many values found in all great art—and which is abundant in the art of Roberto Fabelo.

. . .

Many of the most notable artists of your generation are from rural backgrounds: Zaida del Río, Nelson Domínguez, Pedro Pablo Oliva, the sculptor Enrique Angulo, and yourself. Is there any relation between these rural roots and the vocation of artist?

I was born in Guaímaro, a historical town in the Province of Camagüey, where the government of the Insurgent Republic was formed and the first Cuban constitution was drawn up during the Ten-Year War. I am one of five children of a poor peasant family, and even though I spent part of my childhood here in Havana, the best part of those years was my contact with the Cuban countryside. Living in the country allowed me to become familiar with nature in an organic and extremely natural way. Like all kids in that town, I liked to recognize the birds by their song as well as the trees by the shape of their leaves and the flowers by their colors. All of that seemed some sort of game to me and unconsciously offered me my first notion, extremely gradually, of course, of the world that I belonged to.

Perhaps what made me different from my friends was my habit of molding little figures out of mud and beeswax. I tried to re-create the animals we saw around us—wall lizards, scorpions, all sorts of insects—and for me it was all a child's game. Perhaps there can be found the origins of my vocation, one for which there was neither incentive nor a lack of stimulus, since it was all just a game for me. And perhaps, too, it would have stayed forever as a game if I had not had—like Zaida, Nelson, Angulo, Pedro Pablo, and so many others—the opportunity to study when I reached adolescence. History favored us by giving us all—poor children, the children of peasants—the chance to study in the magnificent National School of Art, a facility which otherwise we never would have been able even to dream about.

And when did that casual game with the mud and beeswax begin to change into a vocation?

Around the end of the 1950s, when my family moved to Havana, I had already shown a certain preference for drawing. But I'm still talking about a preference and not really a vocation. At that time I used to draw on all sorts of materials: the blackboard at school, school notebooks, and even on the street with a piece of chalk. I remember that I used to ask older people to draw things so that I could try to imitate them. Nobody, though, would ever have thought that this would lead to a vocation. You have to understand that my family was extremely poor, and none of us had the luxury of worrying about the future. We lived day to day. My father was a sugar cane cutter and a miner, and when we moved to Havana he became a bricklayer, at that time one of the poorest trades in Cuba.

After the revolution my father went as a bricklayer to rebuild the town of Levisa in Oriente Province, and all of us went with him. That town had been destroyed on the orders of one of Batista's army officers during the war, and all the construction workers received a house there. Soon afterwards, however, my father fell ill, and we had to return to Havana, where we settled in 1963. At that time I spent many hours drawing, and I was very aware that I wanted to study painting. But I was also in the middle of my adolescence and wasn't particularly well focused, as is true of so many kids at that stage.

By chance I found out that there was a competition for students wanting to attend the School of Art, and so I showed up there with a folder full of my drawings. They gave me a scholarship, and I enrolled to study there. When I started at the School of Art, I felt extremely out of my depth, because although I did draw a lot, I had read very little, and I was fairly inexperienced. But I was now entering a world where, in addition to painters, there were also musicians, actors, and dancers. We were all in an environment that was ideal for us to develop our intellect, and it was there that I began to acquire new concerns about life and my work. I also got the impression that the world held an infinite number of possibilities.

How did your stay at the School of Art most help you?

I came into contact with important professors like Antonia Eiriz, Servando Cabrera, Adigio Benítez, Yáñez, Luis Martínez Pedro, and others who, while not famous artists, were excellent teachers. I always remember what a major influence Antonia left in all of us, because she was a delightful woman with a powerful artistic personality and an influential spirit. It was she who helped us to begin to appreciate culture, and she was extremely incisive in her analysis. Her own work had a marked critical character, and I use the term *critical* in the broadest sense of the term, both because of her imagery and in terms of her work style.

The opportunity to appreciate these professional approaches to art was extremely important for us students. Another marvelous professor was Servando Cabrera, who had a gift for developing a love for culture in us as well as making us think. His erotic paintings excited us, because in addition to being highly artistic, they were considered risqué and aggressive. It resulted in his being ostracized to a certain extent, but for us young students it offered the additional attraction of dealing with the "forbidden fruit."

Tell us some more about that young Fabelo, a person with very little cultural knowledge but a great love for drawing. As he began to study art, what models did he have in mind?

I was very taken with the work of the classic artists of the Renaissance for the simple reason that they were the most universal in their work and the best known. But as soon as I started to study, I was immediately influenced by those people in the artistic vanguard who were active at the School of Art. As I began to learn more about the painting styles that were being taught, I discovered—and greatly admired—the work of Raúl Martínez. He was working in the pop style at that time, a style which just amazed me. I became extremely interested in it in 1967 when the Salón de Mayo exhibit was organized in Havana, and among other advantages this was an exhibit that opened my eyes to the world of contemporary art. At that time I was young, learning as much as I could. I wanted to absorb as much information as I could. I was hungry for knowledge of art. . . . And there came a moment when I felt that I knew it all. I even came to believe myself!

Can you tell us about the artistic atmosphere in the 1960s?

The 1960s was a revolutionary decade in all senses of the term. The action and image of Che Guevara were the crowning point of those years. I will never forget how I used to participate, with a small group of students from the school, in a voluntary and secret manner, in training activities to become guerrilla fighters and set off for some country in Latin America. On the other hand, we had all the problems and contradictions that were inherent in the radicalism of those times.

Even in the School of Art, where an extraordinary atmosphere of artistic creativity—which has not been repeated since then—was in full swing, things were not easy. It was a time of great amazement for us, the first artistic creators formed by the revolution, but we also began to feel the symptoms of change when some professors and students had to leave the school, expelled because of some extremists' intolerance and lack of vision. It is important to recognize that those errors damaged the creative atmosphere and the desire for new approaches. It is good to remember such errors so that they will never again be committed.

When did you hold your first exhibit? And when did you receive your first prize?

That would be in 1972, when I graduated from the School of Art and participated in some collective exhibits. At that time, when you graduated you were immediately recognized as a professional and overnight had a different status from that of a student. Fortunately, things aren't like that today, but when I was a student, we even had to ask for permission before entering a competition, and we had to limit ourselves to certain student competitions. And it was also in that year that I won my first prize.

How did your name become related to that of the other "promising young artists" here in Cuba? Were you at first linked with those artists connected with the socialist realism tendency?

I was always interested in figurative elements, and I believe that people were interested more in my drawings, because of the emphasis on virtuoso techniques, than in other aspects of my art, which were not particularly novel. It was in 1978, after I had won some national competitions, that I was awarded my first international prize, and it was in India. At that time I was working on various themes, but basically I concentrated on historical and openly political deeds, which had full institutional support. Many others were working in this area, and I also participated in this tendency.

It is not lying to claim that I felt extremely close to this subject matter, and I assumed these themes as being organically linked to my own interests. As a result, I produced a series on the images of sugar cane cutters. Later in the decade I produced another series related to the question of identity. But I don't remember anybody being pressured to create any form of art related to the aesthetics of socialist realism. What pressure did exist was rather more subtle. For example, the preference for certain themes in artistic competitions led artists to concentrate on these themes and employ a realistic approach—to such a degree that some artists thought that it was the form in which they should work.

But let me develop this, because the process was very complex. Ever since the 1960s, artists like Servando, Antonia, and Raúl—who were extremely influential for many people of my generation—have dealt with explicitly revolutionary themes but in a form that is also very revolutionary. Their influence, especially that of Servando, has been evident in figures that at the time were just beginning to emerge but are now clearly established. I am referring to Nelson Domínguez, Eduardo Roca (Choco), and Ernesto García Peña. This influence came through those works, which were linked in such an obvious manner to the new reality of the country. For example, the images of the militia members, the heads of peasants or women that Servando drew—these had a natural influence on our work and brought us so much nearer to a form of art that was so evidently revolutionary in its outlook. Because of this, my work in the 1970s was part of a natural process in my evolution. I drew exactly what I wanted to draw, without ever being directly pressured by anybody, although as I mentioned there was indeed pressure resulting from the surrounding environment in which we all lived.

Your work has gone through interesting stages—initially more realistic figures that later evolved into a more unreal, dreamlike approach, which has come to characterize your work definitively. How did this transition come about?

After I graduated from the School of Art, I went to work for two years in Matanzas, where I did my social service program. When I returned to Havana, I began to work as professor of drawing at the San Alejandro Academy, and in 1976 I registered at the Higher Institute of Art (ISA). The ISA had opened that same year. I believe that it is in my experience there that I can see an important change, not only in my own work but also in Cuban art in general.

To a large degree, the ISA was able to recover the essential spirit that had been frustrated several years earlier in the School of Art, and immediately the ISA became a space for artistic speculation and experimentation. It was there that the proposals of a newer generation made themselves heard, and this generation would influence Cuban culture in the 1980s. In essence, the ISA was a reply to a certain stagnation in Cuban art that can be traced to the late 1970s. But soon afterwards, more contemporary styles appeared and a thirst for information developed. There were many controversies surrounding this new generation of artists, and their work provoked many reactions, including some negative ones. I felt very enthusiastic about this new creative atmosphere. I believe that it shook up my own artistic philosophy and made me reformulate my aesthetic beliefs. I did not join fully all of its approaches, perhaps because I felt so strongly about drawing human figures. As a result, I recognize that it silenced that part of me which would like to experiment with my art more, and I have not projected this potential.

Nevertheless, I believe that one of the most interesting stages in my work was born during this period, influenced by the new approaches to art that were in the air here. An important step in this process was my graduation thesis from the ISA, "The Image of Popular Elements," which drew me closer, although from a more critical perspective, to the image of the Cuban identity. In the thesis I tried to analyze this identity as seen in Cuban attitudes and forms of behavior. This research was extremely helpful, and I soon produced a series called "Fragments of Life," with which I won the Havana Biennial Festival in 1984. This was a series made with pieces of drawings in which I broke with traditional formats, employing very creative drawings from all perspectives. With those works I believe that I developed significantly, and in doing so I fulfilled the need to escape from my earlier work. It was clearly a turning point for me.

After this series, I changed my concept of images, and my whole work was transformed, too. My interest in drawing human figures remained constant, but I believe that it took on a more universal and less local value. Because of this I then produced a series called "Mundo 3" (World 3), which dealt with problems of the Third World. In it I presented expressionist images of violence and hunger and paid little attention to local topics.

Even though you may blush when I say it, many people consider you to be the best sketcher ever to have lived in Cuba. So why is it, then, that for several years now you have concentrated on painting?

It is difficult to categorize artists, and even more difficult to determine who is the best where there have been so many sketchers, all of great quality, from Menocal in the nineteenth century to Eduardo Abela, Servando, Masaguer, Juan David, and a long list of others. Now, it is true that at present I prefer to paint. At the same time I believe that I remain profoundly and intimately connected with the world of drawing—almost in a depraved fashion. It is upon my drawings that I have based all the images of my work and because of this foundation that I have been able to reach certain conclusions about the role of the image. I have undertaken my drawings in the most diverse and adverse conditions. And drawing has also allowed me access to an immediate means of expressing my feelings. Finally, it has given me the opportunity to communicate my ideas, especially to myself.

Drawing has provided me with a foundation, a bank of images that are neither mock-up sketches nor previous studies. Rather, they are a form of practice, a permanent exercise, and the reply to a need. That is why I don't always use those images as ideas or previous solutions to final works of mine, although eventually I may decide to use them. The important thing to note is that, by means of this technique, which comes to me so naturally, I am producing an infinite number of images that are extremely useful to me and that I frequently consult.

It is true that I am sketching less and am devoting my efforts to painting, because of a simple (or complex) demand for this stage of my work. As a result I look back with a certain nostalgia on those times when I used to draw a great deal, among other reasons because I did not have sufficient space to paint. At that time I always fell back upon my drawings because they were so easy to handle. This even allowed me to carry around a folder with cardboard and paper, so that I could sit down anywhere and start to sketch. . . .

In recent years I began to paint with watercolors, which requires techniques similar to drawing because of the use of paper. And then I felt the need to paint on canvas and to introduce colors as a major element in my work. I also started making three-dimensional works, with carved wood and small figures, perhaps in response to a more complex need to express my feelings.

Whenever critics speak of your work, they mention the possible influences of Velázquez and Goya. How can any communication be established between those painters and a man from the late twentieth century?

Perhaps it has to do with the complexity of the creative process, which of course is one of the most interesting and tremendous features of all artistic developments. Probably this all started when I was studying at the School of Art and a North American came to visit us. I remember that I was sketching. She stopped and asked me if I liked the work of Goya. I had seen some works of his, like those in the National Museum, and I replied that I liked his work. We spoke for a while, and finally I gave her a sketch of mine. As she was leaving, she asked me if she could send me something, and I asked for a book on Goya, which she sent. It was a book on the democratic tradition in the work of Goya, and it proved to be very useful in my early stages of drawing figures.

The fact of the matter is that from the beginning of my work I have had a fairly close connection not only with Goya but with Spanish painting in general. Unlike other Cuban artists who have accepted or worked African influences, I have always felt closer to Spanish elements than to the African side of our Cuban identity. Perhaps an example of this link can be seen in the grotesque, which is so close to us, or in the acceptance of picaresque elements—both of which connect me with these pictorial and literary antecedents in the Spanish tradition, since they also belong to our own culture.

Besides, Velázquez seems such a model example of what a painter should be. The more that I have come to appreciate his work, the more I have come to understand his artistic proposal, in which the search for human figures is present. Of course it goes without saying that Velázquez, Goya, and other great masters who have produced such great figures are still our contemporaries in so many issues.

Do you think that this strong attachment which you have to depicting the human figure could limit or typecast your work?

Absolutely not. I believe that the contemporary understanding of art is that in fact it allows an infinite variety of proposals, all of which are acceptable. Besides, I am not interested in knowing whether my work fits into the modern mainstream or not, whether I belong to some sort of artistic vanguard or not. And this, despite the fact that I consider myself open to new cultural expression. All artists should follow their own cultural tempo, their personality, their own angels and demons. . . . These are my own, and I prefer to continue with them. It has been very important to obtain a definite personality in my work. I don't believe that it makes any sense to break with the artistic impetus of my work. It is better to support the evolution of something that already exists and, without any major breaks, continues to evolve in a consistent manner.

Tell us about your obsession with heads. When did it start? And what explains it?

In artistic circles this interest in drawing heads is so ancient that I don't know what its origins are. I was always interested in seeking out human expressions in my work, and I constantly did so by seeking out the inner qualities of my subjects while sketching portraits. I was trained to sketch not just the head but the entire figure of my subject. But the idea of concentrating on just the heads as an important expressive symbol came about during my artistic maturity.

I believe strongly that it is in people's faces, in their heads, that you can really see a good part of the struggles in their lives, the mystery and pleasures of people, their most hidden thoughts. The head is a visual spectacle of what is happening right in front of you, indeed, in front of your own head. And the head of a subject offers you the opportunity of commenting upon life itself, and every face has a story to tell you. And so, given the enormous number of possibilities offered by any head, with this diversity of expressions, I have felt the need time and again to create different human beings, different characters. Maybe because of this, it has become a sort of obsession, since it has become the most visible—and most constant—form of my work.

I note that your recent work frequently uses the representation approach, with theaters, altarpieces, the Malecón sea wall as a backdrop, various altars all appearing. Why have you included these?

If the head can be taken as a stage setting, then the dreams of those heads are a form of greater representation. And from these dreams there spring new characters, symbols, and those fantastic animals that appear in the series that I have been working on recently. This series is entitled "Small Theater," and it is a continuation, or perhaps a derivation, of my earlier work. But it is true that in this series there appear many of the things that you mention: the Malecón, altarpieces that could appear as altars or simply meeting places for all these characters and beings who in one way or another have been appearing in my work for many years, and which now appear in a recognizable space. Among these various meeting places, I am particularly interested in the Malecón sea wall in Havana, because it is a truly extraordinary place where the sea and the shore merge.

In many ways that wall is almost a duty-free zone! If we take a look at the things that happen there, we realize that it is a sort of theatrical representation of real life, complete with an inexhaustible world of images, always very suggestive. It is for all these reasons that I feel trapped and need to use it so frequently. That area of Havana is extraordinary—the salt air blown onto the people, buildings, and the wall itself. Besides, it is a special kind of salt, Cuban salt, that has accumulated over the years.

When I was a child, I used to live near the Malecón, and it seems as if that memory has been forever recorded in my memory. When I use that theme now, I feel as if I am going back in time, although I never use it as an exact representation of that place. Rather, it constitutes a means of inquiry for me, allowing me to speculate or to bring to the surface that world of fantastic characters—and to place them in this specific setting where the sea and the land come together. And that is why we have so many people from Havana in these works, alongside the fish, the fruits, the mermaids, the snails, and the sea urchins. Almost everything is there, including the sky.

Do you ever wish that you had started painting full time at a younger age?

The 1970s was a very intense decade for me, and I had many things to do. As a result I think that I did not spend all the time that I should have done on my work. Perhaps my work did stop so that I could fulfill other commitments. During that time, in addition to painting, I was studying and teaching art. I also worked with the Hermanos Saíz Brigade of young creators, did my fair share of guard duty, and went to all sorts of meetings.

But while all of these things took me away from my work, I believe that the capacity to participate in such varied tasks did help me to develop an impressive versatility. Of course, nobody can deny that it was an intense stage, as it was of this country. I have no regrets about my work during that time, because that's simply the way that we lived in Havana during those years, in the midst of a rich process and with many contradictions and problems. The decision I made later to devote myself full time to my work is the result of that stage, and now many of us are extremely keen to recover that time and to complete projects that we had postponed, even though many of them simply cannot be done now.

To what extent has the appearance of a new market influenced these new possibilities, both artistically and financially?

I remember clearly how in that earlier romantic period money had a completely different meaning and indeed a different value. We weren't interested then in money, because it was possible to live with very little money. In the 1980s, we felt a certain satisfaction because we could meet our material needs on our salaries alone. The concern with selling was not particularly important, and so there were more opportunities for experimentation and the search for new approaches. Because of this we were less inhibited in creative terms. Everybody had a job somewhere as a professor or teacher, as an adviser, and we had salaries that were enough for us to live on and that allowed us certain small pleasures. But then things changed drastically, and the marketplace made itself felt. We are still in the initial stage of this process, one which has come into conflict with the revolutionary and polemical zeal of the 1980s. There had been a fair amount of resentment concerning the possibilities of marketing our art back then, and this has affected all levels of cultural creation. In any event, I think that it is important for people to have sufficient autonomy to finance their projects. Besides, I believe that the state cannot always be expected to worry about resolving difficulties for everybody. The role of the state is to create the conditions for the artist, to open doors and to assist, but without the excessively paternalistic conditions that existed in Cuba for many years.

How is this incipient market making itself felt in Cuba?

The first development came when people started to travel to Cuba. Some became interested in Cuban art, and the painters started to sell directly to these buyers. Faced with this mounting evidence, the Cuban Fund of Cultural Property, which was in charge of the sale of art on the island, took on the responsibility of marketing the works. Yet when the works were sold, even in dollars, they paid the artists in Cuban pesos. In the 1980s, the foreign buyers began to buy directly from the artists. There were also stores exclusively for tourists and diplomats where works of poor quality were exchanged for dollars.

Curiously enough, while it was illegal for Cubans to hold dollars, it was not illegal to sell your work. And so when this informal market started working on a daily basis, the state realized that it was simply unrealistic to keep harassing people to find out if they were selling their work for dollars or not. What they have done recently is to establish mechanisms to avoid the illegal export of art. In my own case, I sell my work to whomever I wish and wherever I want. Then I pay the established taxes, like any citizen.

In your opinion, what does the Cuban art market need to make it truly competitive and efficient?

I think that we need to introduce standards in technical, professional, and economic terms (which currently do not exist in the art market here), as well as the spaces and the means to promote them. I believe that it is this lack of capacity which most distresses and frustrates Cuban artists, for since there is no professional rigor in the promotion and sale of our art, our cultural products are either devalued or not competitive. There are also things that could—and should—be done better, such as providing some stimulus to gallery owners and specialists so that they do a better job in promoting and selling our work. Cuban artists can compete, and what therefore makes no sense at all is that we don't do so simply because of a lack of appropriate mechanisms. Indeed, if many artists have remained in Cuba, it is because they have managed to create their own mechanisms to sell their work. That annoys me, because I believe that it devalues both the art in my country and the training of those artists. Another development that I would like to see is that we encourage art collections here in Cuba, even when it is known that the financial resources available are limited.

You have had a notable commercial and artistic success in important European exhibits. Have you ever considered living outside Cuba?

When I'm painting in the studio and the electricity goes off because of another blackout, and I begin to melt in the heat, I often feel like heading off somewhere else—as happens to all Cubans. But I have never thought about such a prospect in practical terms. For both myself and my work, it is so important to be connected with this reality. And so I can say with absolute sincerity that I have never thought about leaving Cuba to work somewhere else. Cuba is mine, because I belong to Cuba. I like traveling very much, because I believe that it is necessary, but at the same time I need to be here and not break the connection with my country. I do not feel alien to daily events in Cuba. I feel that I am a full participant in what is happening. I am not, however, an uncritical participant, although I have not been as critical as I should have been.

In any event, I would like my work to be seen and sold here, to see magnificent art galleries here (which are so clearly lacking), and for us all to be able to work here in Cuba, to promote our work and sell it according to its quality. Until this happens, however, I prefer to remember that I have had here some very important stimuli both for my work and for my life. In some matters I am a very proud person, and that's precisely why I will stay here in Cuba.

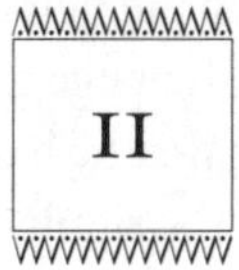

Frank Fernández

From Mayarí to Artistic Glory

Frank Fernández has long been considered one of the major figures on the contemporary Cuban piano scene. His frequent concerts and awards, both at home and abroad, bear witness to the high quality of his musical interpretation and composition skills. Fernández is both a citizen of the world and a man who is proud of his humble peasant origins, since it was in the distant town of Mayarí, in eastern Cuba, that he acquired his first notions of what music really is.

It is also important to point out that in Cuban intellectual circles (and perhaps in the political sphere as well), he is widely seen as an "official" figure. His regular attendance at official ceremonies, commemorations, and other celebrations concerned with the revolution help to support this claim. According to the pianist, his decision to participate in these fora is an attempt to pay back symbolically the benefits that he has received throughout the development of his artistic career. At the same time, thanks to his considerable talent and the opportunity to ply his artistic trade abroad, Fernández appears to live in a very different fashion from the majority of Cubans as they struggle to survive the "Special Period."

The most evident example of this privileged lifestyle came when I interviewed him in February 1998. The interview took place in his new studio located in Miramar, the district of Havana where the wealthy bourgeoisie lived in the 1950s. Nowadays it is the site of many embassies, diplomats' residences, shopping centers, and joint ventures that have changed the social and economic panorama in Cuba. The studio is simple but tastefully decorated, and a large window allows Frank to look out on an exuberant garden while he plays.

Also present at the interview were Fernández's wife, Alina, herself an accomplished musician, and his personal secretary, Abelardo García. He had requested a copy of our questionnaire beforehand to use as the basis for his replies. Perhaps because of that, he began the interview very formally, expanding upon the printed replies that he handed me. He seemed rather nervous initially, wishing to explain the significance of his answers so that they would be properly understood. Soon, however, he appeared more relaxed, perhaps due in part to the excellent añejo rum that he served. When the formal interview had ended, we went to a beautiful patio to which the carpenters were putting the finishing touches. Sculptures and glass mosaic, many trees, and a calm, welcoming environment were immediately apparent. There, surrounded by carpenters and electricians, Fernández continued to develop the ideas we had been discussing previously, possessed by the same vehemence that he shows when he attacks the piano keys.

. . .

Could you tell me something about your family origins and your first interest in music?

My parents were Altagracia Tamayo and Francisco Fernández, and I was born in Mayarí, a small town on the north coast of the easternmost part of Cuba. My family was fairly poor. My father worked as a public accountant, and my mother, who had studied piano and guitar, ran a small music academy. There she taught the piano, along with musical theory, sol-fa, and the basics of harmony.

Thanks to my mother, the earliest memories that I have revolve around music. She taught from morning to night, and all of my uncles and aunts played some instrument or other. Some of them had taken courses at an elementary level in piano, clarinet, flute, and guitar. Thanks to them, music was always present at all major events of my childhood. I am told that when I was four years old I sat down at the piano and reproduced by ear some of the pieces that my mother's students had played.

So, since I was clearly interested in music, my mother began teaching me piano and theory when I turned five. I received enthusiastic support from all my family, although nobody ever thought that I'd become a professional musician, since at that time the musical profession didn't offer much in the way of an economic future. Indeed, almost all the people who played music in my home town had other professions.

Given these circumstances, how did that vocation become a profession for you?

My musical education continued after the death of my mother; she died when I was six years old. It continued because of the support of other family members, as well as some of my mother's more advanced students. Together they helped me to reach what could be termed an elementary level in music. That would be when I was thirteen years old.

At that time I decided to move to Havana, where the famous Municipal Conservatory was located. It was the oldest of its kind in Latin America and had some exceptionally qualified professors, some of whom had been trained in Europe and the United States. I traveled to Havana when I was only fourteen years old, after convincing my father—who wanted me to be an accountant like him—that I would indeed follow his wishes and study accounting in Havana. I never did so, however, because as is obvious it was difficult to take accounting classes as well as to develop my career as a professional musician.

I managed to attend the conservatory here, where I studied harmony, counterpoint, composition, and choral directing. The most important development was my participation in the piano class of Professor Margot Rojas Mendoza, who had been born in Mexico. She had taken advanced courses in New York with Alexander Lambert, a student of Franz Liszt, and then settled in Havana. She was the key link in the chain of my studies, one that allowed me to focus my attention—until that time without a solid academic basis—on the studies that had begun back in Mayarí.

I worked for six years with Margot. I will never be able to thank her enough for the wisdom, generosity, and love with which she developed my artistic talent. It was she who taught me that, however great the technical and intellectual development of an artist might be, the music itself was always far more important. As a result, it was always necessary to assume a humble, respectful perspective. She also provided me with a profound understanding of each musical style in which she was a true specialist. Perhaps it was because she had been indirectly in contact with Liszt.

Finally I finished my studies at the conservatory. At that time it was impossible to go any further here in Cuba. And so I entered the first competition that had been organized by the Union of Writers and Artists in Cuba (UNEAC). The first prize was a sum of money, the opportunity to play a concert with the National Symphony Orchestra, and—most important of all—a scholarship at the famous Tchaikovsky Conservatory in Moscow.

And you won that competition.

Yes, but it was not at all easy, since I didn't have a piano of my own. And so, in order to prepare for the competition, I had to practice at the conservatory or at the house of some friends, who let me use their piano. I was fortunate enough to be awarded first prize at the competition, and so went to study at the Moscow Conservatory under Professor Victor Merzhanov, an eminent pianist and teacher who had himself won—together with Swietoslav Richter—first prize among all Russian pianists in 1944. I finished my studies there in 1971, and then began my career as a concert pianist, one which has taken me to almost thirty countries in Europe, the Americas, and Asia.

Turning to your extensive recording career, how many recordings have you made? Among them, do you have one that is your favorite?

I have made fifteen professional recordings for various labels, among which the last seven are in the CD format. Do I have any particular favorite? Well, each one of these recordings—the three with my own compositions as well as the others that have my work as a concert pianist—has a very personal attraction, as well as a very specific professional focus. Each recording is like one of my own children, a piece of my body even, a work to which I have given all my love at the moment that I performed it. So perhaps the best thing would be to ask the public which recordings they prefer.

There are several recordings that I do remember very clearly, like the first one dedicated to Ignacio Cervantes with his wonderful Dances for the Piano, which I think is among the best that I have done. But when I think about Tchaikovsky's First Concerto, which was recorded in Smetana Hall, when I celebrated the hundredth anniversary of that concerto, which a century ago had been directed by Tchaikovsky himself, I also believe that too is extraordinary. But so is the music of Lecuona that I recorded. And, of course, the same thing occurs when I think about my recording of music by Liszt, Mozart, and Schumann. . . . As you can see, it is very difficult to answer this question, because all of the recordings have an exceptional value for me.

How about your concerts? Which ones do you remember most clearly?

The same phenomenon occurs here, too. I remember clearly the first occasion that I played with the National Symphony Orchestra. I was only nineteen years old, and on that occasion I played for the first time in Cuba Beethoven's Choral Fantasy for choir, orchestra, and piano. It is a wonderful memory. But it was also an unforgettable moment when I was invited—the first Cuban concert pianist ever—to give a professional performance in the Major Concert Hall of the Tchaikovsky Conservatory. Just as important was the concert I gave in Berlin's old concert hall, the Schauspielhaus, since on that occasion I gave the first concert in the Chamber Room following the building's reconstruction. The acoustics there are among the best in Europe.

I have some other wonderful memories. The concert that I gave in the Dominican Republic, sponsored by the Hearts United organization, comes to mind. Some $60,000 was raised to pay the travel expenses of children with congenital heart problems who were to be operated on in the United States. Or the concert in Panama, to raise funds for poor children there. Or the many occasions that I have given concerts for young people in Cuba. Or for university students and factory workers, who usually do not have a solid background in appreciating classical music. I could also mention the concert that I gave at the UNESCO headquarters in Paris during the closing ceremonies to celebrate the fiftieth anniversary of that organization. And, finally, just as moving was the concert that I gave in Mayarí, some twenty years after the last one in the town where I was born. As you can see, it is not easy to recognize which of all these concerts is the most important.

Which activity do you prefer: to compose music, to record, or to perform in a public concert?

I like doing all three, but perhaps the one that I enjoy most is playing for the public. It is then that, if the performer is able to communicate well with the audience, they can receive an extraordinary and immediate stimulus. And just as important as the applause, I also appreciate that magical silence from the audience—almost as if it were an accomplice—that you sometimes sense in concerts.

How do you become inspired to compose? What motivates you?

I fully believe in inspiration. And so I think that any sound produced by nature, any emotion whatsoever, can be turned into music. It is an unconscious act, one that cannot be premeditated. And I also spend a lot of time working, studying the works of the masters, and looking over the musical themes that appear, without any deliberate attempt to seek them out, when there is no concert or particular commitment to compose. So if inspiration comes, it is most welcome, indeed. That said, I believe fully in the concept outlined by Edgar Allan Poe, for whom "cultural perspiration," the effort and work that have to be invested on a daily basis, was extremely important.

How important is traditional Cuban music to your music?

Both in my work as a composer and as an interpreter, traditional music of Cuba has had an enormous influence on me. You have to understand the influences on me during my childhood. There were two major cultural influences in Mayarí: my mother's piano academy and the Municipal Musical Band of which Martín Meléndez was the director. There were all sorts of celebrations at Martín's house, especially concentrating on the old troubadour tradition. It was there that I first got to know and appreciate the purest and most beautiful elements of that rich Cuban troubadour tradition. It was there that I discovered the work of Sindo Garay, Matamoros, Rosendo Ruiz, Pepe Sánchez, and so many others.

I mention this to emphasize that for me there were no differences between popular music and classical music. That may well be the great legacy that I took from my early life in Mayarí—this easy, spontaneous acceptance of all kinds of music. Don't forget that before musical theory there was always the basis of sound and feelings. It was afterwards that the actual theory evolved.

Turning to piano music in Cuba, can it be said that there is a Cuban school of piano?

I definitely think so, even though it clearly does not have the same level of development that we can see in some European schools, like the French or Russian ones. The Cuban school is influenced by three basic elements. The information that the Great Cuban Masters had acquired from the French school, where our first great pianist, Ignacio Cervantes, had studied. Indeed, it was he who received the gold medal for his studies at the Paris Conservatory. A little later we see the influence of the Russian school, which is perhaps the school that had the best teaching precepts.

I believe it is the blend of these two major influences, combined with the spontaneity of our own Cuban character, which is the basis of our music. Indeed, it is this innate musicality, which results from the African and Spanish tradition and which has permeated our national cultural identity, that has allowed Cuban pianists to develop a very specific Cuban form of playing and composing.

Turning to the contemporary situation here in Cuba and the financial difficulties in the 1990s, what impact has the Special Period had on the development of young Cuban pianists? Is it true, for example, that many have left their studies because of financial difficulties and have gone to play the piano in hotels and other tourist centers?

The development of our young pianists is very closely related to what I was saying to you earlier about the Cuban school of piano. The Special Period has had a negative effect on all activities, including cultural matters. More specifically, in the case of teaching music, we see this clearly in the lack of musical instruments and also in the lack of resources to repair and maintain them. It is only with tremendous effort that we have been able to continue teaching music. At the same time our students continue to receive good results and have even received prizes in some international competitions. But there are other problems, too. Even in theaters and concert halls it is difficult to get good equipment nowadays. And the situation in smaller cities in Cuba is even more complicated.

It is because of these circumstances on the one hand, and the growth of tourism and hotels (with fairly substantial resources) on the other, that a great interest has arisen among tourist managers to contract pianists to play at such tourist centers. It is possible that some young people do not finish their studies and prefer to work in these hotels, where they are well paid. The students with genuine talent, however, those who really love their professional musical development, generally make major sacrifices in order to complete their studies. After they graduate, they have to balance their professional careers as concert pianists, or pianists playing popular music, or professors of music.

On the cover of your album Desde la música (From the Heart of the Music), the poet Guillermo Rodríguez Rivera refers to your capacity to play, and to identify with, various types of music: "In the work of Frank Fernández we find classicism and European romanticism, our own nineteenth-century nationalism, the discoveries of contemporary musical vanguards, all of which suddenly lead into the lyrical strains of a troubadour's lyric. At that point Chopin and Bela Bartok come to embrace Ignacio Cervantes and Alberto Villalón." How did this interest in so many different genres of music arise? Where do these notably eclectic tastes originate?

It really isn't that difficult to understand, particularly if you reflect upon the way in which I have come to know and appreciate music since my early childhood. At that time I knew no boundaries between one form of music and another. I didn't understand, for example, what was "classical" music or "popular" music. For me as a child growing up in Mayarí, the only difference was in the names of the musicians. I remember, for example, that the names of the Great Masters were more difficult to pronounce than those I heard at the house of the director of the Municipal Band. At Martín's house the names were Pepe, Sindo, Miguel. . . .

For me these local musicians were, and continue to be, great classical musicians, too. Back at my home with my mother, the only difference was that it was more difficult to pronounce the names of the other classical musicians, such as Ludwig and Wolfgang. But now that you mention it, I don't believe that this possibility of bringing together radically different genres of music is really a deliberate act on my part. Rather, it corresponds to a spiritual need to give back to people my appreciation of all music, to convert my work in the same way that it originally came to me.

Which are the most important musical influences upon your work, both as a composer and as a concert pianist? And who are the composers whom you most admire, both in classical and contemporary music?

There is no doubt that the most important influences upon my work are the result of the musical environment in my home town, which I have already described, and the contact with the music of the nineteenth century, which came through my teacher, Margot Rojas. Concerning the question about my favorite composers, that is very hard to say. As we have already seen, I have recorded a wide variety of music, from the French clavichord to electronic acoustic music. And I think that the reason for playing both is the same, since for me the possibility of communicating with the audience, the music's ability to transmit emotions and to captivate the audience, is of prime importance, whatever type of music is being played.

As a result, I believe that this form of communication can be achieved by playing one of Bach's moving preludes or fugues, or a piece by Couperin or Rameau, as well as a beautiful song of Sindo Garay like "Perla Marina" or "La Bayamesa." I believe that the most important component of all music is this faithful communication of the composer's emotions, since there is the appropriate and exact sound for each emotion. It is clearly not the same, for example, to express a tranquil image of nature's beauty as it is to depict the atrocities of the concentration camps of World War II. I believe therefore that the most important aspect is to be able to understand precisely which sound is needed for each spiritual situation.

I'd like to ask you about your approach to work. What is a typical day like in the life of Frank Fernández?

I get up very late, and I go to bed late, too. Generally I go for a walk and then sit down at the piano to play, or else I compose. I can spend hours and hours without even realizing that the time for lunch or dinner has gone by. Then, once I have reached my goal and feel satisfied with my work, I generally take a break and relax, and then I continue with my work at night. I find that I am at my peak during the night, and at times I wake up in the early hours of the morning with the solution to a musical query that has been bothering me for several days. Once I'm awake, I can spend hours on end studying, oblivious to everything else.

How does it feel to be living in a family with such musical talent?

It is a real privilege. My wife, Alina, graduated from the Higher Institute of Art here in Havana, as did my daughter, Liana María, who graduated in 1997. My son, Frank Ernesto, studied piano and oboe at the National School of Music. Alina has played with me on several occasions, as was the case I mentioned earlier of the concert in honor of the UNESCO anniversary. My daughter, who has just started her career, gave her first concert with the Symphony Orchestra of Matanzas, and it was extremely well received. And finally my son recorded with me one of the pieces for the sound track of a television series that I have just finished.

Tell us something about the life of a concert pianist in Cuba. What kind of a salary do you receive? What do you need to do in order to be paid?

There are different forms of payment for people in the cultural sector. You can work for a fixed income, which means that you have to perform in a set number of concerts or compose an agreed number of pieces. Another scenario is that you can work for a salary that varies according to the category of musician that you are considered to belong to. If, for instance, you have received awards either in Cuba or especially abroad, then your salary will be higher. In exchange for this type of salary, you do not need to perform a set number of concerts. You can work, for example, one, two, or three months without having to give a performance, study a new repertory, make a recording, or prepare for a concert tour abroad. And finally there is the category of what we term an "independent artist," a person who does not receive a fixed salary and whose salary depends on the number of concerts performed. These concerts are paid according to the category of the artist and of the concert hall where the concert is given.

And what happens to the money that you earn abroad? Since the legalization of foreign currency in Cuba, how are you paid?

With regard to the money that the artist receives abroad, the situation is exactly the same as you find in most other countries. If your concert or tour is promoted by the state or by your manager, then obviously you have to pay a certain percentage that is agreed upon beforehand. Generally this varies between 10 and 25 percent. The rest of the fee paid goes to the artist. And if the artist manages to arrange the concert without using the services of any intermediary, then all of the proceeds go to him or her. These different forms of payment have been in place since the recent law on personal income tax, and the system has been gradually improved in the artist's favor.

And how does the royalty system work on record sales?

It's basically the same system. Our royalties are paid both in Cuban pesos for sales made in our currency and in dollars if they are sold in dollars. The system abroad works in much the same way as with other record distributors, and the royalties are usually between 8 and 18 percent, according to the contracts. In terms of all the effort that is put in, I believe that this is a fair system of payment.

Where do you record?

I have made records with several Cuban labels such as EGREM and ARTEX, which distribute them in Cuba, as well as other foreign companies based in Cuba, such as Caribe Productions. I have also recorded with Fonomusic in Spain and with Polygram, and I have made recordings in France, Germany, Moscow, the former Czechoslovakia, Madrid, Colombia, Mexico, and Venezuela. These recordings consist of live concerts that I had given in those places.

In your work, do you have artistic freedom to write what you want, or are suggestions made to you concerning the type of music that you should compose? On a related note, are you free to travel abroad and give a concert, or do you have to request permission from the government?

There have never been any official limits on my work, whether this concerns the themes I choose or the techniques that I employ in the process of artistic creation. The only exceptions to this were when I had accepted a special commission, such as the musical score for a film or a composition for a ballet or theater work. Understandably, in these cases it is understood that, after reading the script of the work, if you accept the commission, then the music needs to reflect the content of the work in question.

In regard to the other question, I am able to accept any invitation to play in any country of the world. I can even work in the United States if they want to contract me. The only limits have to do with the contract between the artist and the impresario. It is a decision that would be absolutely mine and mine alone.

Two questions about money. As a Cuban citizen, do you have a privileged lifestyle compared with others who do not receive part of their salary in hard currency? And when you see concert musicians from other countries, don't you envy the high salaries that they earn?

I do not have a privileged lifestyle in economic terms. Rather, I have an exceptionally privileged lifestyle here in my country because I have received the recognition and the affection of my people. That cannot be measured in dollars and cents.

Concerning the question about possible envy that I might feel toward colleagues from other countries who have reached a similar level of music, but who receive higher salaries, I feel no envy toward them. Indeed at times I feel pity for them, since they lack the spiritual compensation that we Cuban artists receive, even though they do indeed receive far higher salaries. But it is also true that, if they are unable to play because of health difficulties or family problems, they may face economic difficulties. Here in Cuba we are fortunate because none of these social or family problems need to influence adversely our work beyond the normal human concern for their well-being, since we are guaranteed free education and health care in our country.

And so, for example, if one of our children becomes seriously ill, we are not faced with financial ruin because of that. By contrast, colleagues from other countries sometimes become desperate when faced with these problems, because they have to keep playing and working excessively to obtain the money with which to pay for the medical care or education of their families. These are tragic situations, since they destroy all spirituality. At the end of the day, whatever kind of difficulty that we face, it is our spirit which ultimately pays the price.

And at this stage of your career, with so much success already achieved, what ambitions do you have?

My greatest ambition is to continue playing and composing as long as I can. I am sure that, when the last day of my life finally arrives, I will still be searching for the precise sound that can express the particular human feeling I am working on. I have long appreciated, with both admiration and nostalgia, that the human being has an infinite capacity of expressing feelings. I would like to continue the search for this quality, and I continue to study and to express each time a little better this expression of the infinite human condition.

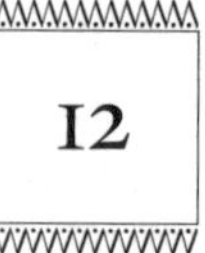

Fernando Pérez

In Search of Happiness

My first impression of Fernando Pérez was that he was thin. After speaking with him, I decided that he was also straightforward and unaffected. The Spanish adjective *sencillo* fits the bill well.

This transparent human quality is very far removed from Fernando's work, where simplicity is nowhere to be found. He has directed numerous documentaries as well as four films. His film themes have varied: from repression and frustration in the days of the Batista dictatorship—*Clandestinos* (The Underground) and *Hello Hemingway*—to the complex situation of Cuba in the grip of the so-called Special Period, as we see in *Madagascar* and *La vida es silbar* (Life Is to Whistle). Significantly, in all cases, Fernando's work is based on a sense of artistic decency, a characteristic that runs parallel with his proverbial unaffected nature.

Pérez was born in Guanabacoa, just outside Havana. Today he lives in a modest apartment in Havana. When the first part of the interview was recorded, he was finishing *La vida es silbar,* which would be the major winner at the International Festival of New Latin American Cinema in Havana, winning in almost every category, including best film and best directing.

It was not casual, therefore, that our conversation should begin at this point, focusing on the present-day reality of Cuba, which has become an obsession for Fernando.

. . .

How do you feel about this recent film, into which you have poured so much emotion?

I believe it is the riskiest project that I have assumed. When you are making a film, you always feel uncertain as to how it will be received, because this creative labor can either be successful or not. And in the case of *La vida es silbar,* I wanted to make a film in which the language of the absurd and the use of metaphors is taken to extreme levels, which makes it a difficult film to appreciate at first. To complicate matters further, I mix drama and humor, without the film ever becoming a comedy, although neither is it a drama. And, of course, it is a film whose central theme is the search for happiness in today's Cuba, at a time when things here are very difficult.

And do your characters find happiness?

In this search for true happiness there are always prejudices or limiting factors—in psychological, political, social, religious, and sexual matters—which we should attempt to overcome in order to find this happiness that we are all seeking. That is the central theme, which is developed in three story lines, two women and a man whose lives are related by another character who is an adolescent. She cannot understand why the others are unhappy, since she owns the secret of happiness but does not reveal it to the audience until the end of the film.

How did you manage to make this film in the middle of so many financial limitations here?

When I completed the script, we began to look for funding. A Dutch institution gave us $25,000. That might seem inadequate, but in fact it helped us considerably. That year, the Cuban Film Institute (ICAIC) participated for the first time in the Sundance Film Festival, in a competition for entries from North America, Latin America, and Japan (in cooperation with NHK Television). They choose a script from each of these regions and then help with the financing. In December 1997, I was informed that *La vida es silbar* had been selected to receive financing. And so in this way we completed the financial arrangements to film it, since ICAIC provided the bulk of the necessary funding.

Being a film director in Cuba seems somewhat exotic. How did your vocation develop?

I believe that my father was responsible. He was a mailman in Guanabacoa, a small town not far from Havana, where I was born. He was a great lover of the cinema, and about 1958—when I was fourteen years old—we used to go together to the movies often, sometimes three times a week. In fact, he loved all forms of artistic expression, although he came from a humble background and never managed to finish his studies, since as a young man he had to leave school and support his family by working as a mailman.

I will never forget the day that we went to see *Bridge over the River Kwai,* directed by David Lean. Both of us were amazed by the film, a truly fantastic work. And as we were leaving he said to me, "That film was very well directed." I asked him what he meant, what a director of a film actually did. And even though he didn't know how to explain the role of a film director, I felt at that moment—and I said so to him—that I too would very much like to be a film director. I remember that experience as being a defining moment in my life. Of course, the idea of being a film director in Cuba at that time was an impossible dream. It was not even a career that could be pursued here. Moreover, the cinema industry here was a disaster, with just a few coproductions undertaken by Mexican directors who came here to develop Cuban themes in their own films. And very little else. Very clearly, then, my interest was a crazy dream but nevertheless a dream that I wasn't ready to renounce.

What kind of films were made in Cuba at that time?

In general they were commercial films, made with the objective of earning money, and definitely not any form of artistic search that contributed to national culture. It was a cinema full of concessions, with an emphasis on folkloric aspects and simplistic plots. There was no interest at all in seeking any meaningful communication with the audience. There were a couple of exceptions, however. For example, the documentary *El Mégano* (The Charcoal Diggers) was one of the first attempts to make a film inspired by neorealist aesthetics and a determination to produce serious cinema. Several young Cubans had come together in order to make it, among them Alfredo Guevara, Tomás Gutiérrez Alea, and Julio García Espinosa. That documentary (which also had some fictional elements) was not shown in Cuba, however, since the Batista authorities prohibited its showing and censored it.

Can you explain how you began your relationship with ICAIC?

It all started in a very strange way. My parents had never made me pursue any particular career at school. It became clear, however, that by studying commerce I would be able to find a job very easily, and in this way I would be able to contribute to the upkeep of our family. By 1959 I had finished my formal schooling and I had started to study IBM technology, which was the predecessor of Internet and computer studies in general. I had also begun to work. But I was interested in none of that.

And so one day I decided to see if I could work somehow with ICAIC. In 1962 I went to their offices. They made me fill out a questionnaire that was fifteen pages long. In it I was asked about my knowledge of cinema, literature, and art and my professional training in general. Of course, my cultural background was poor, since I had never taken literary or artistic courses. I remember that I lost all notion of time while I was filling in the form. I thought that I had been there just a short time, but in fact I had arrived at one o'clock, and when I looked next at the clock it was already six.

Some six months went by, and finally they called me to begin work. I remember that they contacted me during the Missile Crisis of October 1962, when they put me to work as a category C production assistant. The people who interviewed me told me that, if I wanted to, I could be directing in just two or three years. After working at this level, I was promoted to category B, and later to A, and finally to director's assistant, since there were many opportunities. Production was increasing, and they were looking for new staff.

I was extremely timid at that time. They placed me in a coproduction with a Czech film director who was making a film called *¿Para quién baila La Habana?* (For Whom Is Havana Dancing?) I was also naive. When I started, I told myself, "Well, let's see how I measure up to the world of cinema, and how the professionals make films." In reality, however, I was practically a messenger boy, and I'm not sure that I ever saw a sequence of the film being made. Many years later I came across the evaluation that they had written on my work record, and whoever wrote it left a clear impression of how I must have been at that time. They had written, "He clearly has a passion for the cinema and talent, but he is not particularly active in his work. He needs to be more aggressive." And it was true: I wanted to watch the film being made, not work as a messenger.

But they didn't kick you out of ICAIC.

No, and when the filming was complete, I was called in to see what I wanted to do. At that time they were talking about opening a cinema school here in Cuba, but first I was told that I had to improve my cultural knowledge. That meant attending college if I really wanted to make films. And since I had some training in Russian translation, I majored in literature. That was in 1963. I was accepted by the university to study Hispanic literature and art history, and that's how my cultural training began.

When I finished my studies in 1970, I had already agreed to participate in that year's sugar harvest. I was called, though, by people at ICAIC, who wanted me to start as an assistant to Tomás Gutiérrez Alea, who was making a film, *Una pelea cubana contra los demonios* (A Cuban Struggle against the

Devils). I can say that it was then that my real training in cinematography began. I learned to know the cinema from within, to work alongside the director. In sum, my schooling as a film director began.

I worked with several directors, including Manuel Pérez, Manuel Herrera, and Manuel Octavio Gómez. Then in 1974 I was offered the opportunity to make my first documentary. It was an idea that started in collaboration with the writer Jesús Díaz, who at that time was also taking his first steps as a film director. We had both seen some things about the struggle of Puerto Rican nationalists and thought that we could do a documentary on the subject. The project was approved, and so we began to work together.

We were absolutely crazy to start filming as soon as possible. Suddenly the project that was to have been about ten or fifteen minutes long became a feature-length production. We even filmed reconstructions of historical events. And in the end we had a documentary that lasted eighty minutes! It was called simply *Puerto Rico,* and here in Cuba it was very well received. As I look back upon it now, it seems to me that it was an expression of the period in which we were living. It is a militant form of cinema, committed to the cause of Puerto Rico and Latin America in general.

What experience did you gain from the first film you directed?

For the first time in my life I had the opportunity to handle a film camera and to stage fictional settings. After this experience I continued making documentaries, until in 1979 I joined the team headed by Santiago Álvarez that made the ICAIC *Latin American News Bulletin.* Until this point I had acquired some general notions about making films, and of course I was familiar with the possibilities of cinematic language. But it was under the direction of Santiago, and with the possibility of filming reality on a daily basis, without any preconceptions and with the need of deciding how best to manage the image and the information contained in the documentary, that I really had my fundamental schooling.

Working alongside Santiago was always an important learning experience, because he allowed us to express freely all our concerns. He never placed any limits upon us, and indeed our very young team managed to develop a workshop that was extremely creative, since we made not only news bulletins but also documentaries. It was an extremely creative stage for me, one where I really came to know and appreciate what it was to be a film director. In all, I spent five years there.

How many documentaries did you make?

About fifteen. After that experience in the *News Bulletin,* we split up and returned to making documentaries. But by now we intended to make the jump to the world of fiction, which was really our true vocation. During those years I made some documentaries that were extremely important for me, since I felt that in them I fully achieved my goals. For example, there was one documentary on a Brazilian singer, Chico Buarque de Hollanda, and I worked very hard on the dramatic construction of the documentary through still photographs, music, and the appropriate montage.

I also remember with some fondness a documentary on Omara Portuondo, where I began to manage certain fictional scenes. In many ways this represented the first step in preparing myself for larger works of fiction. And I also directed a documentary called *Cuatro mil niños* (Four Thousand Children), which I liked very much. It is an example of spontaneous cinema concerning a celebration in which four thousand children participated. I began to film three months before the actual celebration took place, and I followed it through the entire process.

On the other hand, I am embarrassed to remember the second documentary that I made, *Cascos blancos* (White Helmets), on the microbrigade construction workers here in Cuba. This documentary was a major lesson for me, since it was such a horrible, disastrous film. It was filled with clichés and with a false, cold structure. I learned through that work that the cinema is a much more complex work, far more difficult and serious than I had imagined it to be.

How did you find the transition from documentaries to fiction?

It was very difficult. Despite the fact that in the 1970s and early 1980s the Cuban film industry didn't face the same economic problems that it does now, at the same time there weren't opportunities for everybody. As a result, there was a large delay in developing a new generation of people in the film industry, not just directors but also editors and photographers. We made lots of proposals but were always told that we weren't ready to do that sort of thing. Indeed, it was only in the mid-1980s that ICAIC finally realized that young film directors were badly needed, that we were getting old while we waited for our opportunity. As a result, they opened a competition for people in the documentary side of things to propose fictional scripts. The objective was to select nine or ten projects. Almost all of the documentary makers offered proposals, and ten directors were chosen. We presented our first works of fiction in the second half of the 1980s.

Was the film Clandestinos your project?

That's right. As you know, it has a story line set in the 1950s and is about the struggle of a group of young people against the Batista dictatorship. It was a theme that several of my colleagues saw as being outdated, especially since there had already been a great deal of coverage of the topic in literature, the cinema, and television series. But that was the project that I had in mind, and it was what I really wanted to do.

And so I wrote the script with Jesús Díaz. It is an original idea but one inspired by real events that I transformed into fiction, since we wanted to have a certain dramatic freedom. I also tried to include all of the themes that I was interested in, but I treated them in a style close to that of an action or even police movie, since I was interested in seeing the spectators' emotions. I wanted very much to see my characters escape from being cardboard heroes and instead become ordinary people. And to a certain extent I think that I achieved this. This therefore allowed the spectators, particularly younger audiences, to come to terms with a theme that had already been treated in a schematic and doctrinaire fashion.

Can you summarize the role of filmmakers in Cuba?

Look, like every human group of creators, we are not homogeneous. Cuban film directors have been influenced by their different upbringing. They have diverse social origins, different experiences and concerns—and all of that is precisely what enriches us as a group. But I also believe that there are some common denominators. . . . A film director in this country, for example, will never be seen as a privileged person, somebody who is very different from most other Cubans. What defines us as a group is that we try to produce a form of cinema that has repercussions on society, that can contribute to the definition of concerns that we have—not just as individuals, but also as part of the collective society at large. And because of this, even though we might employ the most diverse of styles, we have developed a form of cinema that seeks to deal directly with our reality. We are not producing a form of cinema with a defined political program or one designed to educate our population. And we do not produce a form of cinema that is designed to earn money. By contrast, our cinema brings us the greatest satisfaction when we see that it has an impact on Cuban audiences, that it enters a meaningful debate to discuss aspects of Cuban reality. It seeks to deal with our history and our reality, our way of life.

How do you feel when you travel abroad and see a colleague who is earning a tremendous salary and has enormous prestige in that society? Don't you make a comparison with yourself and your colleagues here?

It is indeed certain that there are great differences between their conditions and ours. But these differences cannot be drawn only between film directors, because the same could be said about any professionals in Cuba and their counterparts abroad, including doctors, scientists, and sports figures. Obviously, all of them could be millionaires outside Cuba and enjoy a standard of living that is clearly superior to life in Cuba. It is a striking difference, and that is precisely why some figures have opted to follow that path outside Cuba.

But speaking for myself, I think that it is only in Cuba that I can direct the type of films that I want to. Here I have had the freedom to produce exactly the kind of cinema that I wanted to, and if it fails at the box office, it doesn't affect me in the least. On the other hand, if I direct a film that is a runaway success, very few benefits accrue to me, apart from the satisfaction that I did a good job. And to a certain degree this system allows one, as an artist, to be more closely linked to a reality that is shared with all Cubans, in a society like ours.

Of course, I don't want this to be interpreted as presenting an image of the Cuban cinema as some sort of paradise. Rather, it is a moral option of the artist—and in my case a personal decision—and it is a path that has been chosen by many of us who have decided to remain here in Cuba. Neither should it be taken as a defense of an argument that our approach is magnificent or perfect, because here in Cuba we clearly have many problems that need to be addressed. For example, I believe that I was lucky because I began my career at a time of great potential, and I believe that film directors of my generation reached a cultural maturity in the 1980s, at a time when a boom in the Cuban cinema seemed imminent.

But that potential was never realized. And now it is so much harder for young people who want to produce good cinema to get their first break, since the selective process is so much more difficult now. In other words, most of those young people who would like to make films now face a future where the possibilities are no longer certain. In fact, this generation has developed into one that has extremely limited possibilities. As a result we are now faced with a situation that has helped to reduce dramatically such a promising dynamic from the Cuban cinema and such great human potential.

I wonder if you could talk a little about some of the practical aspects of film directing here in Cuba. For example, do you benefit if your films are shown abroad? Or do all the benefits go directly to ICAIC?

We film directors have a basic salary, which is about four hundred Cuban pesos a month. If it is judged solely in terms of the U.S. dollar, that is a very low salary. And we do not receive any form of royalty that results from our films being shown abroad. All of that money goes to ICAIC, as the producer and distributor. Even when we are all working on a coproduction, the technicians and actors receive most of their salaries in pesos, with just a certain percentage paid in dollars. This is a very difficult situation, because we all have to survive on these salaries and to face many difficulties on a daily basis. What has changed recently is the distribution of prize money: if a film is awarded any money at an international festival, the director is awarded the prize money, which is then shared with those who have contributed most to the film's success.

How about the issues of censorship and self-censorship? Do these phenomena exist here in the Cuban cinema? Are there any parameters given by ICAIC concerning topics that should not be dealt with in Cuban films?

No, there are no such guidelines at ICAIC. It is always possible that a director could present a script that dealt with a controversial topic. In that case we would see as a team how we could present the material most effectively and how the topic could be dealt with artistically. But there are no directives that tell you that, for example, this particular theme could not be dealt with, that something was prohibited, that a topic could not be done in a particular way. In my own case, I have always directed the films exactly as I wanted to. Of course, there have always been discussions, but in the end I have always made the films that I wanted to.

Is the same true for your colleagues?

I believe that here in Cuba we need to confront problems dealing with the management of information. For example, I believe that the press, television, and radio, as mass media, are subject to a form of control that is much stronger than we face in the cinema, theater, literature, and other arts. The cinema is a means of mass communication, but it does not have the same level of consumption that television, radio, and the press do. In addition, as the result of a policy that ICAIC has been able to maintain for many years, the cinema in general here is a far more complex phenomenon.

That is not to say that everything is ideal with the cinema. The most serious problems that have arisen have to do with showing films. ICAIC has occasionally come up against restrictions on the showing of certain films. Moreover, in those areas of the country that have to do with cultural matters, other approaches—often held by far more conservative bureaucrats—have at times considered films as being inappropriate. As a result, there have indeed been discussions. On some occasions things have reached the point where the debut of a film has been postponed and in other cases where the showing of a film has been prohibited. I could give some concrete examples.

Such as Alicia en el pueblo de Maravillas (Alice in Wonderland)?

Exactly. Before that, however, there was a film called *Techo de vidrio* (Glass Roof), which was filmed in the 1980s by Sergio Giral, a Cuban director who later left for the United States. His film deals with the theme of a bureaucrat who commits acts of corruption. At that time, such a topic was unheard of. And so, when it came time to show the film, it was decided by the bureaucrats that it was not appropriate to do so.

I saw the film myself at that time, and I believed that its major problem was not what it criticized but the manner in which it did so. The film was really full of good intentions, although the artistic result was somewhat schematic. The characters were not particularly well developed, and the story line was somewhat ingenuous. The film's premiere was postponed, until finally the film was shown some five or six years later in local cinemas. But in the meantime, so much had happened, and Cuban society had witnessed cases of corruption and other problems that were so much more notorious than anything seen in the film. So when the public finally was allowed to see the film, they asked with surprise: "What was so negative about this film that it was not shown all these years?"

I had thought that the case of *Techo de vidrio* was going to be a lesson to us all—that we should not be afraid of such discussions that dealt with the negative aspects of our reality. Now, however, I think that we will always see a struggle between those in favor of an open culture, welcoming constructive criticism and unafraid of controversy, and those conservatives who prefer a more programmed culture, more carefully planned and with a dose of propaganda.

And then in the 1990s we saw the clearest case of that confrontation in a film made by the director Daniel Díaz Torres, who was a member of our group. I personally believe that *Alicia en el pueblo de Maravillas* is a film with great artistic merit that seeks to deal with problems in our society that had not been dealt with. But the film caused a tremendous uproar here.

I believe that the way it was handled was truly disastrous and mistaken. At first the film was shown for just two or three days and was referred to as a counterrevolutionary film. A press campaign was unleashed in which film critics did not participate. Rather, there were other journalists who led a violent and, I believe, inappropriate attack on the film. This in turn raised the level of invective about it. An attempt was made to direct the public, and members of the Communist Party of Cuba were mobilized to ensure that no demonstrations in favor of the film were organized.

All of this provoked a crisis between those working in the film industry and those levels of the government with whom we disagreed about the film. Indeed, things reached such a point that the very existence of ICAIC as an institution was in danger. It was proposed, for example, that because of financial difficulties during the Special Period, ICAIC should cease being an autonomous institution under the auspices of the Ministry of Culture and should instead become part of a conglomerate composed of Cuban television and other groups affiliated with it. This would have led to the destruction of ICAIC.

This decision led to a great deal of discussion, and although the situation became very tense, in the end I believe that it enriched and strengthened ICAIC as an institution. It was then decided that Alfredo Guevara would return to ICAIC, since he was the only mediator capable of resolving the crisis. And although a clear agreement was not reached, it was established that ICAIC would be retained as an independent institution. There then resulted a period of renovation for the film industry here, with films like *Fresa y chocolate* (Strawberry and Chocolate), *Guantanamera,* and *Amor vertical* (Vertical Love) being produced—all of which showed the direction being followed by this necessary, mature cinema.

Agreed. However, in light of what had happened with Alicia, it is surprising that Cuban film directors decided to confront further controversial themes for their films.

That depends on the character of every director, for self-censorship is indeed an option. I believe that in periods when those in power decide to exercise censorship, self-censorship is a logical choice for many. But there also exists the option of fighting to defend the values and ideas in which one believes.

Have you censored your own work to avoid difficulties?

I have always done as I wished in my films. Indeed, at a time when they asked me to consider making a more critical film, I really wanted to make something set in the 1950s. And so I directed *Hello Hemingway.* Later, when I felt that it was time to develop a more complicated theme about what was happening around me, my artistic reply was *Madagascar.* The fact of the matter is that I never stopped to wonder if they were adequate stories or not. Nor did I ever ask myself if they would provoke official reactions, because if I begin to think like that, then I am deforming a creative process in which sincerity and the ideas in which one believes simply disappear. And that is unacceptable.

I believe that this is a responsibility that one needs to respect. If I am to say something that concerns or bothers me, that perhaps are the obsessions which one holds as an artist and citizen of this country, then I try to express my thoughts just as I feel them. I've always found very useful that observation of the American filmmaker Nicholas Ray, who said that, while there is no formula for success, there is one for failure—trying to make everybody happy. I think any art that makes everybody happy runs the risk of being a failed art. That is the challenge which we all have to face.

Looking at the type of films that are being made in Cuba, what impact has the Special Period had on the Cuban cinema?

I spoke earlier about the boom of the creative spirit in ICAIC. But the times have changed, and nowadays ICAIC—if it is to survive—has had to pursue directions that would have been inconceivable several years ago. I think, though, that it is an act of intelligence to be in tune with the changing times. Indeed, if it had not been for the foreign investments and the coproductions, ICAIC would not have survived. It has become a great institution that does not depend on the state. Rather, it finances its operations and even makes a financial contribution to the state. At the worst moments of the crisis, in 1993 and 1994 when I made *Madagascar,* it was with money that came from coproductions and services provided to foreign film projects.

If we had not sought that solution, the Cuban film industry would not have survived. I also believe that, if there had been a different political system and with the economic conditions that Cuba faced at the time, the Cuban cinema would simply have disappeared. Yet we remain alive, almost miraculously, but we are alive.

What impact has the crisis had on individual projects?

The possibility of making a film every two or three years is no longer very secure. Now, in order to make a Cuban film, we need financial support in hard currency. If we don't have that financing, we can't obtain resources that are absolutely indispensable to make a film. To make an average feature-length film in Cuba now, you need no less than $200,000. In comparison with other countries, that is a ridiculously small sum. For us, however, it is a considerable amount, especially since you need to find producers, whose goal is to recoup their initial investment and who often impose conditions that we never had to consider before.

What can you tell us about your most recent film, La vida es silbar?

Its theme is the search for happiness in today's Havana. The film was shown for the first time in 1998 at the Havana Film Festival, and its participation there has been encouraging for me, not just because of the recognition which it received from the critics but also because of its impact on the public.

The film, of course, has been controversial. It was very risky to make, basically because of its narrative style. Moreover, I blend humor and drama, breaking all the laws about true dramatic development. And it is a film in which metaphor, symbols, and oblique language are all of fundamental importance. Because of all of this, to a certain extent the spectator has to become a participant in the film, something which many people are not prepared to do.

You must feel very pleased with the film's success.

It is true that the film was well received by the critics. It received four prizes from the jury and seven other prizes. And, of course, I love to receive awards, since it indicates that the film might continue to be successful. At the same time, this question of awards is somewhat relative. It depends on many variables: the composition of the jury, the competition from other films in the festival, the historical context surrounding the film. . . . For me, the most important facet is when the film begins to establish its own dynamic and to create its own relations with the public.

Do you feel realized as a film director, or is there some professional challenge that you still would like to fulfill?

I feel that I have realized my potential as a film director in the sense that it is extremely difficult to make films in Cuba—and in making four films to that extent I have indeed realized my potential. This is especially true when you consider that there are many talented people here who have never made a film. And because of that, when I look at the context here in Cuba, I would be foolish to say that I do not feel realized. I have clearly had opportunities that other people simply have not received.

I am not a very prolific film director. I am not one of those people who always have an idea and who, the minute after they have finished a film, hurl themselves into another project. Between one film and the next I need time to reflect, to assimilate the results of the film that I have just finished, and to weigh future directions. In other words, I don't make a film for the sake of making it. Rather, I try to make a film in which I can recognize myself, and it is true that in every film of mine I have left a piece of myself. And when you work like this, you need a certain time afterwards to reflect. That is why there are still so many films to make, so many things to say and ideas to express. And there is simply not enough time to do all that.

13

Jorge Perugorría

Climbing Up a Mango Tree

Jorge Perugorría is the latest in a long line of actors to gain international fame because of their success in Cuban films. He played the lead in the most important Cuban film of the last fifteen or twenty years, *Fresa y chocolate* (Strawberry and Chocolate), directed by the late Tomás Gutiérrez Alea.

It is curious, and perhaps contradictory, that the image with which Perugorría began his successful film career should be the exact opposite of the stereotypical Cuban. For, in a country that is viscerally and culturally the defender of macho values, homosexuals have traditionally been shunned. And yet Perugorría (Pichi to his friends) triumphed in a film in which he portrayed an openly gay man who overcomes prejudice.

It is thanks to a previous short story of Senel Paz and a film inspired by that text that the traumatic drama of a homosexual caught in the midst of revolutionary rhetoric has become such an artistic success. In it we see the symbol of the need for tolerance, the possibility of understanding people with widely differing views, and the urgent need for all Cubans to come together, including those separated by the historically rigid barriers of homosexuality and exile. A heady message indeed, and one that had not previously been developed in the Cuban cinema.

. . .

Can you tell us how you first got interested in the idea of acting?

Everything began the day that I saw a play that had been staged by some friends of mine at high school. At that moment I had this very strange feeling, because right away I knew that this was exactly what I wanted to do. It was a feeling of such a great need that from that moment on I never wanted to do anything else other than be an actor.

Could it be because there was some family influence when you were a child?

No way! I was born on August 31, 1965, in a district on the outskirts of Havana known as El Wajay. I was brought up there and had a rather pleasant, quiet childhood. El Wajay is very close to the countryside, and it has a somewhat rural pace of life, and so it was very pleasant to grow up in that environment. My parents divorced when I was a child, and I was raised by my grandmother and my mother, who worked in the offices of a warehouse. All of my family were from humble backgrounds and had no relationship at all with the artistic milieu.

What happened after you saw that high school play?

Until then I had been keen on studying medicine, and even in my last year my career seemed pretty clear. I was to study medicine. Indeed, I never even knew that there was an entrance exam at the Higher Institute of Art that I could have gone to. That was the normal way for students interested in drama to seek admittance to the program. But after I saw that play, everything changed. When I graduated from high school I did not register for medicine, but instead took a course as a building technician. This was not because I was interested in buildings but because it bought me some time while I found out how to study acting.

It was then that I entered the theater group of that technical school, and things started to work out really well. I even won some student awards for my acting in a play directed by Eduardo Novoa, *Historia de un flemón* (History of a Gumboil). It was in one of those festivals that the director Humberto Rodríguez saw me. At the time he was working with the Olga Alonso amateur group, and he suggested that I act in *Romeo and Juliet.* I spent about four years in that group, until I finished my program as a building technician. I then had my first major opportunity in 1984, when there was a competition for a professional group, the Popular Art Theater directed by Eugenio Hernández Espinosa.

After I entered the group as a professional actor, I began to evaluate myself seriously. Besides acting in the theater, I also did some work on television and a few parts for the International Film School here. Then came the opportunity to work in *Fresa y chocolate,* which was my first film. It opened a new direction for my acting—in the cinema—and also for my life.

When you were working in the theater, what kinds of plays did you act in?

I acted in several plays, but perhaps the most important was when the director Carlos Díaz invited me to act in a trilogy of North American plays, and it turned out to be one of the major theatrical events of 1990. Under his direction I acted in *La bacanal de los sentidos* (The Orgy of Senses), *Zoológico de cristal* (The Glass Menagerie), and *Té y simpatía* (Tea and Sympathy). Afterwards I worked with the Rita Montaner group in such plays as *Juana de Besiel, Electra Garrigó,* by Virgilio Piñera, and *Hablo bajo si no grito* (I Speak Deeply If I Don't Shout), and from there I went back to work with Carlos Díaz. We then founded El Público theater group and staged *Las criadas* (The Maids) by Jean Genet. That was the last play in which I acted before making *Fresa y chocolate.*

Of all the roles that you have played, which are the ones that you remember most fondly?

I think that I'd have to say those of the North American trilogy, which were the most important roles that I'd done until then. That particular project was well received by the critics here and had a fairly major impact. That success was not due as much to my contribution as it was to that of Carlos Díaz, who is one of the most highly regarded directors in Cuba today. And his group, El Público, is well respected indeed. I also remember other characters like the one I played in *Hablo bajo si no grito* or in *Perra vida* (Miserable Life).

During this period of developing yourself as an actor, was there anybody who influenced you or assisted you in particular?

My career as an actor has been based upon all that I have learned from each of the directors with whom I have worked. Many of them were professors at the Art Institute, people with a great deal of experience who passed along their ideas to me. If I had to mention specific names, I would obviously begin with Humberto Rodríguez, who was the director of a group of amateur actors and a real professor to me. Thanks to him, I came to understand the Stanislavsky method and theater techniques in general.

Your life has changed since Fresa y chocolate. How did you meet Tomás Gutiérrez Alea, and how did he come to offer you the part of Diego in the film?

When Titón [Gutiérrez Alea] was casting roles for the film, I was recording a television series called *Shiralab,* in which Mirta Ibarra was also acting. She mentioned the film to me. I had read the story by Senel Paz and knew that it was an extremely beautiful work with two excellent characters, and so I turned up at the audition. I was really interested in the character of David, which was the role that I believed I understood best. The character was very much one of my generation, in fact quite close to me, but Titón already had several options, and so he told me he was now casting the role of Diego. He gave me several scenes to study, and after I had auditioned I received a call from ICAIC a few days later to say that I had the part.

How was your relationship with Titón?

During the entire time that I was involved in this project— from early preparations for the film until we were shooting it—I always felt that I was in the presence of a true maestro of the cinema. Clearly I was living out the greatest dream of any actor in Cuba, which was to work alongside the great master of Cuban cinema, Tomás Gutiérrez Alea. From the very first moment that I began to work with him, I was fully aware that I had to be a sponge, absorbing everything that Titón said and did. It was therefore a relationship which from the very beginning was exceptionally clear: I was determined to learn all that I could. And in fact I continued to do so after the film, when we went to various places where it was shown or to several festivals. In other words, I learned from him, not just as an actor but also in the way that I came to see Cuba and to understand my country, asking the right questions and answers about its reality. Later, when I made *Guantanamera* with him and Juan Carlos Tabío, I continued along these lines, and I believe that all of that experience with Titón helped me enormously as an actor and as a human being.

People also speak so highly of Titón and often seem to forget about the contribution of Juan Carlos Tabío.

That's right, but the fact of the matter is that Tabío helped all of us, including Titón. Personally I have always liked the films that Juan Carlos has made. My relationship with him was more personal, although I also learned a lot from him in professional terms.

In professional and human terms, what do you owe to the character of Diego?

I remember that when I began to work with Titón, one of the exercises that we did was simply to walk through the streets of Havana. Of course, I had done this on thousands of occasions, but without looking at it in detail. I had never really examined its streets. I was not aware of its beauty or its exceptional qualities. However, when I saw the city alongside Gutiérrez Alea, and through Diego's eyes, I began to see into its soul, to recognize all the beauty that this city has, despite so many problems that it faces. While he was looking for locations for the various scenes, I discovered buildings that had always been there but which I had never really looked at. I have always found Havana to be a pretty city, but I had never assimilated its beauty in this fashion, feeling a responsibility toward it and learning that it is a city that needs to be defended, that we need to struggle to save.

In a country where macho values are promoted so often, was it difficult for you to play the role, and convincingly so, of a homosexual?

When I took on the character of Diego, I knew that I had a beautiful role, but I also knew how challenging it would be. At first I thought that if it turned out poorly, I would simply look ridiculous. It clearly was a challenging role, and if I failed, then my career as an actor could have gone downhill very quickly. Later, when the film was first shown, I was living in the Lawton district of Havana together with Elsa, my wife, and my children. When my friends went to see the film, they often got angry because people in the audience said that the actor had performed the role so well that he simply had to be gay. People in this district got very angry because they knew that I was straight. I then had to try and convince them not to get so upset, that it didn't really matter what people thought. In fact, if people thought that I was gay, they were just supporting me, since my acting had apparently been so convincing. This was probably the clearest evidence that I had passed the test of trying to play the role of a gay man.

Would it be fair to say that to some degree Diego changed your own perspective on homosexuality?

Not really. In my work as an actor I have always had close contact with colleagues who are gay, and we have worked and lived together for many years. I have never had any feelings of discrimination toward them. In that sense the character of Diego did not help me to develop any new understanding, because I had never experienced those prejudices. Having said that, the character did help me in that, despite the deeply rooted machismo which is widespread here, it allowed me to feel a great deal of affection for those people who congratulated me on my acting and the beauty that I tried to contribute to the role of Diego. This was the first time that I have played a truly great role, one that had so much resonance with the public and one that resulted in recognition from my peers in the cinema who began to consider me as a true professional. And it was all because of the role of Diego.

Fresa y chocolate is a film that can be read on many levels. What do you think Titón was seeking to achieve when he made this film?

Titón was far too intelligent to tell us actors what he was trying to show with this film. I understood, however, that what he wanted was to provide us Cubans with a message, a very simple one, but one that for him was extremely important: namely, that Diego and David's final embrace represents a call for tolerance. His message is that we Cubans can embrace one another and live together, accepting our various differences, whatever they may be. We need to work together, and all of us should think about Cuba, and our peculiar Cuban spirit.

Were you surprised by the international success of the film?

Of course. I had absolutely no idea that it would be so successful. While we were making the film, I was well aware that we were talking about ideas that were taboo within Cuban society, that we were talking about extremely important matters, with a very profound meaning. I also thought that this was clearly a film intended for a Cuban audience. Yet I was still surprised at the great success of the film here in Cuba. And as for the success abroad, I don't think that even Titón himself had imagined that.

What did this film represent for the Cuban cultural environment?

I believe that the film was of tremendous importance in changing the rather simplistic image of Cuba, particularly at a time—following the fall of the Berlin Wall—when the world had changed dramatically. At that time the image of Cuba was rather one-dimensional. The film helped to change that: *Fresa y chocolate* was released, and people had the opportunity to see a country in all its complexity. Many people even asked aloud whether the film had actually been made in Cuba. They simply didn't understand it, since this film broke all the established views about culture in Cuba.

Would you say, then, that the film meant a new opening in Cuban cultural policy?

To a large extent Cuban cinema had clearly been heading in the direction of *Fresa y chocolate*. Indeed, this particular film is the result of our cinema, which for many years has been committed to the goal of defining our Cuban reality and not giving in to mere entertainment. These goals have been achieved, to a greater or lesser extent, in terms of artistic quality, but this has always been the artistic goal of those people employed in the Cuban film industry.

After Fresa y chocolate, you made Guantanamera, with almost the same film crew. What did this new experience in Cuban cinema mean for you?

Although it is not a film of the same artistic quality as *Fresa,* in terms of the story line or the characters themselves, I also enjoyed making this film. It was like making a film about local customs, based, of course, on the surreal reality that we find here in Cuba.

Yet the film was criticized here in the Cuban political context. What do you think about the opinions that Fidel Castro has expressed about the film?

I disagree completely with those opinions. I have been asked this question on several occasions, and I have always replied that I disagree with the idea that this is a counterrevolutionary film. I wish that I could have the opportunity to meet Fidel and tell him that and to explain why I feel that way. I believe that it was a mistake to reduce the film to that idea, because it is definitely not the goal that Titón set for the film, nor is it the result of the finished product itself. By contrast, I believe that it is a story with a very distinctive Cuban flavor, which comes from the ability which we Cubans have of making fun of our own tragedies. I believe, therefore, that *Guantanamera* very much springs from its deep Cuban roots.

How greatly do you feel that Cuban cultural policy has evolved? Even though there are films like Fresa y chocolate and Guantanamera, do you believe that there is censorship in the Cuban cinema?

I believe that in all artistic expression there is a form of censorship, whether that be in Cuba or anywhere else in the world. I also believe, however, that the worst form of censorship is self-censorship, when the very creators of this cultural expression apply it to themselves. Within the cultural context of Cuba, many things have changed, as one would expect, largely because the world has changed a great deal, as has Cuba. It is therefore logical to suppose that intellectuals in Cuba will also have changed, and this has been the case. I think that right now our culture has tremendous responsibility toward the Cuban people and toward the government. We artists in Cuba—and indeed in any place in the world—have the obligation to ask questions, while the politicians have to respond.

What do you think about the present and the future of the Cuban cinema?

I see the present circumstances as being very difficult for the Cuban cinema, although I am one of those people who believe that we can do far more than we are doing at present. At the same time I admit that I don't know how this can be done. I do believe that we have to come up with a new approach to making films, staging coproductions, injecting support to the way that we have traditionally worked. Perhaps we need to revisit the whole structure of ICAIC, since it is still functioning in a different fashion than I believe it should be, particularly given the times we are now living in. Right now I believe that we have to learn a lot, and more quickly, if we are to come up with new approaches to save the film industry and our art here in Cuba. There are many people with talent and possibilities here, many directors who haven't been able to make films for many years, and with excellent projects to work on.

Do you see the exodus of members of the Cuban cultural community as a cultural bloodletting or as a personal need of those artists?

I see it as an individual need. I respect the right of anybody to pursue the path that they believe they need to take. In any event, at this moment I think that people are not really thinking only as members of a collective but also as individuals. People have learned that they can't sit on their hands and wait for somebody to call them, tell them that they have talent, and invite them to make a film. They have learned that, as individuals, they have to go out and make themselves known, both here in Cuba and abroad. Increasingly we see how people have come to realize that their destiny lies in their own hands, based upon their own efforts. And so in many cases they have to leave and work wherever they can find employment and to do whatever it takes. Fortunately, we understand increasingly here that the option to work abroad is not a political decision, just an option to make a living.

Ever since Fresa y chocolate, you have been swamped with work both here in Cuba and abroad. Which roles have you played that have been most satisfactory on an artistic level?

In recent years I've been very busy in the Hispanic film industry and have made films in Spain, Argentina, and Brazil. I've played many roles, but I remember in particular the ones I played in *Bámbola* with Bigas Luna, as the character of "Cachito" by Enrique Urbizo, the role in Jorge Alí Triana's *Edipo alcalde* (Oedipus the Mayor), in *Cosas que dejé en La Habana* (Things That I Left in Havana) by Manuel Gutiérrez Aragón, and in *Amor vertical* by Arturo Soto.

Since your success in Fresa y chocolate, have you ever thought about living outside Cuba?

No. And it is something that I have become increasingly sure about as I have grown, both as a Cuban and as a human being. Being born in any given place is an accident. You can be born anywhere in the world, and it just so happens that I was born here. But as I have developed as a human being, and as I have been able to work outside Cuba, I have felt increasingly attracted to my country, its culture, and our people. I feel extremely proud to be Cuban, and it has never seriously occurred to me to live outside here. In fact, just the contrary is true: staying here to work is an idea that has steadily grown as the years have gone by. I have my roots, a sense of belonging here, that I want to preserve. Moreover, I have met so many Cubans who live abroad that I have come to realize that, even if you physically leave here, you never really break ties with Cuba. I have seen so many Cubans abroad. Some of them have done very well for themselves, and others not so well. What is common to all of them is that no matter how far away or how near they are to Cuba—or want to be—they remain spiritually here in Cuba. If they are not connected with their land, they have no roots at all, because Cuba is a sort of phantom that is always right alongside them.

I would not want that to ever happen to me. And that is why it is so absurd and so terrible that some four decades later the worst enemy that a Cuban can have is just another Cuban. In my own case, I need to feel connected with my country. When I wake up, I need to be able to choose between going down and sitting on the Malecón sea wall, or walking around Old Havana, or going to talk with a friend in my neighborhood. And it is precisely because of these ties that I dream about the possibility that one day there will be real understanding, that we can all live together and one day give the embrace to each other that David and Diego did in the film.

What are your goals as an actor? And the dreams that you would like to fulfill? Would you be interested in working in Hollywood?

That's a good question, but really I don't like to set myself long-term goals. Life has already brought me so many surprises, and there have been so many developments flashing by me at a dizzying speed that I really haven't had time to sit down and plan my future. But the question of working in Hollywood is easy to answer: If I went there, it would be just the same as if I had gone to work in Colombia, Argentina, Brazil, Spain . . . or for that matter to Burundi, if someday they invite me to make a film there and I am interested in the project. In order to get to Hollywood, however, there are only two paths: one is to pack your bags and head there, waiting to see if you can develop your career in the North American cinema industry. Quite frankly, that option doesn't interest me. The other way is to follow that of several outstanding actors, like Marcello Mastroianni, who really founded the cinema in his own country. Yet he was able to work later in many places around the world, including Hollywood. That is what I would like to do. I am certain that he was always attracted by the legendary reality of Hollywood, in the same way that Hollywood was attracted by his reputation as an actor. But Mastroianni was able to develop his artistic career in a marvelous fashion, as several other actors who have also contributed to their own national culture and their own cinema have done.

Are there any specific directors with whom you would like to work?

There are many interesting directors with whom I would like to work, but there is no one in particular. What most interests me is to work in films that are intimately connected to real-life situations, films—to give some examples—like *Il Postino* (The Mailman). Whenever I see it, I tell myself how much I would have liked to act in it. I have always preferred the cinema that has a profound human dimension, as is the case with Italian neorealism or the work of Buñuel, which form part of that same aesthetic. Someday I would like to make a film that is within that current, and in so doing contribute to the most authentic goals of the Latin American cinema.

You say that you don't have any long-term plans, but you have said that at some point in the future you would like to direct films.

You're exactly right. I would love to direct films. I have thought about it a lot, but I know that I am still not ready to do that yet. But I would like to tell a story in one of these films. I already have the basic story line, and it is becoming increasingly clear to me.

Nowadays, because of your success, you have far greater economic opportunities than most Cubans. Yet until your success you lived a very ordinary life, like any other Cuban. How do you feel about your changed circumstances, particularly at a time when this country is in the midst of a general crisis?

Ever since my success started, this has put me in a rather difficult situation. At first it really bothered me, because it meant that in financial terms I could leave the reality of Cuba and be somewhere else. I never wish to feel separated from my homeland, however, just because of this luck, and I will fight tenaciously to keep in touch with my country. I know that it is difficult to take on some individual identity. I also know that I am not a good example of anything, not even of a lucky person. As an individual I cannot claim to be any kind of exemplary Cuban. All of this, as you can see, is very difficult to assume—and even more difficult to explain, and especially to explain to me. And so I do all that I can so that this success that I have had does not go to my head. I do not want to feel in the least different or change my ideas or the way I am. And so when people tell me that I'm in a privileged position in Cuba, I disagree. I tell them that I hold a privileged position in the world, because there are so many actors not only in Cuba but also in many other countries who would love to be able to work professionally in the cinema. And there are so very few who can do so.

Success, good luck, fame and fortune. . . . How greatly has the Pichi of ten years ago changed during that time?

Even though some people may see me in a different light, I am the same person that I was ten years ago. Indeed, I make a conscious effort to be the same Pichi who grew up in the Lawton district. Instead of two children, I now have three. I have been able to improve my life in material things, but from the spiritual point of view I have tried hard not to change. I want to continue to be the same kid who grew up in El Wajay, who used to climb up a mango tree and eat the mangos and suck the skin. That Pichi is the person I never want to stop being.

Epilogue

Living and Creating in Cuba

Risks and Challenges

Leonardo Padura Fuentes

My friend and colleague John Kirk is correct when he states that one of the problems facing Cuban culture is that it is significantly greater than the country from which it springs. This gigantic culture, whose origins can be traced back to the nineteenth century when national culture as such was just beginning, has been with us Cubans for so long that we scarcely notice it now. In the nineteenth century we were fortunate to have had three distinguished and influential poets: José María Heredia, the first great Romantic poet in the Spanish language, and José Martí and Julián del Casal, founders of Modernism in poetry. But there was also an extraordinary early expansion of Cuban music, inspiring various musical genres and fashions, as well as dances and distinctive forms of musical expression in several other Latin American countries and even in the distant Spanish metropolis.

Already in the nineteenth century, then, Cuban culture had managed to project itself in an astounding fashion, thanks to numerous personalities based in this small Caribbean country. We should remember that in his 1994 book, *The Western Canon: The Books and School of the Ages,* Harold Bloom includes five Cubans among the thirty authors he considers the mainstays of the Spanish language.

If we consider the exceptional world of Cuban music, we should also remember how in the 1940s the percussionist Chano Pozo changed the direction of North American jazz. Just as important was the contribution of his mentor and close friend, the band director Mario Bauzá, who created Latin jazz, so important in contemporary music. Shortly afterwards, Dámaso Pérez Prado was to surprise the world by creating the mambo, and Enrique Jorrín invaded the dance floors and even Hollywood with his delightful cha-cha-cha. It was at this time, too, that Alicia Alonso was triumphing on the international ballet scene, Cuban actresses were all the rage in the Mexican cinema, and painter Wilfredo Lam had become one of the leading figures in the field of surrealism, due to his clearly Cuban and indeed Caribbean style.

And so, when the revolution of Fidel Castro succeeded in 1959, Cuba was already an important cultural presence in the western world, with its creators and protagonists receiving recognition in the most diverse artistic circles. There can be no doubt that, from that point on, this solid artistic potential and this major cultural thrust received a tremendous boost in their development in Cuba. Government support helped to multiply that potential, turning it into a clear cultural reality that spread rapidly. Moreover, because of government support, culture was now available to all levels of society (as producers and consumers of our culture) and it achieved new levels of international prestige.

Other measures taken by the government helped to support and develop this new cultural reality. The 1961 Literacy Campaign was key to cultural development in the 1960s, as were the creation of schools of art and cinema, the production of books, and the development of music and theater. That decade had as its backdrop the cultural policy drawn up by Fidel Castro: "Within the revolution, everything is possible; outside it, nothing is," he noted in October 1961. An atmosphere of genuine creativity exploded, full of enthusiasm and massive participation. Its first discordant note sounded with the closing down of the weekly cultural supplement *Lunes de Revolución,* its first major schism came with the Padilla affair, and the process of officially imposed "cultural parameters" that ushered in a period of profound dogma following the 1971 Congress of Education and Culture.

If the 1960s was a decade of expansion, vitality, renovation, and open commitment with the revolutionary process on the part of Cuban artists, the 1970s have been judged as a dark, repressive period, one in which numerous cultural figures (the most notable being Lezama Lima and Virgilio Piñera) were officially marginalized. Artistic parameters similar to the inauspicious dogma of socialist realism were imposed in a more or less visible fashion. It is not by chance, for example, that out of nowhere there should appear the new genre of the "revolutionary police novel." This tendency was of dubious artistic value, presenting everything in terms of us vs. them, and clearly written with the intention of defending the goals of the revolution while ignoring general aesthetic principles.

Nor is it coincidental that drama, traditionally set in theaters, should be forgotten in favor of an intensely realistic theater that was the result of a process of "collective creation." This was conceived and indeed staged in rural communities, with the intention of influencing social problems and seeking solutions with community involvement. A similar comment could be made about films made during the 1970s. One finds in them the omnipresent dramatic conflicts between slaves and masters, men and women, and revolutionaries and counterrevolutionaries. There were scarcely any other themes to be found in films of the era and even fewer nuances in the presentation of issues or characters.

In the second half of that dark and somber decade, the Ministry of Culture was created to redirect Cuban culture. This came in the wake of several grave political errors by the government, both in the treatment of intellectuals and in the very definition of what artistic expression should be. Just a few years later, however, these new state structures began to assimilate the need for a more profound change of policy. This was not the result of a new interpretation of the cultural phenomenon per se. Rather, it was demanded by artists themselves, who expressed their feelings clearly in their work.

As a result, from the early 1980s on, we can see the definitive rehabilitation of so many artists who had been marginalized by Cuban officialdom for almost ten years—and for a variety of reasons (perhaps because they were practicing Christians or homosexual; because their art was more of a questioning nature than one that reaffirmed official positions; or because in their literature they included clear social criticism). It was a time when a generation of Cuban cultural figures emerged. They brought a new approach to the traditional insular reality. They also felt relatively angst-free, an important development, since many of their predecessors felt burdened with the original sin of not having fought more directly in the revolution.

If the Cuba of the 1960s was a country in the midst of social and political effervescence, a country in which socialist institutionalization was taking its first steps in the midst of the struggle for control over the cultural apparatus, the 1970s was a period when the socialist cultural project was implemented with few concessions upon a population that had mainly shown its support for the revolutionary struggle. The result of this approach, however, wreaked havoc in cultural circles: artists were repressed, and culture was taken over by an official bureaucracy.

Despite this current, however, the internal dynamic of the country, together with its deeply rooted, potent culture, ended up showing a fair degree of independence in the 1980s. At that time painters, writers, dramatists, and even dancers and people involved in the cinema took fairly substantial risks and began opting for a less inhibited cultural expression. This decision was based more on an identification with the aesthetic function of art than on any direct political expression of the content.

The maturation of this process actually took place during one of the most convulsive social and economic periods of Cuban history and indeed the most dynamic era of the revolutionary history since the 1960s. It constituted the first clarion call, and a dramatic one at that, of significant changes in Cuba. This led to the dramatic 1989 court trials that would end in the execution of important figures of the armed forces and the Ministry of the Interior, the imprisonment of other officials, and the firing of dozens more.

As the Berlin Wall was tumbling down and the Soviet Union was collapsing, Cuba experienced a terrifying political and economic solitude. The government introduced the "Special Period in Times of Peace," a title with which it baptized the harshest economic crisis that the country had ever lived through. Just a few years later, as the crisis worsened, the government felt obliged to introduce major economic changes—with immediate social repercussions—changes never before imagined. The country was opened up to international tourism and foreign investment, the dollar was legalized and circulated freely throughout society, the farmers' markets were reopened, people were allowed to work independently, an incipient income tax system was introduced, travel abroad became far easier, and religion became acceptable once more.

Many of these benefits also brought significant social change. Prostitution and a network of pimps reappeared; some social sectors suddenly became extremely wealthy; Cuban society became divided between those holding dollars and those without; an exodus of professionals moving to work in the tourist sector became visible; Cubans moved to the far corners of the earth; and religious faith and religiosity noticeably increased, as did violence and delinquency. Symbolic of these changes was the disappearance of the term *compañero* (denoting solidarity and classlessness) in favor of the more traditional expression *señor.* All of this occurred in a society that lacked the most basic materials and where the U.S. embargo had drastically affected the economic and social life of the country.

In such a convulsive (and truly special) period, artistic and literary production could be no less convulsive and special—as in fact proved to be the case. As a result there was a distinctive change in the relationship between the cultural creator and the state. If I were asked to define the cultural characteristics of the 1990s, I would name three: the crisis of cultural production, the winning of space by the creators to express themselves, and the massive (voluntary) exile of Cuban artists.

The first of these factors has been analyzed on several occasions. It includes a drastic reduction in the number and types of Cuban books published, television programming and films produced, art exhibits mounted, and plays staged. It is true that in the late 1990s these difficulties were steadily overcome. Nevertheless, we have been faced with a crisis of such magnitude, a crisis in which institutions were simply unable to respond with support to the productive demands of culture. This had a special connotation in a country like Cuba, where government support had been crucial. It provoked a stagnation and a fundamental rupture of the artistic growth that had been obtained in the 1980s. At that time there had been a significant growth in quantitative, and indeed qualitative, terms in several areas of cultural expression.

Closely linked to these economic difficulties of the 1990s is perhaps the factor that has proved most important of all the cultural changes of this decade, namely, the necessary opening up of space for artistic expression. It is true that there was always a certain level of ideological support for this phenomenon and not for reasons solely linked to the economic crisis. Institutions like the Ministry of Culture, the Union of Writers and Artists of Cuba (UNEAC), and the Cuban Film Institute (ICAIC) have traditionally supported the need for their members to have access to a greater space for reflection, analysis, and criticism of themes that previously had been either censored or treated in a superficial manner.

With the economic crisis, however, the lack of institutional support to finance their projects meant that cultural figures actually gained in independence. This allowed them greater freedom of expression, and they responded with the badly needed sounds to fill the silent void that existed before. Their situation had cried out for artists and writers, film directors and singers, to voice their feelings. Yet in the midst of the previous institutionalization, this had been impossible. Now things had changed. All of this process can be seen very clearly in the interviews found in this book.

As a result, several alternative projects have emerged and have dealt head-on with areas previously ignored. This is seen most clearly in the Cuban cinema. To appreciate this development, one must remember that since the historic scandal surrounding the 1961 documentary *P.M.,* the cinema industry has been centralized under the auspices of ICAIC and two or three smaller production houses controlled by trusted institutions such as the Ministries of Education and the Armed Forces. Now that these state institutions were unable for financial reasons to take on any further projects, this created the possible space for some initial efforts by independent filmmakers—a phenomenon that previously would have been inconceivable—to produce their work in video format. Just as important, however, is the fact that even within the traditional structures Cuban cinema has developed an aesthetic vision of reality that it has been struggling to present for many years. In short, it now dealt openly with themes that it would have been impossible to examine even a decade earlier.

One film in particular clearly revealed Cuban filmmakers' urgent need to express themselves: *Fresa y chocolate.* This film, directed by veteran Tomás Gutiérrez Alea in collaboration with Juan Carlos Tabío and based on a script of Senel Paz, has proved to be a truly significant aesthetic benchmark. It has staked out, like no other film, the claims and possibilities of Cuban art in the 1990s, one that is very different from the epic romanticism of the 1960s, the simplistic ideological presentation of the 1970s, and the critical stammering of the 1980s.

It is around this film that several others have developed, such as the controversial *Guantanamera* (at which Fidel Castro publicly lashed out) also made by Alea and Tabío; the most recent films by Fernando Pérez (*Madagascar* and *La vida es silbar,* both of a distinctly existentialist flavor); *Amor vertical* by Arturo Soto; and what was without a doubt the film that generated the bitterest controversy in recent years, *Alicia en el pueblo de Maravillas* by Daniel Díaz Torres. *Alicia* was condemned in the local media as a counterrevolutionary work and snatched from Cuban cinemas just three days after its premiere. Even during its limited showing, the cinemas were filled with "revolutionaries," sent there to avoid any demonstration that might support a film with such perverse political intentions.

Something similar has happened with Cuban literature. Again, the lack of editorial support because of the economic crisis, changes in mentality in certain spheres of the state direction, and the need for writers to reflect upon a complex and difficult reality have all combined to mold a new form of literary production. This is particularly evident in the narrative, which has contributed to the destruction of several previous taboos, as well as to the literary treatment of several topics which previously had been either totally disregarded or not "well regarded." It was thought in official circles that there was never an opportune moment to deal with such themes, including exile, narcotics, homosexuality, corruption, desperation, and suicide. What is curious about many of these works is that they have arrived on the Cuban scene already possessing the pedigree of recognition from several international, and occasionally national, literary competitions. As a result, they were well known before they were distributed on the island.

And so what in happier economic times (albeit under more rigid ideological parameters) would have caused rumors and quarrels (if not full-blown scandals and possible punishment) has now been accepted as being a natural ingredient of a more open and flexible creative environment in Cuba. Perhaps the best adjective to describe this new policy is *intelligent.* And significantly all of this has come about despite the position of political protagonists (both outside and within the so-called cultural sector) who have openly expressed their opposition to this form of reflection and cultural expression, which to a certain extent they consider alien and indeed harmful to the goals of the Cuban government.

None of this means that the traditional phenomena of censorship and self-censorship have disappeared from Cuba. The freedom for all cultural figures on the island, as Antón Arrufat explained, is conditioned by the political and social reality of the country, which in turn imposes rules of the game that those in the cultural world have learned well. That said, it is indeed true that the levels of permissiveness and the ceiling of tolerance have grown. Now, thanks to the economic crisis of the 1990s, Cuban culture has gained space: cultural workers now possess increased possibilities both to reflect and to express themselves, possibilities that simply did not exist before. These possibilities now extend as far as dealing with the thorny ideological and aesthetic challenges of working "within the revolution," a process which for many years had been reduced to working "in favor of the revolution"—and nothing else.

The economic context has also brought about another feature of Cuban culture that previously did not exist: the possibility of commercializing cultural work. As a result, several writers now publish their manuscripts in

Spain, Mexico, and Italy before they appear in Cuba. Dozens of artists hold exhibitions of their work throughout the world and sell it through foreign galleries, often without the slightest involvement of the state apparatus. And Cuban actors work abroad for international companies.

The most complicated and heartrending of these end-of-the-century problems, however, against which the only bureaucratic measure has traditionally been repression, is undoubtedly the mass exodus of members of the cultural sector. This has notably impoverished Cuban cultural life. This fact of life, which, given the significance of the numbers involved, could perhaps be compared with the impact of the 1959–61 exodus, is really quite different. Early in the revolutionary process, several key figures in the cultural realm left Cuba, including intellectual Jorge Mañach, popular singer Celia Cruz, ethnologist Lydia Cabrera, and television magnate Goar Mestre. The political process at that time, however, produced a dynamic of such tremendous artistic growth, supporting the development of a radically new culture, that it was possible to overcome the loss of these figures.

The exodus of the 1990s was very different, however. It was produced by people who had been formed within the revolutionary cultural tradition, and it included some of its most notable representatives (the great historian Manuel Moreno Fraginals, the novelist and film director Jesús Díaz, the extremely popular painter Tomás Sánchez, musicians like Arturo Sandoval, the journalist and writer Norberto Fuentes, almost the entire generation of plastic artists trained in the 1980s, and finally a legion of television and film actors including Reynaldo Miravalles).

It is worth noting, however, that for the first time since 1959, cultural workers have left for both economic and political reasons. This is also seen in the public attitude toward the revolutionary process of these intellectuals. The "economic" exiles are able to maintain links with Cuban cultural institutions, to enter and leave the country, and to exhibit their work here in Cuba, a development which has meant that they have not broken completely with Cuba, even if their work is for the most part produced and distributed outside Cuba. By contrast, their "political" counterparts, definitively distant from the Cuban system, have become the last legion of political dissidents who are officially recognized as such. A significant part of their work—if not all of it—supports this definitive rupture, since it appears irreconcilable, at least given the parameters being debated at present.

Within the island an attempt has been made to build bridges between state institutions and Cuban exiles who do not maintain political positions that are hostile to the government. An example of this happens with the so-called Cuban Americans who left the island during their childhood. On the other hand, the tension is maintained, and indeed it has sharpened, between Cuban authorities and those who could be considered political dissidents. The official position toward them is the same as it has always been: to ignore them totally and, if possible, to alienate them from their cultural roots. Such an approach goes above political affiliations or political will. Guillermo Cabrera Infante is clearly a Cuban writer, even though government officials may not admit it, publish the fact, or even recognize him in Cuba. And even though Cabrera Infante himself might state that he doesn't want to be considered a Cuban writer, or denies the fact (as he has done), he is clearly a Cuban writer.

The basic option of these dissidents, meanwhile, has been more or less the same: They increase their political opposition to the government in response to the system. In some cases, too, in works of doubtful artistic merit, they have condemned the Cuban government. This tactic is clearly the quickest way to develop an audience, and it is an approach that has led to their work being distributed widely and to a fairly substantial income.

It is a fact that, for any nation in the world, the departure from circulation of a notable percentage of those working in the cultural sector leads to a serious loss for the country's spiritual life. And Cuba is clearly no exception. The surrounding cultural atmosphere is made up of figures who grow in that country, producing work that is inspired by daily experiences there, and leaving a legacy through their words, their work, by means of a necessary accumulation of visions and opinions. The absence of such figures, whatever their cultural stature, produces a vacuum that is combined with the other vacuum stemming from the crisis of production by national institutes. The end result is that Cuban culture is suffering the presence of both these blows, different but at the same time complementary.

Despite the complex and dramatic features of the actual situation of Cuban culture, I believe that the country is living through a period of special creative effervescence. We see in Cuba today the flowering of the results of this small space that is now available for reflection, for creation, and for debate. If it is true that some sectors, and especially the newspapers and television, are little more than instruments of propaganda instead of information, we also need to recognize that today many people in the cultural sector are expressing themselves with greater depth within the space of "conditional freedom" that they have been winning in recent years. Doing so, of course, is not without its risks (which can range from censorship to deliberately ignoring them or their work in the media). That said, risks and censorship can also be a challenge to the imagination.

Because of this complex context, it is no coincidence that Cuba has once again created a culture that is so much larger than the small insular territory from whence it springs. People in several Spanish-speaking nations are increasingly speaking about the boom of the new Cuban novel, thanks to the work of a dozen or so authors from several generations whose work has received a number of prizes in international competitions. In addition, Cuban music (both traditional and modern) is at a peak in terms of creativity and financial return. This can be seen in international prizes being awarded at the highest levels, concerts given at the most desirable venues in the world, and impressive record sales, even in the United States.

The Ballet Nacional de Cuba has recently celebrated its fiftieth anniversary by touring Europe and North America, revealing in its productions its continuing vitality. The plastic arts, too, are now obligatory points of reference on the artistic and commercial circuits in Paris, Geneva, and New York, with Cuban artists increasingly winning international competitions. And finally the Cuban cinema, still badly affected by the economic crisis, continues to produce miracles, with prizes piling up in many international film festivals.

And so, in the midst of tensions and risks, with artistic expression produced both in Cuba and abroad, often with virtually no resources, Cuban culture has returned, larger in so many ways than the relatively small country that produced it. This process over the last forty years has been hard and complex, as the preceding interviews demonstrate. The rigors of censorship, the effects of being marginalized, the current presence of a voracious marketplace for these talents—all have blazed the trail for today's cultural expression. Above all, however, and with so many of its talents living abroad, the cultural creativity of this small Caribbean island continues to be one of the greatest riches of the Cuban nation and, why not, of the entire world.

Suggested Additional Reading

Arnold, Sandra Martin. *Alicia Alonso: First Lady of the Ballet.* New York: Walker, 1993.

Behar, Ruth. *Bridges to Cuba/Puentes a Cuba.* Ann Arbor: University of Michigan Press, 1998.

Bejel, Emilio. *Escribir en Cuba: Entrevistas con escritores cubanos, 1979–1989.* Río Piedras: Puerto Rico Press, 1991.

"Bridging Enigma: Cubans on Cuba." *South Atlantic Quarterly* 96, no. 1 (winter 1997), special issue.

Cabrera Infante, Guillermo. *Mea Cuba.* Mexico: Editorial Vuelta, 1993.

Camnitzer, Luis. *New Art of Cuba.* Austin: University of Texas Press, 1994.

Casal, Lourdes. *El caso Padilla: Literatura y revolución en Cuba.* Miami: Ediciones Universal, 1971.

Cassaus, Víctor, and Luis R. Noguera. *Silvio: Que levante la mano la guitarra.* Havana: Letras Cubanas, 1996.

Chanan, Michael. *The Cuban Image: Cinema and Cultural Politics in Cuba.* Bloomington: Indiana University Press, 1986.

Daniel, Yvonne. *Rumba: Dance and Social Change in Contemporary Cuba.* Bloomington: Indiana University Press, 1995.

Davies, Catherine. *A Place in the Sun? Women Writers in Twentieth-Century Cuba.* London: Zed Books, 1997.

Desnoes, Edmundo, ed. *Los dispositivos en la flor. Cuba: Literatura desde la revolución.* Hanover, N.H.: Ediciones del Norte, 1981.

Díaz Ayala, Cristóbal. *The Roots of Salsa: The History of Cuban Music.* Westport, Conn.: Greenwood Press, 1993.

———. *Discografía de la música cubana.* San Juan, Puerto Rico: Fundación Musicalia, 1994.

———. *Cuando salí de La Habana, 1898–1997: Cien años de música cubana por el mundo.* San Juan, Puerto Rico: Fundación Musicalia, 1998.

Díaz Pérez, Clara. *Sobre la guitarra, la voz.* Havana: Editorial Letras Cubanas, 1994.

Espinosa, Belkis, and Jorge Luis Llópiz. *Cine cubano: 30 años en revolución.* Havana: Centro de Promoción y Estudio del Cine "Saul Yelin," 1989.

Fleites, Alex, and Leonardo Padura. *Sentieri di Cuba: Viaggio nella cultura, nelle tradizioni, nei personaggi.* Milan: Pratiche Editrice, 1998.

Fornet, Ambrosio. *En blanco y negro.* La Habana: Instituto Cubano del Libro, 1967.

Giró, Radamés. *Leo Brouwer y la guitarra en Cuba.* Havana: Editorial Letras Cubanas, 1986.

González Echevarría, Roberto. *The Pride of Havana: A History of Cuban Baseball.* New York: Oxford University Press, 1999.

Ibarra, Jorge. *Un análisis psicosocial del cubano, 1898–1925.* Havana: Editorial Ciencias Sociales, 1985.

López Sacha, Francisco. *La nueva cuentística cubana.* Havana: Ediciones Unión, 1994.

Martínez, Juan A. *Cuban Art and National Identity: The Vanguard Painters, 1927–1950.* Gainesville: University Press of Florida, 1994.

Martínez, Mayra. *Cubanos en la música.* Havana: Editorial Letras Cubanas, 1993.

Menton, Seymour. *Prose Fiction of the Cuban Revolution.* Austin: University of Texas Press, 1975.

"Miradas a la cultura popular cubana." *La Gaceta de Cuba,* no. 5 (Sept.–Oct. 1998), special issue.

Moreno Fraginals, Manuel. *Cuba/España, España/Cuba: Historia común.* Barcelona: Grijalbo Mondadori, 1995.

Orovio, Helio. *Diccionario de la música cubana.* Havana: Letras cubanas, 1996.

Padura Fuentes, Leonardo, ed. *El submarino amarillo (Cuento cubano, 1966–1991).* Mexico City: UNAM, 1993.

Pérez, Louis A., Jr. *On Becoming Cuban: Identity, Nationality, and Culture.* Chapel Hill: University of North Carolina Press, 1999.

Pérez Sarduy, Pedro, and Jean Stubbs, eds. *Afrocuba: An Anthology of Cuban Writing on Race, Politics, and Culture.* Melbourne: Ocean Press, 1993.

———. *Afro-Cuban Voices: On Race and Identity in Contemporary Cuba.* Gainesville: University Press of Florida, 2000.

Pérez Stable, Marifeli. *The Cuban Revolution: Origins, Course, and Legacy.* New York: Oxford University Press, 1993.

Vázquez Díaz, René, ed. *Bipolaridad de la cultura cubana.* Stockholm: Olof Palme International Center, 1994.

———. *Voces para cerrar un siglo (I y II).* Stockholm: Olof Palme International Center, 1999.

Vázquez Montalbán, Manuel. *Y Dios entró en La Habana.* Madrid: El País-Aguilar, 1998.

Vega, Jesús, ed. *El cartel cubano en el cine.* Havana: Letras Cubanas, 1996.

Yáñez, Mirta, ed. *Cubana: Contemporary Fiction by Cuban Women.* Boston: Beacon Press, 1998.